The Bra

International Studies in Folklore and Ethnology

VOLUME 1

EDITED BY Anne O'Connor

PETER LANG

Oxford · Bern · Berlin · Bruxelles · Frankfurt am Main · New York · Wien

The Brahan Seer

The Making of a Legend

Alex Sutherland

PETER LANG
Oxford · Bern · Berlin · Bruxelles · Frankfurt am Main · New York · Wien

Bibliographic information published by Die Deutsche Bibliothek
Die Deutsche Bibliothek lists this publication in the Deutsche Nationalbibliografie; detailed bibliographic data is available on the Internet at <http://dnb.ddb.de>.

A catalogue record for this book is available from The British Library and from the Library of Congress.

ISBN 978-3-03911-868-7

Printed in Germany

Contents

Acknowledgements

The writing of this book would not have been possible without invaluable help from many people and organisations. The staff of various libraries and archives provided unstinting help in answering my numerous questions and guiding me towards appropriate material. Thanks to those in the Queen Mother Library, the Elphinstone Institute and Special Collections at the University of Aberdeen; Aberdeen City Archives; the National Library of Scotland with a special mention to Eoin Shalloo, Curator, Rare Books Division, for his help in tracing Gaelic chapbooks; the National Archives of Scotland; the audio archives of the School of Scottish Studies, University of Edinburgh; the British Library, the John Rylands Library at the University of Manchester, University College, Dublin; the public libraries of Aberdeen, Elgin, Forres, Dingwall and Inverness.

Various individuals took an interest in my research project and I am very grateful to the following for their time in discussing ideas, corresponding with me and in guiding me towards invaluable material. I thank especially Professor Michael Hunter of Birbeck College, London for identifying and discussing the Henry Baker Correspondence at the John Rylands Library; Professor Fiona Stafford and Dr David Shuttleton for identifying and discussing Romantic writers on second sight. I am grateful to Dr Shari Conn and Dr Margaret Bennett for highly informative discussions on second sight and being invited to participate in the latter's practical demonstration of waulking songs. My thanks are extended to Professor Colm O'Boyle for translating an Irish text for no other reward than the pleasure he derived from doing it and to Miceál Ross in Dublin for his patient and instructive discussions on Irish oral tradition. Daibhidh Ailein, Aonghas Mac Coinnich and Fionnlagh Mac a leathainn all provided invaluable assistance with Gaelic translations.

Many people gave of their time and knowledge while I was making enquiries in Easter Ross, before, during and after the Brahan Seer Festival, in September, 2001. The festival director, Lizzie McDougall, the writers Christian Innes and Elizabeth Sutherland, Pat and Ian Macleod at the Dingwall Museum, Andrew Matheson, owner of the Brahan Estate and Susan M. Belford and Frank McConnell at Conon Bridge Primary School are among those who helped me. Bob Pegg; Mhairi McArthur; the traveller Alec John Williamson; Iain Thomson from Lewis; Linton Rogers and Davy Macleod from Easter Ross, are just a few of those who provided versions of prophecies attributed to the Brahan Seer. Several people shared their personal experiences of second sight and I am particularly grateful to Jean Mackenzie and Lesley-Anne Thomas for taking the time to provide me with detailed manuscript accounts. I am also indebted to Dr Elizabeth Hallam and Dr Phil Withington who provided words of wisdom and support during the period of my doctoral thesis on which this book is based.

Many members of my family and friends provided support in different forms during the preparation of this book. This included the discussing and sharing of ideas, lending moral support or providing accommodation during field trips to the Highlands, Edinburgh and Manchester. To all those who provided help in whatever form, I express my sincere thanks. There are many whose names are not mentioned. They know who they are, and have not been forgotten.

Abbreviations

APS *Acts of the Parliament of Scotland* (12 vols, London, 1814–1875)
BL British Library
BSF Brahan Seer Festival
CSP *Calendar of State Papers Relating to Scotland* (13 vols, Edinburgh, 1898–1969)
ERS *Exchequer Rolls of Scotland* Vol. XX (1899)
NAS National Archives of Scotland
NLS National Library of Scotland
RPC *Register of the Privy Council of Scotland,* First Series, 1545–1625, (14 vols, Edinburgh, 1877–1898). Second Series, 1625–1660 (8 vols, Edinburgh, 1899–1908)
SPR Society for Psychical Research
TGSI *Transactions of the Gaelic Society of Inverness*

Stylistic Conventions

The central individual of this book is Coinneach Odhar, the Brahan Seer. His surname is variously spelt Our, Ower, Oyer, etc. in different sources while his forename Coinneach is subjected to similar variations. The spelling of a particular source has been used when citing that source; otherwise Coinneach Odhar is used as standard.

The earliest references to Coinneach Odhar are contained in Latin texts. These have been translated and any quotations rendered in Standard English. Some of the records, including those of the Inverness Burgh Court, are in the vernacular Scots. Many cases formally begin 'Ane brocht strukin be …' – A dispute brought by – followed by a named plaintiff. Standard English equivalents have been substituted for Scots words and little used or archaic terms, although quotations from such sources have been rendered in the original. Later Gaelic sources have been translated into English. Original spelling is retained for quotations in English unless otherwise stated. Where ampersands or *thorns* are used, these have been replaced with the words 'and' and 'the'. No effort has been made to standardise the frequent interchangeability of 'u', 'v' and 'w' and the Scots' tendency to replace 'w' with 'qu'. Words in square brackets have been inserted where documents contain lacunas. Any additions to quotations have been inserted between square brackets; for example, to identify an individual more fully, '… Mr [Thomas] Mackenzie of Applecross …' and [*sic*] has been inserted on those rare occasions where there may be doubt as to the accuracy of the quotation.

Scots words for weights and measurements have been left in the original. The following have been used in the text:

Ell – for measuring lengths of cloth = 0.94 metres.
Firlot – for dry measuring grain, meal, etc. = 52.91 litres.
Mutchkin – for measuring liquid = 0.21 litres.

See Mairi Robinson (ed.), *Concise Scots Dictionary* (Polygon, Edinburgh, 1999), pp. 817–19.

In accordance with convention, the 'historical year' is taken as beginning on 1 January and not (as in Scotland until 1600 and in England until 1752) on 25 March. Dates have been 'silently' adjusted where necessary.

CHAPTER 1

Introduction

The legend of the Brahan Seer

There is a legend circulating in the Highlands of Scotland and beyond concerning the Brahan Seer – a figure so celebrated for his prophetic gifts that books have been written about his prophecies, songs have been sung, plays have been performed and standing stones have been erected to commemorate his deeds and the manner of his death. The legend in its current telling encompasses historical events, folklore, oral tradition and literary romance. Each blends into the other to create an account of the past that defies orthodox historical explanation. The legend has been created over time, each enhancement being shaped from within the world-view of those making the additions. Facts and myths intermingle to create a fluid account of the past. This relates to the more general point that we more fully understand an event's significance by placing it in context, in its time and place, in relation to other events upon which it encroaches, and by studying the beliefs and actions of those determining the events. The Brahan Seer legend is a representation of cultural flux within a particular, relatively small, geographical region. The legend serves as an example of how a cultural production, once created, continues to influence conceptions of the past while being viewed from an ever-changing present. At the heart of the Brahan Seer legend are witchcraft, second sight and prophecy each of which relies on beliefs and practices that can best be examined through a methodological framework associated with 'cultural history'.

This book is concerned with the legend of the Brahan Seer and with placing the seer-figure and its story within the cultural, political and social contexts that shaped its development between the sixteenth and twenty-first centuries. These contexts include the practice and prosecution of witchcraft; the phenomenon of second sight; the rise of Romantic literature; and the perennial use of prophecy. The Seer legend is considered in relation to each of these contexts to show how a cultural production is created and transmitted over time. It is a story that has significant implications for our understanding of the relationship between 'popular' and 'elite' culture. It is also one that requires us to try and understand the past as it was experienced by those involved.

In contrast to oral tradition, which only enters into the historical record when, long after its origin, someone decides to write it down, events are usually fixed in time and place by being written down when, or soon after, they happen. On 18 March 1875, Alexander Mackenzie, secretary and founding member of the Gaelic Society of Inverness, read a paper entitled, 'The Prophecies of Coinneach Odhar Fiosaiche, the Brahan Seer.'[1] He did so because the prophecies existed among the people and he thought that, by placing them on record, he would allow future generations to test their faith in second sight – by comparing events with unfulfilled prophecies. After the success of his talk, Mackenzie serialised an extended version of the paper in *The Celtic Magazine*, of which he was editor, before publishing a slim volume entitled *The Prophecies of the Brahan Seer* in 1877, containing all the richness of language associated with Victorian Romantic literature.[2] A second edition appeared in 1878, it was revised in 1899 and subsequent editions appeared in 1903, 1907, 1912 and 1925. A second impression appeared in 1972 to be followed by a centenary edition, with a commentary by Elizabeth Sutherland, which has been reprinted nearly every year since.

According to Alexander Mackenzie, the name of the Brahan Seer is Kenneth Odhar, derived from the Gaelic *Coinneach Odhar, Fiosaiche* –

1 A. Mackenzie, 'The Prophecies of Coinneach Odhar Fiosaiche, the Brahan Seer', TGSI, 1875, Vol. III, pp. 196–211.

2 A. Mackenzie, 'The Prophecies of Coinneach Odhar Fiosaiche, the Brahan Seer', *The Celtic Magazine*, no XIII Vol. II (1876).

'Sallow Kenneth,' 'the one who knows.'[3] Possibly because his fate was so closely entwined with the family of Seaforth Mackenzies the Seer is also often referred to as Kenneth Mackenzie.[4] Although there are several versions of Coinneach Odhar's origins, the version which holds greatest currency is that some time in the seventeenth century he was born in a small community called Baile na Cille on the westerly shores of the district of Uig on the island of Lewis.[5] One night before he was born his mother was tending her cattle overlooking the village graveyard. Around midnight she was horrified to see many of the graves open and the occupants fly away in all directions before returning at different times. Eventually, only one grave had not been reoccupied and Coinneach's mother – curiosity giving her courage – resolved to speak with the returning spirit. She placed her distaff across the entrance and the presence of this worldly object made it impossible for the spirit to pass so that Coinneach's mother was able to question her.

She was a princess from Norway who explained that she had been drowned at sea and buried by those who had found her body on the nearby shore. She was fated to make continual visits to her homeland until such time as somebody satisfied local custom and purchased her grave, thus allowing her spirit to rest in peace. She begged Coinneach's mother to purchase the grave on her behalf. A sheaf of corn sufficed and as a reward the spirit gave her a stone with a hole in it which she was to give to her unborn son when he reached the age of seven. With this stone he would have the gift of prophecy. Eventually the child was born and one day, when he had reached the required age, his mother asked that he call his father to the house. The boy refused; his mother remembered the stone and offered it as a reward. Peering through the hole Coinneach made his first prophecy – seeing a whale stranded in the bay. This rich find of

3 A. Mackenzie, *The Prophecies of the Brahan Seer* (London, 1977 (1877)), p. 25 and Elizabeth Sutherland's commentary therein, p. 141. E. Sutherland, *Ravens and Black Rain: The Story of Highland Second Sight* (London, 1985), pp. 225–226.

4 Mackenzie, *Prophecies*, p. 27.

5 Ibid., p. 27.

meat and oil was welcomed by the community and laid the foundation for Coinneach's reputation for having the gift of second sight.[6]

By the time his fame had spread Coinneach Odhar had moved to Brahan in Easter Ross where he was employed on the estates of Kenneth of Kintail, third earl of Seaforth and chief of the Clan Mackenzie. When the earl visited Paris some time after the Restoration of Charles II in 1660, Countess Isabella called upon the seer at a large gathering of the nobility at Brahan Castle to tell her how her husband was faring.[7] The seer at first declined but the Countess persisted and eventually he relented and told her what he saw. 'My lord seems to have little thought of you, or of his children, or of his Highland home. I saw him in a gay-gilded room, grandly decked out in velvets, with silks and cloth of gold, and on his knees before a fair lady, his arm round her waist, and her hand pressed to his lips.'[8] Enraged at this public humiliation the Countess ordered that the unfortunate seer be seized and dragged to the Chanonry of Ross at Fortrose on the Black Isle where, with the complicity of the church, he was found guilty of witchcraft and condemned to die in a barrel full of burning tar.[9]

Realising that no mercy was to be shown, Coinneach Odhar, the Brahan Seer, made a lengthy and detailed prophecy predicting the downfall of the Seaforth Mackenzies. The last Lord Seaforth would be surrounded by four great lairds each of whom would have some distinguishing physical characteristic by which all would know that the prophecy was coming to pass. Burdened by debt, beset by ill health and premature death, the once great family did come to an end through the direct male line in the first decades of the nineteenth century. The last Lord Seaforth, both deaf and dumb in line with Coinneach Odhar's prediction, was predeceased by his four sons. Coinneach had also said that the remnants of Seaforth's estate would be inherited by a white hooded lassie from the

6 Ibid., pp. 28–29.

7 Ibid., p. 106.

8 Ibid., p. 108.

9 Ibid., p. 114. A.B. McLennan, 'Traditions and Legends of the Black Isle No XII,' *The Highlander* November 22 (1873) p. 7.

east who would kill her sister.[10] This could be taken to refer to the tragic death of Lady Caroline Mackenzie in April 1823 following an accident that occurred when her sister, Mrs Stewart-Mackenzie – who had returned from India in widow's weeds but had since remarried – lost control of the pony that was pulling the 'little garden chair' in which they were travelling.[11] The historical events surrounding the Seaforths' demise are well documented and form the fulfilment of the prophecy.

It is said that on leaving Brahan Castle, on the way to his execution, the seer threw his stone into nearby Loch Ussie, predicting that it would one day be found by one who would inherit his powers.[12] While these events were taking place, moreover, the Earl returned unheralded to Brahan and on hearing what had happened he rode as never before to prevent the execution. His horse, driven beyond endurance, died on the way so that the Earl arrived at Chanonry on foot; moments after the seer had been consigned to the flames.[13] The Countess had goaded Coinneach Odhar to the last, telling him that he was bound for hell. The seer replied that he was bound for heaven though she was not. As a sign that this would be so a raven and a dove would circle the burning pyre and the dove alight on the smouldering embers. And so it proved, the symbol of hope alighting as foretold, the harbinger of doom flying away.[14]

There is no historical evidence that a Coinneach Odhar existed during the seventeenth century or that anyone was put to death for witchcraft by Isabella, Countess of Seaforth. Moreover, early in the twentieth century W. M. Mackenzie found the name of Coinneach Odhar charged with witchcraft in state documents dating from 1577, a century before the

10 Mackenzie, *Prophecies*, p. 110. McLennan, 'Traditions and Legends of the Black Isle,' p. 7.

11 *The Seaforth Muniments*, NAS GD 46/15, f.135,12. A narrative of the accident and the illness of 'our dear angel' in the hand of Mr Stewart-Mackenzie but told partly from the viewpoint of his wife.

12 Mackenzie, *Prophecies*, pp. 109–110. McLennan, 'Traditions and Legends of the Black Isle,' p. 7.

13 Mackenzie, *Prophecies*, pp. 116–117.

14 Ibid., p. 115.

Brahan Seer's fateful encounter with Countess Isabella. These documents, found in a Munro of Fowlis family chest, implicate Coinneach Odhar in a plot by Lady Munro of Fowlis to kill her stepson by witchcraft so that her natural son could inherit the family title. Mackenzie dismissed the legend on the basis of the discrepancy of nearly a century between the witch's *floruit* and that of the Countess.[15] William Matheson, emphasising the connection between the sixteenth century Coinneach Odhar and Gaelic oral tradition, argues that Alexander Mackenzie's account in *The Prophecies of the Brahan Seer* is not 'sober history' but 'a mere congeries of folklore motifs, devoid of historical content.'[16] However, several writers of folklore accounts, including Otta F. Swire and Alastair Alpin Macgregor, have concluded that the Coinneach Odhar of the Fowlis affair and the Coinneach Odhar who carries the appellation of the Brahan Seer must be two different people.[17] Elizabeth Sutherland surmises that even if the Countess did not condemn a man by the name of Coinneach Odhar she may have condemned some other man. She 'ventures to suggest' the name of Kenneth Mackenzie on the grounds that people of that name claim descent from the seer in the present day.[18] 'Sober' historians dismiss the legend on the basis of documentary evidence while folklorists and popular historians accept it by the mere fact of its existence.

15 W. M. Mackenzie, 'The Truth About the Brahan Seer.' *Glasgow Herald*, 25 January 1936, p. 4. C. T. McInnes (ed.), *Calendar of Writs of Munro of Fowlis* (Edinburgh, 1940), No. 92.

16 Wm. Matheson, 'The Historical Coinneach Odhar and Some Prophecies Attributed to Him,' TGSI Vol. 46 (1968), pp. 66–88. p. 71.

17 Among them are R. C. Macleod in *The Island Clans During Six Centuries* (Edinburgh, 1930); Otta F. Swire in *Skye, the Island and its Legends* (Glasgow, 1961) and again in *The Outer Hebrides and their Legends* (Edinburgh and London, 1966). In *The Scots Magazine* of October, 1969, Mairi MacDonald asks 'Were There TWO Brahan Seers?' It is a rhetorical question; she answers in the affirmative. Alastair Alpin Macgregor in *Over the Sea to Sky* (London, 1926) concurs. MacLeod, p. 164; Swire (1) p. 112 and (2) pp. 56–57; MacDonald, pp. 34–38; Macgregor, p. 115.

18 E. Sutherland in her 'Commentary' in A. Mackenzie, *Prophecies of the Brahan Seer* (London, 1977), p. 141.

This book, in contrast, adopts an approach loosely based within 'cultural history' in order to combine historical evidence and oral tradition. Although reliant on documentary proof from primary sources, it goes beyond their 'factual accuracy' to examine cultural productions, such as patterns of belief, which may be transmitted orally.[19] It is 'intended to be realistic and honest' in its treatment of the legend, without allowing contemporary value judgements to cloud our understanding of past beliefs and practices.[20] This need not imply a lack of discrimination in seeing all practices and beliefs as equally valid. Rather, it requires that the writer report events as they are presented by the evidence without introducing descriptive statements or drawing inferences that are not already explicitly stated in the material, thus 'providing insights into the way the world is experienced in other times and other places.'[21] It is an approach that, as Peter Burke has argued, requires 'a cultural translation from the language of the past into that of the present, from the concepts of contemporaries into those of historians and their readers. Its aim is to make the 'otherness' of the past both visible and intelligible.'[22]

Early approaches in 'cultural history' relied on elite conceptions of culture and on elite primary sources.[23] 'Culture' equated to the intellectual life of the educated elites. This approach often looked at culture as if it were unitary and ignored different attitudes and beliefs, especially those held by people at the bottom of the social scale. In the pursuit of factual objectivity the recording of myth, anecdote, personal and fictional accounts were relegated to a secondary place. To overcome these problems historians have increasingly looked to anthropology for methodological support and I draw on this approach here in order to study the narratives of oral tradition and legend associated with the seer.[24] To this

19 J. Baxendale and C. Pawling, *Narrating the Thirties: A Decade in the Making, 1930 to the Present* (Basingstoke, 1996), p. 8.

20 L. Jordanova, *History in Practice* (London, 2000), p. 94.

21 Ibid., p. 203.

22 P. Burke, *Varieties of Cultural History* (Cambridge, 1997), p. 193.

23 Jordanova, *History in Practice*, pp. 32–33.

24 Ibid., pp. 39–42, 170 and 203.

end, a key term of analysis has been invoked. 'Appropriation,' as Burke puts it, explains the receipt of a cultural production by different groups while removing the focus of attention from the giver(s), who may invest the production with particular meanings, symbolism and significance, to the receiver(s) who may invest it with the same, or totally different meanings, symbolism and significance.[25]

Despite Burke's sensitivity in identifying differences within and between cultures, John Mullan and Christopher Reid refer to his model as 'bi-polar' because it focuses on differences between popular and elite culture, rather than on interrelations between them. They also criticise the model for playing down the degree to which there may be differences between groups within either culture.[26] As Bob Scribner also points out, appropriation occurs between different groups within the same culture and blurs the edges of the distinction between 'elite' and 'popular.'[27] The complex system of relations between groups in the *ancien régime* led Roger Chartier to conclude there was no such thing as 'the people' and that what was required was to study 'the systems of representations' through which individuals choose to articulate what gives meaning and value to their world.[28] These might include literature, mode of dress and other cultural forms and practices. The criticisms of Mullan and Reid and the findings of Chartier and Scribner are central to the contemporary debate over differences between elite and popular culture. They suggest that a more nuanced approach is required to the examination of culture as a whole to see if the distinction between elite and popular culture is justified. This study of the Brahan Seer legend provides one contribution to the

25 Burke, *Varieties of Cultural History*, p. 196. Michel de Certeau (trs. by S.F. Rendall), *The Practice of Everyday Life* (Berkeley, Los Angeles, London, 1984 (1980)), pp. xvi, xxi, 33, 36.

26 J. Mullan and C. Reid (eds), *Eighteenth-Century Popular Culture: A Selection* (Oxford, 2000), pp. 2–3.

27 B. Scribner, 'Is a History of Popular Culture Possible?' *History of European Ideas* Vol. 10 (2) (1989), pp. 175–191. p. 179.

28 R. Chartier, *The Cultural Uses of Print in Early Modern France* (Princeton, 1987), p. 11.

debate by examining the beliefs – relative to witchcraft, second sight and prophecy – of different groups within a society at different times over the past four centuries. The interrelation between beliefs of educated elites and popular culture – what German social historians describe as folk culture – indicate little difference at a fundamental level, with the latter continuing to have a reciprocal relationship with the former.[29]

Until the advent of widespread literacy a significant part of 'popular culture' was transmitted orally, and oral tradition, which had once played a key role in Scottish Highland culture, was sustained especially in rural and island areas until the mid-twentieth century.[30] Oral tradition played a significant role in the creation of the Brahan Seer legend by providing regional accounts of how the Seer acquired his supernatural powers and by acting as a source for the myriad prophecies he is alleged to have uttered. Jan Vansina defines oral tradition as 'verbal messages which are reported statements from the past beyond the present generation.'[31] The content of the message must extend beyond the lifetime of the narrator. For this reason he excludes oral history, the recollection of contemporary events from personal reminiscences, hearsay or eyewitness reports.[32] However, the act of meeting to impart information was seen as an important aspect of Highland culture and this practice requires a broader definition than the one offered by Vansina. The dictionary definition of tradition is 'the handing down from generation to generation of the same customs, beliefs, etc. especially by word of mouth.'[33] This, in turn, raises the problem that beliefs, by their very nature, are often unverifiable in terms of their provenance. As Eric Hobsbawm and Terence Ranger have pointed out, a person or a people can believe that something is traditional when it is of relatively recent origin, including productions created within the life-

29 Scribner, 'Is a History of Popular Culture Possible?' pp. 179 and 182.

30 T. A. McKean, *Hebridean Song-Maker: Iain Macneacail of the Isle of Skye* (Edinburgh, 1997), p. 93.

31 J. Vansina, *Oral Tradition as History* (Madison, 1985), p. 27.

32 Ibid., pp. 12–13.

33 *Collins English Dictionary* (London, 1995).

time of the narrator.[34] The approach adopted by Richard Bauman would appear to overcome this problem. He points out that tradition has, until recently, always been construed as both the process and the content of something transmitted from the past. However, by reinterpreting tradition 'as symbolically constituted in the present,' scholars facilitate a greater understanding of 'the social need to give meaning to our present lives by linking ourselves to a meaningful past.'[35]

It is Bauman's approach that is used in following chapters when considering the need of recorders and collectors of oral tradition to link their 'present lives' to a meaningful past as perceived from their world-view. This should provide a clearer understanding of their beliefs and how they viewed their traditions in the context of their time. Bauman's interpretation accommodates the inclusion of recently invented traditions believed to be true such as local events of significance which may become part of oral tradition when they are retained and repeated beyond the original telling. For present purposes the definition of oral tradition is 'the transmission by word of mouth of any anecdote concerning the past which at some time was held to be true and contained common meaning and values for narrator and audience.'

This book is concerned with a particular type of oral tradition, namely legend, which, together with myth and folktale, constitute the main forms of oral narrative (epics, sagas, riddles and proverbs being others). The terms have generated much controversy among scholars partly because they are not always used to mean the same thing and partly because the content of an oral narrative may refuse to sit neatly within the confines of a single definition.[36] William Bascom has provided a generally accepted

34 E. Hobsbawm and T. Ranger (eds), *The Invention of Tradition* (Cambridge, 1983).

35 Richard Bauman, 'Folklore,' in R. Bauman (ed.), *Folklore, Cultural Performances and Popular Entertainments* (New York and London, 1992), pp. 31–32.

36 R. Finnegan, *Oral Tradition and the Verbal Arts* (London and New York, 1992), p. 142.

model for defining the terms.[37] Myths are believed to be true and are set in the remote past and in another world, either the earth before its present state or the underworld or the heavens. The characters in myths are supernatural beings and they provide an explanation for the phenomena of the natural world. Legends are also believed to be true. They relate to the recent past and although concerned with identifiable persons, times and places, their human agents may interact with supernatural powers or beings. Folktales are believed to be fiction. They are set in indeterminate time and place, are populated by humans and non-humans, they are told for entertainment.

These definitions centre on the concept of what people believe. However, the difference between fact and fiction, even if this could be ascertained, provides insufficient grounds for separating belief in one narrative from another, especially when a narrative contains elements of the natural and the supernatural. The difficulty of identifying differing levels of belief in regard to legends has been explored by Linda Dégh and Andrew Vázsonyi.[38] They argue that although legends are believed to be true it is not an objective truth about the particular content of a particular legend that is believed but a truth more generally assumed concerning the concept about which the legend is told. A legend about a ghost is about ghosts, and the narrator may be trying to convince her audience that there are ghosts, that there are no ghosts, or perhaps that there used to be ghosts somewhere. The level of belief in the concept by teller and audience can vary from total acceptance to outright scepticism and is not relevant to the telling of a legend. However, some overall belief in the concept would have a bearing on the success or otherwise of a particular legend's continued appeal. The demise of one legend would entail the creation of a different legend, or legends, about the same gen-

37 W. Bascom, 'The Forms of Folklore: Prose Narratives,' in *Journal of American Folklore* No. 78 (1965) pp. 3–20. Also cited in Finnegan, *Oral Tradition and the Verbal Arts*, pp. 146–149. See also Dan Ben-Amos, 'Folktale,' in Bauman (ed.), *Folklore, Cultural Performances and Popular Entertainments*, pp. 101–118. pp. 101–102.

38 Linda Dégh and Andrew Vázsonyi, 'Legend and Belief' in Dan Ben-Amos (ed.) *Folklore Genres* (Austin and London, 1976), pp. 93–123.

eral topic if such topic continued to be an object of belief. The central point of any legend is that it is an instance of a more general belief held '*sometime*, by *someone*, *somewhere*' (original emphasis).[39] For completeness Dégh and Vázsonyi could, and should, have added 'about *something*.' On this reading a belief in the Brahan Seer is less important than a belief in witchcraft, second sight and prophecy. Belief in these, especially the effectiveness of prophecy, is what has sustained the legend of the Brahan Seer over the centuries.

The Scottish context

Among the few to specifically treat of the elite/popular relationship in a Scottish context is Edward J. Cowan who discusses popular culture in an all-inclusive sense in a number of places. He does so most notably when examining 'The Covenanting Tradition in Scottish History' with reference to the 'killing times' of 1679–1689 when the persecution of Presbyterians for the sake of their conscience gave rise in oral tradition to tales of saints and martyrs prepared to die for their cause.[40] He looks in particular at the case of the Wigtown Martyrs, Margaret Wilson and Margaret McLachlan, who, legend has it, were tied to stakes between the high and low water mark and drowned when they refused to abjure.[41] Wilson's gravestone in Wigtown churchyard and monuments to the martyrs as far afield as Stirling and Toronto attest to the executions despite strong historical evidence against them ever having taken place.[42] The 'people's history', derived from oral accounts, was committed to print by, among others,

39 Ibid., p. 119.

40 E. J. Cowan, 'The Covenanting Tradition in Scottish History,' in E. J. Cowan & R. J. Finlay (eds), *Scottish History: The Power of the Past* (Edinburgh, 2002) pp. 121–145.

41 Ibid., p. 132.

42 Ibid., p. 137.

Rev. Robert Wodrow some thirty years after the events, and countered propagandist pamphlets which showed the Covenanters in a poor light.[43] Although the case represents an example of ongoing tension between oral tradition and documented corroboration it would be an oversimplification to suggest that it represents a dichotomy between elite and popular culture. Historical dispute about the incident continued. In the nineteenth century Mark Napier was only the most passionate in his condemnation, not only of Wodrow, but also of Thomas Babington Macaulay – calling them 'two of History's most "incorrigible calumniators"' – for perpetuating the martyr legend.[44] Using historical evidence in the form of legal precedent and parallels he engaged with his contemporaries in a robust and convincing defence of the Crown against the execution of the Wigtown Martyrs.[45] The persecutions also attracted the attention of nineteenth-century Romantic writers such as Sir Walter Scott and James Hogg who added their own gloss to events. Scott, his head perhaps turned by the dashing, cavalier images of their persecutor, John Claverhouse of Dundee, condemned the Covenanters in *Old Mortality*. However, after that work had received an anonymous review (its author was in fact Thomas McCrie) accusing the writer of 'violating both truth and probability,' Scott's later output was more sympathetic to the Covenanters' cause.[46] What is clear is that the Covenanting tradition is robust and what has come down to the present is a mix of oral tradition, historical

43 R. Wodrow, *The History of the Suffering of the Church of Scotland,* 4 Vols. (Glasgow, 1721–2 (1823)) Vol. I, pp. xxvii–xlii; cited in Cowan, 'The Covenanting Tradition,' p. 127. See also John Howie, *The Scots Worthies, Containing a Brief Historical Account of the Most Eminent Noblemen, Gentlemen, Ministers, and Others Who Testified or Suffered for the Cause of Reformation in Scotland, from the Beginning of the Sixteenth Century, to the Year 1688* (Glasgow, 1775 (1845)).

44 Cowan, 'The Covenanting Tradition,' p. 129.

45 M. Napier, *Memorials and Letters Illustrative of the Life and Times of John Graham of Claverhouse, Viscount Dundee*, 3 Vols. (Edinburgh, 1862), Vol. I pp. 145, 148, 155; Vol. II, pp. 43, 59, cited in Cowan, 'The Covenanting Tradition,' pp. 133–137.

46 [Thomas McCrie], *A Vindication of the Scottish Covenanters: Consisting of A Review of the First Series of the 'Tales of My Landlord,' Extracted from the Christian Instructor for 1817* (Glasgow, 1824), pp. 4, 33–34, cited in Cowan, 'The Covenanting Tradition,'

events and literary romance based on the world-view of reporters from different times. It also highlights the complex interrelation between folk tradition and elite culture and demonstrates that any account of the past that chooses to ignore that relationship is imbalanced.

The relationship between folk tradition and elite culture in the history of Scotland has been explored in the context of examinations of ballad texts from a historical perspective. Seen as the preserve of folklorists and literary critics, they have been currently overlooked by historians according to Cowan, because '[r]ecord-thirled historiography has scant regard for oral or popular tradition.'[47] Ballad texts, he argues, are worthy of study for their historical content because it is possible they have preserved events of local significance that have otherwise been lost.[48] Charles Duffin points out that this is not to suggest we will find objective historical 'truths' but 'we could expect to find the kind of culture-bound "truths" that emphasise group consciousness and cement the world-view of a traditional, oral community.'[49] However, ballads, he laments, are no longer passed down by word of mouth so they cannot be subjected to the authority and democratic criticism of the singer's audience. It was this, he argues, that formerly ensured the historical integrity of the message, irrespective of artistic merit. Instead, ballads have become fixed in literary texts where they have been subjected to the editorial refinements of the writer.[50] Oral tradition no longer mediates its own history; collectors and writers have intervened and placed themselves as arbiters between the ballad singer and audience. Despite this, Lizanne Henderson argues that ballads remain a valuable historical source for the investigation of

---

p. 139. See W. Scott, *The Bride of Lammermuir* and 'Wandering Willie's Tale' in *Redgauntlet* for examples of Scott's sympathetic treatment of the Covenanters.

47 E. J. Cowan (ed.), *The Ballad in Scottish History* (East Linton, 2000), p. 1.

48 Ibid., p. 11.

49 C. Duffin, 'Fixing Tradition: Making History from Ballad Texts,' in E. J. Cowan (ed.), *The Ballad in Scottish History*, pp. 19–35. p. 21.

50 Ibid., pp. 20–21.

fairy belief as they can contain factual and emotional truths not otherwise found in the records.[51]

Elsewhere, Henderson and Cowan investigate the nature of Scottish fairy belief from the fifteenth to the nineteenth centuries. Their study overlaps in so many ways with the present area of interest in that it discusses belief in witchcraft and second sight and touches on some similar issues and some of the same personalities. They are not concerned to prove or disprove the existence of fairies but what their study does show is that from the mid-fifteenth to the mid-eighteenth centuries many Scots believed that fairies were real.[52] Belief, as they point out 'is not the easiest of subjects to study,' because it forms part of a person's mental world and may be expressed through the spoken or written word and then perhaps through the mediation of others.[53] Cowan and Henderson point out that testimonies from witch trials are essential to their study as they seek to hear the voices of witches through the mediating language of their persecutors. Only when their voices cease to be trivialised is it possible to hear what the witches believed and recognise that this included belief in fairies who were thought to be 'guid neighbours' from a supernatural world with whom it was possible to interact. They had human characteristics and so could be good as well as bad. This belief became demonised under the witch prosecutions instigated by King James VI whose slim volume *Daemonologie*, published in 1597, helped the elite and the pious suppress the beliefs and practices of the majority and give greater worth to the cultural beliefs of an elite minority.[54] By redefining fairies as hallucinatory agents inspired by the Devil to do his work, the elites ensured that all who believed in them were at risk of prosecution.[55]

51 L. Henderson, 'The Road to Elfland: Fairy Belief and the Child Ballads,' in E. J. Cowan (ed.), *The Ballad in Scottish History*, pp. 54–69. p. 69.

52 L. Henderson & E. J. Cowan, *Scottish Fairy Belief: A History* (East Linton, 2001). pp. 2 and 12.

53 Ibid., p. 3.

54 Ibid., pp. 106–107.

55 Ibid., p. 138.

Despite the attack on folk culture, learned men of the late seventeenth century believed in the existence of fairies. Rev. Robert Kirk believed in, and wrote extensively and authoritatively about, a distinct order of God-created beings living in a subterranean world, generally invisible but with whom 'seers or men of the second sight have verie terrifying encounters.'[56] Kirk's account stands as a bulwark against the advancing Age of Reason and shows that the elite minority was not homogenous; believers in fairies could still be found among their ranks. It need hardly be said that Romantic writers such as Scott and Hogg seized on fairy lore to nourish their art, although Scott, late in life, observed that men of breeding could no longer sustain such beliefs which had been 'banished to the cottage and the nursery.'[57] Judging by the practice of leaving cloth offerings at Doon Hill, Aberfoyle, where Kirk died, fairy belief, with or without men of breeding, continues to the present day.[58] For good measure, as Cowan and Henderson point out elsewhere, belief in witches has also persisted through the twentieth century among the 'peasantry' and the 'educated.'[59] These various works in Scottish popular culture show the difficulties of treating elite and popular culture as dichotomous entities. They parallel the present work on the legend of the Brahan Seer and provide a context in which it can be viewed.

56 R. Kirk, 'The Secret Commonwealth: Or a Treatise Displaying the Chief Curiosities Among the People of Scotland as They Are In Use to This Day, 1692' in M. Hunter, *The Occult Laboratory: Magic, Science and Second Sight in Late 17th-century Scotland* (Woodbridge, 2001), 77–106. p. 79.

57 J. Hogg, *The Three Perils of Man: War, Women and Witchcraft*, D. Gifford (ed.), Edinburgh, 1996), p. xvii, cited in Henderson & Cowan, *Scottish Fairy Belief*, p. 198.

58 L. Henderson & E. J. Cowan, *Scottish Fairy Belief*, p. 214.

59 E. J. Cowan & L. Henderson, 'The Last of the Witches? The Survival of Scottish Witch Belief,' in J. Goodare (ed.), *The Scottish Witch-hunt in Context* (Manchester, 2002) pp. 198–217. p. 217.

CHAPTER 2

The Fowlis Affair and the 'Real' Coinneach Odhar?

Introduction

The origin of the Brahan Seer legend can be traced to events that took place in and around Easter Ross in the vicinity of Inverness during the last quarter of the sixteenth century. An examination of the historical records from the time provides documentary evidence for the existence of a Coinneach Odhar. He is named in state papers dealing with witchcraft trials in 1577 and 1578, and Inverness Burgh Court records of 1576. These are the only official records so far traced which bear his name and show that he did not live in the latter half of the seventeenth century as the Brahan Seer legend relates. This suggests that there has been a temporal dislocation of the legend surrounding him, one of 'several respects,' according to William Matheson, in which Alexander Mackenzie's book *The Prophecies of the Brahan Seer* 'misrepresents Gaelic tradition.'[1]

Aside from the name of Coinneach Odhar the records reveal several key constituents of the legend that further point to its genesis in the sixteenth rather than the seventeenth century. These include the involvement of a woman from the most powerful family in the region; the burning of witches at Chanonry of Fortrose; and the use of magical stones. Matheson has noted some of these similarities but this chapter examines the Fowlis affair more closely as it considers the politics of witchcraft that provided the immediate context for Coinneach Odhar's appearance in official records. In so doing it seeks to shed further insight

1 Wm. Matheson, 'The Historical Coinneach Odhar and Some Prophecies Attributed to Him' in TGSI Vol. 46 (1968), pp. 66–88, p. 86.

into Scottish witchcraft in this period. The chapter engages with King James VI's knowledge and early interest in witchcraft, the involvement of the church, the devil's pact as popular belief, and witches' identities and networks.

The events in Easter Ross took place at a time when the young King James VI was emerging from rule by regency and anxious to exert personal control over a kingdom riven by religious division and lawlessness and when church and state were vying for control over the moral conduct of the people.[2] Historians generally agree that witchcraft played an integral part in this struggle, though there are different emphases. P. G. Maxwell-Stuart argues that initially there was no sign of any intention on the part of the king to prosecute witches and applies this same relaxed attitude to the Kirk.[3] On the other hand Jenny Wormald speculates that the inspiration for pursuing the Easter Ross witches must have been initiated by local authority in the shape of the 'watchful, worried and very devil-conscious body, the Kirk.'[4] This chapter contends that there was minimal church involvement in the pursuit of the Easter Ross witches and that they were prosecuted on the insistence of local lairds. Witches found guilty by a local assize were executed by burning as the law demanded. Most executions took place at the Chanonry of Fortrose on the Black Isle where, according to legend, the Brahan Seer met just such a fate.

The incidents of witchcraft in Easter Ross took place before King James's departure for Oslo where he married marry Anna of Denmark on 23 November 1589 before going on to Elsinore.[5] The visit was thought to have prompted James's interest in continental demonology because it was

2 P. G. Maxwell-Stuart, *Satan's Conspiracy: Magic and Witchcraft in Sixteenth-Century Scotland* (East Lothian, 2001), pp. 88–89.

3 Maxwell-Stuart, *Satan's Conspiracy*, p. 143 and 143n.

4 J. Wormald, 'The Witches, the Devil and the King,' in Terry Brotherstone and David Ditchburn (eds), *Freedom and Authority: Scotland c1050 – c1650* (East Lothian, 2000), pp. 165–180. p. 173.

5 CSP Vol. X (1589–93), p. 179 and 479. L. Normand and G. Roberts (eds), *Witchcraft in Early Modern Scotland: James VI's Demonology and the North Berwick Witches* (Exeter, 2000), p. 34.

only after this time that charges against witches began to include accusations of witches' Sabbaths and pacts with the devil.[6] Maxwell-Stuart has found no evidence that the king discussed demonology during his visit and has suggested that educated men in Scotland were already engaged in this study.[7] Lawrence Normand and Gareth Roberts suggest that the king would have been unable to persuade them 'to accept those ideas if there was not already some knowledge of them, and if they did not fit into existing beliefs about witchcraft, however vague or undefined.'[8] Notwithstanding this argument, the king's relationship to the concern with witchcraft is usually still presented as falling into three distinct phases; a period when he was uninterested, a period when he was very interested and a period of declining interest in the years leading up to his move to England as king of Great Britain in 1603.[9]

Part of the reason suggested for the king's apparent early disinterest in witchcraft is that he had no meaningful personal experience other than seeing it presented as the object of black humour in a lengthy flyting poem.[10] The catalyst for his changed perception, it is argued, was the threat to his person posed by the North Berwick witches who were accused of raising the storms which imperilled him and his new queen on their return from Denmark.[11] James examined the witches in 1589/90 and while Wormald argues that the king was influenced by his visit to the continent, Maxwell-Stuart suggests that his early 'intermittent curiosity'

6 C. Larner, *Witchcraft and Religion* (Oxford, 1984), p. 5. S. Clark, 'King James's Daemonologie: Witchcraft and Kingship in S. Anglo (ed.), *The Damned Art* (London, 1977), p. 157. J. Simpson, '"The Weird Sisters Wandering": Burlesque Witchery in Montgomerie's *Flyting*', in *Folklore* 106 (1995), pp. 9–20. p. 17. Wormald, 'The Witches, the Devil and the King,' p. 166.

7 P. G. Maxwell-Stuart, 'The Fear of the King is Death: James VI and the Witches of East Lothian,' in W. G. Naphy and P. Roberts (eds), *Fear in early Modern Society* (Manchester and New York, 1997), pp. 209–225. pp. 211–213.

8 Normand and Roberts (eds), *Witchcraft in Early Modern Scotland*, p. 35.

9 Larner, *Witchcraft and Religion*, pp. 5, 8–15. Clark, 'King James's Daemonologie,' p. 157. P. G. Maxwell-Stuart, *Satan's Conspiracy*, p. 143.

10 Simpson, "The Weird Sisters Wandering," p. 17.

11 Maxwell-Stuart, 'The Fear of the King is Death,' pp. 209–210.

in witchcraft was derived from purely Scottish sources. Wormald and Maxwell-Stuart both agree, however, that the king's first meeting with a genuine witch took place in Aberdeen in 1589 when he there examined one of the Easter Ross witches out of nothing more than 'interested curiosity.'[12] This chapter argues that the king had first hand knowledge of the witchcraft in Easter Ross having presided over a Justiciary Aire held there in 1589, and that he personally influenced the course of events when he demanded the prosecution of a prime suspect after proceedings against her by lesser authority had been allowed to lapse. This significantly revises the chronology of the King's evolving interest in the subject.

Crucial to the pursuit of witches was the concept of the devil's pact. Maxwell-Stuart has shown that the devil's pact was known in Scotland prior to the king's continental visit. There is no evidence that it was introduced into the country by the king.[13] Continental theories of witchcraft included the pact, witches' Sabbaths and sexual orgies. After an examination of Aberdeenshire trials of 1596–97, Maxwell-Stuart suggests that witches contributed to their own fate by admitting to dancing round the major crosses of Aberdeen '[U]pon Hallowe'en last bypast, at twelve hours at even or thereby ... under the conduct and guiding of the Devil present with you.'[14] Although he does not argue the point, the inference is implicit that such practices were introduced into witchcraft by the witches themselves. Julian Goodare, in a critique of Maxwell-Stuart's essay, argues that references to the devil and witches' Sabbaths did not appear in the original testimony of witches but only after confessions had been prepared prior to their appearance in court. Since such confessions would not have been provided voluntarily, he argues that they must have been obtained under

12 Wormald, 'The Witches, the Devil and the King' pp. 171–172. Maxwell-Stuart, *Satan's Conspiracy*, p. 142.

13 Ibid., pp. 211–213.

14 P. G. Maxwell-Stuart, 'Witchcraft and the Kirk in Aberdeenshire, 1596–97.' *Northern Scotland: the Journal for the Centre of Scottish Studies*. Vol. 18 (1998), pp. 1–14. p. 4.

torture.[15] He musters evidence to show that the Hallowe'en dance had gone unseen by independent witnesses and concludes, therefore, that it did not happen. The notion of the devil, in this and other Aberdeenshire cases of the time, must have been implanted into the minds of the witches by their inquisitors.[16] However, the evidence from the Easter Ross trials show that witches were eminently capable of absorbing into their practices rituals and beliefs appropriated from cultures other than their own. The devil as master and advisor to at least one Easter Ross witch makes his first recorded appearance in January 1589 and there is no evidence to suggest that this was other than because the witch perceived him as such.[17] Only after the risk to the King's own life posed by the North Berwick witches, does the devil's pact feature as a central plank in royal policy towards witchcraft with the implication that the notion was borrowed from witches and then used against them, demonstrating that elite' and 'popular' culture were inter-mixed and related.

The records of the Easter Ross trials challenge, finally, the notion of a stereotypical Scottish witch who, like her English counterpart, is often perceived as 'an old, poor woman who lived alone.'[18] Witchcraft was endemic in the region. There existed a community of witches, many of whom had close family ties. They included several men and were drawn from the whole social and generational spectrum.[19] Witches met regularly, engaged in group activities and drew upon the expertise of fellow witches when the need arose. Their expertise was called upon by rich and

15 J. Goodare, 'The Aberdeen Witchcraft Panic of 1597.' *Northern Scotland: the Journal for the Centre of Scottish Studies.* Vol. 21 (2001), pp. 17–37.

16 Goodare, 'The Aberdeen Witchcraft Panic,' pp. 19, 23, 24 and 28.

17 R. Pitcairn (ed.), *Ancient Criminal Trials in Scotland* Vol. I, Part II (Edinburgh, 1833), p. 203.

18 J. Goodare, 'Women and the Witch-hunt in Scotland,' *Social History* Vol. 23. No. 3 (1998), pp. 288–308. H. V. McLachlan and J. K. Swales, 'Stereotypes and Scottish Witchcraft.' Contemporary Review Vol. 234. part 1357 (1979), pp. 88–94. Keith Thomas writes of English witches that 'at her most malevolent [she] was an isolated individual'. K. Thomas, *Religion and the Decline of Magic* (London, 1973), p. 627.

19 R. J. Adam (ed.), *Calendar of Fearn* (Edinburgh, 1991), pp. 135–136. Pitcairn, *Trials*, p. 203.

poor alike. Many, including educated lairds, shared belief in the efficacy of their practices. They were, in effect, the embodiment of the intersection of 'elite' and 'popular' culture. The Easter Ross witchcraft trials introduce the historical Coinneach Odhar and it is very likely that his activities – and those of his associates – and the events depicted are the provenance of the Brahan Seer legend.

The Fowlis trials: witchcraft practice and belief

On 22 July 1590 two separate trials involving charges of witchcraft were held before Justiciary Aires in Tain, a small coastal Royal Burgh some thirty-five miles to the north of Inverness.[20] They were the culmination of events, spanning a period of some fourteen years, which occurred in and around Easter Ross and the Black Isle. The first trial involved Katherene Ross, Lady Munro of Fowlis, the second trial her stepson, Hector Munro of Fowlis. Katherene was the daughter of Alexander Ross of Balnagown. She became the second wife of Robert Mor (elder) Munro of Fowlis, contracting to marry him while his first wife was still alive.[21] From his first marriage Robert Mor had two surviving sons, Robert (younger) and Hector, who, as the younger son, trained for the church.[22] After studying at St Andrews University he was appointed chaplain at Obsdale in 1570 and was Dean of Ross from May 1583 to August 1589.[23]

By his marriage to Katherene, Robert Mor had seven children.[24] Under the terms of the contract he agreed to invest male heirs with title

20 Pitcairn, *Trials*, pp. 192–204. Adam, *Fearn*, p. 144.

21 R. W. Munro (ed.), *The Munro Tree (1734): A Genealogy and Chronology of the Munros of Fowlis* (Edinburgh, 1978). p. 17 and Notes on the text R.

22 Munro, *Tree*, p. 19 and Note S. p. 19 and R/39 and p. 17 and R/1. C. T. McInnes (ed.), *Calendar of Writs of Munro of Foulis* (Edinburgh, 1940), No 77.

23 Munro, *Tree,* Note S.

24 Munro, *Tree*, pp. 17 and Note R/3; 18 and R/23; R/24 and R/39.

to any lands he bought during his wife's lifetime but despite their union having 'been perfected' by the arrival of a lawful son, George, he failed to abide by the terms of the contract.[25] Katherene's alleged response can be gauged by the evidence which came to light during her trial. Her prosecutors were Mr David McGill the King's Advocate and her stepson Hector. The dittay accuses her 'of unnaturally abusing yourself, contrary to the laws of God, and exercising and using yourself most ungodly and wickedly, by perverted Inchanmentis, Wichcraft, Develrie, Incantatiounis and Sorcerie, with the craft of poysoun in manner underwritten ... against Robert Monro, heir apparent of Fowlis, and Marjory Campbell, spouse to George Ross heir of Balnagown, at the times and places specified, in company with Christine Ross Malcolmson, and others hereafter specified ... '[26] George Ross, heir of Balnagown, was Lady Fowlis's brother. Her alleged plan was to dispose of those Munros who stood in the way of her son (also George) and to dispose of young Lady Balnagown so that her brother would be free to marry the widow of Robert, younger.[27]

Lady Fowlis faced a total of twenty-nine charges, most of them derived from the confessions of less fortunate co-conspirators who had already been convicted. The earliest event with which she was charged and which may reflect her initial involvement in witchcraft is that, in midsummer, 1576, she arranged for Agnes Roy, 'ane of the Vichis,' to fetch Marion McKane McAllister alias Laskie Loncart to speak with her.[28] Laskie Loncart's advice that Lady Fowlis should go to the Hills to speak

25 McInnes, *Calendar of Writs*, No 100.

26 Pitcairn, *Trials*, p. 192.

27 According to Alex Mackenzie, Robert had had several wives, some of whom had died within a few months of marriage and one of whom had died on the eve of her wedding. At the time of the plot his wife was most likely Marjory, from the Mackenzies of Kintail, forebears of the Seaforths. A. Mackenzie, *History of the Munros of Fowlis* (Inverness, 1898), p. 60. However, her name suggests she was from the Campbells of Cawdor, a family with whom the Munros were on good terms.

28 Pitcairn, *Trials*, p. 196. The Gaelic *Losgadh-lùchairt* may be translated as 'burn the castle' a nickname very probably endowed following her involvement in some prior escapade. Matheson, 'The Historical Coinneach Odhar,' p. 69.

to the 'elf folk' would have been meant literally, confirming a belief in the fairy world as a source of knowledge and inspiration.[29] The plotters made continued use of flint arrows from antiquity. Known as elf-shot, they were believed to be influenced by malicious fairies and were fired at clay images – *corp creadha* – the plotters thinking that if these were hit their intended victims would be destroyed.[30]

However, Lady Fowlis was too pragmatic to rely on supernatural agencies alone. She was accused of giving William MacGillivrey five ells of linen cloth for a consignment of poison in September 1576. She ordered him to consult the Gypsies on what would be her best course of action and possibly as a result of their advice he travelled to Elgin in the following spring to buy rat poison from an Aberdeen merchant. William also bought poison in Tain and delivered it to Lady Fowlis at the house of a relative, William Munro of Culcraigie. Present when William delivered the poison was a kinswoman of Lady Fowlis, also named Katherine Ross, daughter of Sir David Ross of Balnagown. She prominently assisted at several of the clandestine meetings.[31] Her servant, Agnes Ross, was also implicated.

According to the dittay the plotters used as a base Christine Ross Malcolmson's house in Tain. Although men and women stayed overnight on a number of occasions, there is no allusion to sexual malpractice in any of the charges faced by Lady Fowlis or her conspirators. One visitor in midsummer, 1577, was John McNilland from Dingwall to whom Lady Fowlis paid four shillings for an elf arrowhead.[32] This was required by Laskie Loncart, who, in collaboration with Christine, Gradache Malcolmson and Agnes Roy fired it at pictures of clay in the likeness of young Lady Balnagown and the young Laird of Fowlis. The plotters also devised a secret hand grip and password to be given only to those who were privy

29 Pitcairn, *Trials*, p. 196. See also Ann Gregory, 'Witchcraft, Politics and "Good Neighbourhood" in Early Seventeenth-Century Rye,' *Past and Present* No. 133 (1991), pp. 31–69. pp. 35–39.

30 Pitcairn, *Trials*, p. 192 et seq.

31 Ibid., pp. 194–196.

32 Ibid., p. 194.

to their secrets.[33] Perhaps they were mimicking journeyman masons who are known to have used this form of greeting at the time in Germany and France. In all likelihood it was being used by their Scottish brethren.[34] The witches' efforts failed and they held a further meeting on 2 July 1577 with reinforcements to their cause. Among those present was Thomas McKane More McAllan McEuoch (or McHenrick) alias Cassindonisch.[35] Under the guidance of Donald and William MacGillivrey they made a picture of butter in the likeness of young Robert Munro. Laskie Loncart fired at it eight times without success. The same conspirators tried again on the morning of 6 July 1577. They reshaped the picture several times with no better results. Christine had provided a quantity of fine linen cloth. Had the picture been hit, it would have been bound in the cloth and buried, as the ritual required, opposite the gate to the Fowlis property.[36]

It was alleged that in August 1577 Lady Fowlis was with Christine and Thomas Cassindonisch in a drying barn at Drumnyne during Fraser of Lovat's *comoning* (a quasi-regal visitation by one chief or laird upon his neighbours). When asked by two men named Mackenzie what they were doing there, she replied that this was her best chance of success, for young Lady Balnagown was in the barn with them. No explanation is given for her presence.[37] That Lady Fowlis should voice her intentions to strangers is inexplicable. There was already tension in the air. This particular *comoning* was to introduce the young Fraser of Lovat who had recently succeeded his father. Several Mackenzies had objected that his entourage had strayed into their territory, and by implication were laying claim to it, while marching round the bounds of his lands. The intervention of

33 Ibid., p. 197.

34 D. Stevenson, *The Origins of Freemasonry: Scotland's Century, 1590–1710* (Cambridge, 1988), pp. 18 and 19.

35 *Cas-an-donais* is Gaelic for 'devil's foot' and may refer to some physical impediment. Matheson, 'The Historical Coinneach Odhar,' p. 70.

36 Pitcairn, *Trials*, p. 199.

37 Ibid., p. 195.

Lady Fowlis's husband and a party of armed Munros was required to diffuse the situation.[38]

Lady Fowlis's brother, George Ross, was reported to have taken part in a meeting in a barn at Drumnyne on 24 August 1577. It may have been the same meeting as took place during the *comoning*. He urged Thomas Cassindonisch to pursue the destruction of his wife and young Robert Monro, promising him a suit of clothes for his labours. George is described as standing with his back to the door, and holding a wand in his hand while he addressed Thomas. It is not clear if any significance can be attached to his position in the room but several male witches used a wand to assist in their rituals and it is generally reported as being used by the person with most authority.[39]

All through the late summer and autumn meetings were held at Christine's house in Tain or in Culcraigie's parlour. 'Christine Miller, daughter to Robert Miller, smith in Assynt,' received payment of a half firlot of meal on one occasion, after haggling over the cost of her services.[40] The sheer length of time the plotters had been at work, the large numbers of witches involved, their numerous indiscretions in front of innocent servants, identifiable tradespeople and other witnesses, some of whom must have been hostile, meant that their conspiracy was an open secret. The king granted a commission, dated 25 October 1577, authorising Robert Mor Munro to investigate and try the witches involved.[41] It is not known how long it took to gather evidence or how long the commission

38 J. Fraser, *Chronicles of the Frasers: The Wardlaw Manuscript etc., 916–1674* (Edinburgh, 1905), pp. 178–180.

39 See the case of John Stewart in Irvine in 1618. W. Scott, *Demonology and Witchcraft* (London, 1868), p. 159. RPC Vol. XI, pp. cxxxix–cxli. See also the case of John Cunningham alias Doctor Fian in *Newes from Scotland* in Pitcairn, *Trials*, Vol. I part II, pp. 221–222, where his report of the devil breaking his wand is reminiscent of the ritual of the king's messenger breaking his symbol of office, his Wand of Peace, if prevented from going about his lawful duties.

40 Pitcairn, *Trials*, p. 198.

41 NAS, Ref.: E1/7 fol. 67(v)–68(r). Exchequer Rolls of Scotland (ERS) Vol. XX (1568–1579) (Edinburgh, 1899), pp. 522–523.

took to prepare. It certainly did not take long to reach Easter Ross and certainly was acted quickly upon once it arrived.

Even as it was being sent north Lady Fowlis persisted with the ritual of firing elf arrows at clay effigies but when these accidentally broke she asked Laskie Loncart to concoct a poisoned drink to be made for best effect at Hallowe'en. This was added to a pail of ale. When this leaked, Lady Fowlis made Donald McKay, her servant lad, taste the residue. He became sick but survived. Lady Fowlis instructed Laskie Loncart to make stronger poison which was delivered to her in a jug. This was in turn sent to Robert, younger, the unwitting messenger being Lady Fowlis's nurse, Marie. Travelling under cover of darkness, she dropped and broke the jug. Innocently, she tasted the poison and immediately died. Although the poison was intended for her stepson, Lady Fowlis was accused of the murder of her own nurse.[42]

Beset by this failure, Lady Fowlis bribed her brother's cook to mix rat poison with part of an evening meal at the home of young Lady Balnagown. One of the conspirators, Katherene Neynday, who delivered the poison, witnessed the vomiting and distress that overcame the lady and her guests. The legal response was swift and severe. On 24 November 1577, Christine Ross Malcolmson confessed to her involvement, being accused in the presence of Mr Martin Logie, notary public, and five (named) witnesses. On 28 November 1577, she appeared before Walter Urquhart and Robert Mor Munro, in a Justice Court held within the Cathedral Kirk of Ross, confessed again, was convicted by a jury, and burnt.[43] William MacGillivrey and Gradoche Malcolmson were 'brunt' on the same day.[44] Before they were led to the stake George Ross and his father, Sir Alexander Ross of Balnagown, obtained point-of-death statements from William and Gradoche in which they confirmed in front of witnesses and a notary public that neither man had been involved in witchcraft. The witches provided the statements because they were about to die and took it upon

42 Pitcairn, *Trials*, p. 194.

43 Ibid., pp. 197, 193.

44 Ibid., p. 195. Adam, *Fearn*, pp. 135–136. Named as [blank] Nyne Gillecallum Garrowe but identified as Gradoche from October 1577 commission.

themselves to tell the truth before God.[45] There is no evidence of any other motivating factor. Of the fifteen men who witnessed this 'declaration in the name of Balnagowyn' only the last three signatories held positions in the church.[46] They also acted as burgh clerk or schoolmaster, so it may be in these civil capacities that they were involved.

According to testimony, Lady Fowlis did not leave her remaining conspirators to the mercy of their pursuers. She arranged for Thomas Cassindonisch and others to be hidden and looked after in Christine Ross Malcolmson's house. They were discovered. Thomas, being accused, confessed, was convicted, and '*suffered the deid*', the sentence being carried out at Dingwall some time in December 1577.[47] According to *The Calendar of Fearn*, in the same month and year nine witches were burnt at the Chanonry of Ross.[48] It is likely that this number comprises the totality of those killed there. Thinking that her accomplices would implicate her, Lady Fowlis declared before two notaries public that although publicly maligned with witchcraft and sorcery nobody had formally accused her. She was prepared to defend herself in court if they did but instead of appearing before a judge she fled to Caithness. There she stayed for nine months until, after the intercession of George, Earl of Caithness, her husband was persuaded to take her home again.[49] Whatever agreement was reached in her absence, Lady Fowlis seemed safe from prosecution, at least for the time being.

Despite the executions that had taken place, Hector Munro, Lady Fowlis's stepson, was implicated in witchcraft some years later. The incumbent Dean of Ross was acting with the best of intentions; he was seeking a cure for his sick elder brother, Robert. It was alleged that in August 1588 he sent for John McConeill-gar and his wife, and John Bane's wife

45 Adam, *Fearn*, p. 135.

46 Ibid., p. 136.

47 Pitcairn, *Trials*, p. 199. Adam, *Fearn*, p. 135. The year is given as 1578. Walter Urquhart is described as 'Sheriff of Cromartie, at that time' suggesting the document was written after the event.

48 Adam, *Fearn*, p. 135.

49 Pitcairn, *Trials*, p. 200.

and sought their advice. The witches cast spells using hair cut from his brother's head and nail clippings from his fingers and toes.[50] They told Hector he had delayed too long in sending for them, as they could do nothing to help Robert who died later that same month. The witches were so afraid that Hector's father would arrest them that he had to organise their escape in the night. When Hector again turned to witchcraft, this time to cure his own illness, neither he nor the witches had anything to fear from Robert Mor who died on 4 November 1588.[51] His father and elder brother both being dead, Hector Munro succeeded to the title.[52]

When Hector took ill in January 1589, he allegedly sent his manservant to look for Marion McIgaruch, 'ane of the maist notorious and rank Wichis in all this realme.'[53] She was conveyed to a house in Alness where Hector was being tended by his wet-nurse, Christine Neill Dalziel, and her daughter. There he sought advice from Marion, hoping to be cured by her spells and witchcraft. She gave him three drinks of water from three stones she carried; and after lengthy deliberation declared that the only way to recover his health was if 'the principal man of his blood' should die in his place.[54] Having considered who this should be, Hector and his accomplices decided that it was his half-brother, George.

Although some of Hector's friends came to see how he was getting on, he and Marion agreed that nobody should be allowed into the house until George arrived. To be certain that George should be the first to see him he sent daily requests that he come and when George answered the summons Hector placed his left hand in George's right hand, as he had been instructed, and did not speak to him for an hour other than

50 Ibid., p. 201.

51 Munro, *Tree*, Note R. Mackenzie, *History of Munros*, also has Robert Mor dying on 4 November 1588 but he has Robert younger succeed his father and die in July 1589 (p. 60–62). The events and dates of the charges against Hector Munro support the date of Robert younger's death as being August 1588, the date given in *Fearn*, p. 141.

52 Munro, *Tree*, Note S and Mackenzie, *History of Munros*, p. 62.

53 Pitcairn, *Trials*, p. 201.

54 Ibid., p. 202.

to answer questions about his health. According to the charges, this was the prelude to a more elaborate ceremony. At one o'clock next morning Marion left the house with accomplices, including some of Hector's servants. Carrying spades, they went to a piece of ground lying at the boundaries of two superiors' lands near the high tide mark where they dug a grave of Hector's length. When they returned to the house Marion explained each one's part in the coming ceremony and what would be the outcome. Several were afraid that if George should die suddenly then a hue and cry would erupt and their lives would be in danger. They urged Marion to delay George's death and she agreed to protect him until 17 April '*nixt thaireftir*' (next but one).[55]

Reassured, Hector's servants put him in a pair of blankets and under Marion's supervision carried him to the grave. Everybody involved was told to remain silent, 'vnto the tyme that [Marion] and [Hector's] foster-moder sould first speik with hir maister, the Dewill.'[56] Hector was placed in the grave; the green turfs were laid on top and held down with staves. Marion remained beside him while Christine Neill, who had her young son with her, was ordered to run the breadth of nine rigs. When she returned to the graveside she asked Marion, 'Which was her choice?' She replied that 'Mr Hector was her choice to live, and his brother to die for him.'[57] This ritual was performed three times after which Hector was carried home in complete silence and put to bed. He celebrated his recovery by taking 'Marioune the Witch' to the house of a paternal uncle where he entertained her as if she were his wife. He then placed her in such favour that she was the lady of Fowlis in everything but name. The flaunting of Hector's consort and the bewitching of George, however ineffectual it may have seemed at the time, intensified the bitterness between stepmother and stepson.

Whatever other legacy Robert Mor had left his wife he had certainly provided for her *teirce,* the income for life (liferent) of one third of his

55 Ibid., p. 203.
56 Ibid.
57 Ibid.

heritable estate to which she was entitled by law.[58] Hector tried to deprive her of part of this by first threatening her tenants with violence and when this failed he purchased a commission against Lady Fowlis and the *spouses* of her tenants, charging them with witchcraft (emphasis added).[59] By a complaint brought before the Privy Council on 4 June 1589, Lady Fowlis and four (named) women strenuously denied the allegations and sought to have the commission discharged. Hector was ordered to desist from proceeding against the women until such time as the case could be heard 'in the nixt justice courtis appointit to be haldin eftir his Majesteis repairing to the north pairtis of this realme in the moneth of Julii nixt.'[60]

The involvement of King James VI

The purpose of the king's visit to the north was to stamp out lawlessness: to demonstrate his dissatisfaction with, and to speed up, the legal process.[61] His visit had been long planned. On 11 October 1587, he had issued a proclamation from Holyroodhouse announcing that he intended to travel throughout the country to hold Justiciary Courts over which he would preside in person. He was scheduled to be at Cromarty some time around 13 February 1588.[62] The trip was postponed due to an outbreak of plague in and around Leith.[63] Had he arrived on that date it is highly unlikely that Lady Fowlis would ever have come to trial for the events of a decade earlier. Her husband and Robert, younger, would still have

58 McInnes, *Calendar of Writs*, Nos. 111, 112 and 123.
59 RPC Vol. IV, pp. 392–393.
60 Ibid., p. 393.
61 RPC Vol. IV, pp. 217–219.
62 Ibid., p. 219. The month is missing from the records but February is most likely based on the timescale of the king's eventual itinerary, CSP Vol. X, p. 117.
63 RPC Vol. IV, p. 238.

been alive and it is only after this date that Hector Munro is known to have involved himself in witchcraft.

Although James was concerned about the high incidence of crime, the proclamation could be interpreted as an attack on Catholicism. He had been involved in a vigorous military campaign against the Catholic earls of Huntly and Errol and had only recently suppressed their rebellion in the northeast.[64] His major concern was curbing 'ydolatrie and mantenance thairof' which took precedence over the 'four pleas of the crown,' robbery, murder, rape and fire raising.[65] '[W]itchecraft or seikaris of responssis or help at witcheis' did not appear to be considered a serious issue, nor is there any reference to it being associated with a pact with the devil.[66] The brief description of witchcraft appears twenty-fifth on a comprehensive list behind such diverse crimes as the receiving and maintaining of Jesuits, injury to and slaughter of domestic animals, the making of and trafficking in false coin, and the failure of law officers to bring accused persons before the courts.

King James's long delayed trip to the north finally took place. He left Aberdeen on 9 July 1589, spent 16 July at Chanonry of Fortrose on judicial affairs and the next few days hunting 'the hart with hownds in a forest called Cromarty' before returning to Aberdeen on 28 July.[67] Among the king's retinue, which included the young Duke of Lennox, were members of the Privy Council; the Earls of Angus and Atholl, Thomas Lyon, Sir Robert Melvin, and the Justice Clerk, Sir Lewis Bellenden.[68] These men, together with the king, heard Hector's case against Lady Fowlis and her female tenants.

It was alleged that even before the publication of Hector's Commission, and before he had time to put it into effect (he was in the north on the king's behalf pursuing Catholic chiefs sympathetic to

64 CSP Vol. X, p. 102.

65 RPC Vol. IV, p. 217.

66 Ibid., p. 218.

67 CSP Vol. X, p. 115, letter from Thomas Fowler, English ambassador, to his superior, Sir Francis Walsingham. CSP Vol. X, p. 117, itinerary.

68 CSP Vol. X, pp. 115 and 372. RPC Vol. IV, pp. xxvii, 33, 293, 385 and 405.

Huntly), Lady Fowlis, knowing herself guilty, and afraid to stand trial, had used her influence to purchase a Suspension of the Commission. She had inserted into it, not only her own name, and those names specified in the Commission, but also other names which were not referred to. The Commission and Suspension were produced before the Privy Council and examined 'at mair lenthe.'[69]

During the enquiry Hector's own participation in witchcraft came to light. The records do not show if he was informed upon. However, he had to explain how he had been cured of his sickness and how the witch Marion had assisted in this by producing water from three magical stones.[70] When ordered to present Marion to the king he denied knowing where she was. Lady Fowlis insisted before the court that she was in his house. The king demanded Hector and Marion's attendance on his return to Aberdeen. Hector, against his will, was forced to take her there; where she was questioned by the king and demonstrated the stones. These were handed into the custody of Sir Lewis Bellenden, of whom it was later said that he died of fright when the devil was raised at his request by Richard Graham, one of the North Berwick witches, in his garden in the Canongate, Edinburgh.[71]

At this stage no legal action appears to have been taken against either Hector or Marion, presumably because the king and his Privy Councillors were satisfied that no harm had been done. However, the Privy Council left Hector in no doubt what they expected of him with regard to his stepmother. Whatever his claims against the property of Lady Fowlis and her tenants – the case appears to have been deserted – it seems clear that the King's intervention re-opened old issues. Lady Fowlis was pursued for her actions of 1576–78. While in Aberdeen, Hector received a caution, dated 1 August 1589, demanding that he prosecute Lady Fowlis to

69 Pitcairn, *Trials*, p. 200.

70 Ibid., p 203.

71 J. Scott, *Staggering State of the Scots Statesmen from 1550–1650* (Edinburgh, 1754), p. 48. Also cited in Chambers, *Domestic Annals*, Vol. I. p. 236 and RPC Vol. IV, p. 730. Bellenden died on 27 August 1591.

the utmost, 'without schift, excuse or delay.'[72] Further, she was placed in ward, with Hector appointed to administer her affairs.

The legal dispute was not allowed to go away. Lady Fowlis appeared before the Justiciary Court on 28 October 1589, when the case was adjourned.[73] Both parties appeared before the Privy Council in Edinburgh on 11 November 1589, in one of the first cases to be heard before the Duke of Lennox, newly appointed President of the Council.[74] Hector complained that his stepmother 'mynding still to hald the said Mr Hector in trouble' had obtained a caution in the sum of £2,000 that he would not harm her or her tenants.[75] He objected that this would cause financial hardship to his guarantor, John Campbell of Cawdor, the very risk he was supposed to accept, and begged to be excused from the need to continue paying Lady Fowlis's daily expenses. The Privy Council insisted that the order remain in force until such time as Lady Fowlis came to trial and declared that Hector would be put to the horn if he failed to comply.[76]

To further exacerbate the already fraught relationship between mother and stepson, Hector's half-brother, George took ill, very likely on 17 April 1590, since the dittay against Hector gives that specific date. He lingered until 3 June 1590.[77] Only then were charges brought against Hector. Lady Fowlis accused him of causing George's death through witchcraft and the magic stones were cited as the means.[78] Hector denied the charges. Contrary to law, the fifteen man jury at his trial was made up of his social inferiors, mostly burgesses from Tain, tenant farmers and

72 RPC Vol. IV, pp. 404–405.

73 Pitcairn, *Trials*, p. 185.

74 RPC Vol. IV, p. 433. The Duke of Lennox first appeared in the Privy Council on 23 October 1589. He was appointed President of the Council for the King's absence in Denmark. RPC Vol. IV, pp. 423–425 and xxvii. The King left for Denmark on 22 October 1589. RPC Vol. IV, p. 423.

75 RPC Vol. IV, p. 434.

76 RPC Vol. IV, pp. 431 and 434.

77 Pitcairn, *Trials*, p. 204. Munro, *Tree*, p. 17, Note R/3 gives the date of George's death as June 1589.

78 Pitcairn, *Trials*, p. 203.

the elder sons of small landowners, many of whom may have depended on Munro patronage for their welfare. They found Hector not guilty. For seven of the fifteen members of the jury it was their second stint in court, since earlier that same they had served on the jury that had sat through the more complex reading of the dittay against Lady Fowlis and being '*throuchlie resoluit*' on each point had declared her innocent of all charges.[79] There is no record of Hector's accomplices having been brought to trial. Despite his infatuation with Marion he had contracted to marry Anne Fraser, daughter of Lord Lovat, on 15 July 1590, a week before the trial.[80] His confidence in the outcome was not in doubt.

Thus ended the legal processes regarding the Fowlis affair. The extent to which James would have been familiar with the minutiae of the events is impossible to know. Among the opening charges against Lady Fowlis, drawn up in 1589 at the earliest, was that she engaged in 'Develrie' but this could simply mean evil doing. The only reference to the devil is Christine Ross Malcolmson's testimony that Lady Fowlis said she would do anything, by whatever means, 'of God in heaven or of the Devill in hell,' for the destruction of the young Lady Balnagown.[81] She appears to be invoking the help of whatever agency would bring her success. The confessions of the witches from the earlier trials of 1577 made up the main body of evidence against Lady Fowlis. They show a belief in magic which is linked to the supernatural. When witches in those trials sought advice from non-human sources they invoked entities from the fairy world rather than the devil. A decade later, however, when Hector was being buried in his mock grave (the ceremony itself a parody of the resurrection) Marion spoke to her master, the Devil.[82] The inclusion of the words 'her master' implies a pact; a master/servant relationship was a formal undertaking. Those bringing the charges may have used the words but the incident is not emphasised, nor does the devil's involvement form part of the formal charges against Hector. It appears to be an account of what happened as

79 Ibid., p. 200.

80 Munro, *Tree*, p. 19 and Note S.

81 Pitcairn, *Trials*, p. 195.

82 Ibid., p. 203.

described by someone taking part. At least one witch in Easter Ross had begun to consult the devil instead of fairies by the year 1589. By doing so she was replacing a traditional and long held belief in the efficacy of one form of supernatural power with another, a process described by Keith Thomas when explaining the decline of traditional beliefs in magic in the face of new ideology and technology.[83] The witch's knowledge of the devil, perverted or otherwise, could only have been derived from religious sources.[84] Whether or not King James knew of this detail, its inclusion suggests that the devil's pact was known to witches before it became the major charge in trials. This suggests that the notion was not imposed upon them by their elite inquisitors.

James appears to have remembered the case when he came to write his *Daemonologie*. Drawn from personal experiences, this book aimed to persuade sceptics that witches existed and to press for their punishment.[85] Although not published until 1597 it is thought to have been written in early 1591 as a response to James's exposure to the North Berwick witches, when the events associated with that affair were still fresh in his mind and could be recounted with considerable accuracy.[86] However, in Chapter V of Book II, Philomathes and the learned Epistemon fall into discourse regarding the actions of witches towards others. Epistemon expounds his thoughts on the devil's role as their master:

> EPI. To some others at these times hee teacheth, how to make Pictures of wax or clay: that by the rosting thereof, the persones that they bear the name of, may be continuallie melted or dryed awaie by continuall sickness. To some he gives such

83 Thomas, *Religion and the Decline of Magic*, pp. 767–800.

84 Gregory, 'Witchcraft, Politics and "Good Neighbourhood"' p. 34, where she writes of witch beliefs 'being a direct inversion' of a societies' values. She cites C. Larner, *Enemies of God: The Witch-Hunt in Scotland* (Oxford, 1983) where this 'anthropological truism' appears, p. 134.

85 P. G. Maxwell-Stuart, *Witchcraft in Europe and The New World, 1400–1800* (Basingstoke, 2001), p. 51. The same point is made in Normand and Roberts, *Witchcraft in Early Modern Scotland*, p. 332.

86 Maxwell-Stuart, *Witchcraft in Europe and The New World*, p 71. J. Craigie, *Minor Prose Works of King James VI & I* (Edinburgh, 1982), p. 110.

> stones or poulders, as will help to cure or cast on diseases: And to some he teacheth kindes of vncouthe poysons, which Mediciners vnderstandes not (for he is farre cunningner than man in the knowledge of all the occult properties of nature) not that anie of these meanes which hee teacheth them (except the poysons which are composed of things naturall) can of them selues helpe any thing to these turnes, that they are employed in...[87]

In this passage James provides a recognisable summary of the key witchcraft practices carried out not only in North Berwick but also in the Fowlis affair he had examined earlier. These include the use of clay pictures, magical healing stones and 'uncouthe poisons'. He believed that poisons worked by themselves through their natural properties which, though not fully understood even by doctors, were understood by the devil. However, other instruments of witchcraft did not work by themselves; they required the active participation of the devil. Reflecting on the use of clay pictures James concludes that the devil causes death by cunningly making his victims ill at the same time as the picture is melting.[88] By introducing the devil as master and participant James made the idea of a pact significant in 'elite' witchcraft ideology. The devil became an integral presence in all witchcraft cases and any tacit distinction between harmful and non-harmful witchcraft was ignored. The devil's pact is seen as an aspect of 'elite' discourse but is likely to have originated from so-called 'popular' practices such as those of the Easter Ross witches.

The historical Coinneach Odhar, leader of witches

The genesis of the Devil in Scottish government attitudes to witchcraft coincides with the genesis of the Brahan Seer legend in 'popular' culture. The Royal Commission issued in favour of Robert Munro of Fowlis,

87 Craigie, *Minor Prose*, p. 31.
88 Ibid., p. 32.

instructing him to pursue those responsible for trying to poison members if his family is dated 25 October 1577. It was issued from Holyroodhouse under the Quarter Seal, an administrative device which required the king's authority but not necessarily his full attention.[89] Written in Latin, it authorised Robert Mor and Walter Urquhart, Sheriff of Cromarty:

> conjointly and severally, to question, investigate, seize and arrest, one and all of the individuals undermentioned, suspected and exercising the diabolical, iniquitous, and odious crimes of the art of magic, incantation, murder, homicide, and other horrible crimes and sins, committed within the boundaries of the earldom of Ross and the Lordship of Ardmanach [The Black Isle] and other parts within the Sheriff's district of Inverness ...[90]

There follows the names of seven men and twenty-four women, drawn from every quarter of the region from Tain to Chanonry, from Dingwall to Nigg. The last named is 'Keanoch Owir, leader or principal "enchantress," to interrogate the same and to administer justice according to the laws of the Kingdom.'[91] This description has led at least one scholar to postulate that the scribe who drew up the document knew no Gaelic and did not know that 'Keanoch' was a man's name.[92] However, although in Latin the grammatical gender of 'enchantress' is feminine this does not refer to the biological gender of the person referred to.[93] Those pursuing Keanoch knew exactly who they were after; at no time was he thought to be a woman.

Several of those who feature in the dittay against Lady Fowlis head the list – namely: 'Thomas McAnemore McAllan McHenrik, alias Cassindonisch, William MacGillivrey in Daan, Donald (Mac)Gillivrey in Daan, Marion Neyne McAllester alias Laskie Loncart, Christine

89 J. Goodare, 'Witch-hunting and the Scottish State' in J. Goodare (ed.), *The Scottish Witch-hunt in Context* (Manchester, 2002), pp. 126–127.

90 NAS Ref.: E1/7 fol. 67(v)–68(r). ERS Vol. XX, pp. 522–523.

91 Ibid.

92 Matheson, 'The Historical Coinneach Odhar,' TGSI Vol. 46, p. 68.

93 Third declension nouns are mostly feminine: my thanks to Dr Frederik Pedersen of the Department of History, University of Aberdeen, for pointing this out.

Miller, daughter of Robert Miller, smith in Assynt, Cradoch Neynane McGillecallum (Gradoche Malcolmson), Christine McColinston (Christine Ross Malcolmson), Katherine Ross, daughter of (Sir) David Ross (of Balnagown), Agnes Ross, servant to the foresaid Katherine Ross, Agnes Roy in Nigg, John McNoullar (John McNilland from Dingwall).'[94] Neither Lady Fowlis nor her brother, George Ross, are named on the commission, nor is William Munro of Culcraigie. Only one of the women named is described as the wife of a (named) man; one, Ibbie Forbes, is described as a materfamilias. Fourteen are described as 'Neyne' or 'daughter of' suggesting that they are single, though this need not imply that they are still young. Lady Fowlis's namesake, Katherine Ross, may have been nearly sixty and very possibly of royal descent.[95] The Malcolmsons were mother and daughter. The MacGillivreys may have been brothers. To become notorious, as some are described, witches would have had to practice their arts relatively openly and for long enough to gain a reputation, it is highly likely that some of them had done so for a number of years. Witchcraft had been widely practised without apparent suppression by either law or clergy. The threat to the Munro family rendered this state of affairs intolerable.

What of the person described as leader and principal 'enchantress,' Keanoch Owir? Other than appearing on this and a later commission he is not mentioned in the surviving records of the Fowlis affair. The evidence that he was involved rests on his inclusion in the two commissions with named others who were involved, and on his description as leader. The records show that ten people were executed in November and December 1577. Of those named in the first commission Thomas Cassindonisch, William MacGillivrey, Gradoche Malcolmson, Christine Ross Malcolmson and Agnes Roy are known to have been among them.[96] Laskie Loncart, Christine Miller and Coinneach Odhar appear to have escaped the net. This would explain the need for a second commission

94 NAS Ref.: E1/7 fol. 67(v)–68(r). ERS Vol. XX, pp. 522–523.

95 Adam, *Fearn*, p. 95. J. B. Paul (ed.), *The Scots Peerage* (Edinburgh, 1904–1914) Vol. I, p. 153; Vol. IX, pp. 354, 361; Vol. IX, pp. 10, 103.

96 Pitcairn, *Trials*, pp. 193, 195, 197, 199. Adam, *Fearn*, p. 135.

issued on 23 January 1578, which names specifically 'Kenneth (Kennitum – no doubt about his gender here) Owir, principal or leader of the art of magic, Marion Neyne McAllester alias Laskie Loncart, and Marjory [sic] Miller, daughter of Robert Miller, blacksmith in Assynt, and all other men and women using and exercising the diabolical, iniquitous and odious crimes of the art of magic, sorcery and incantations, who shall be named by the ministers within the bounds foresaid, each for their own parish.'[97] The area of search was extended to 'other parts within the Sheriffdoms of Inverness, Elgin, Forres and Nairn' because the fugitives could not be found in their native haunts.

The search now included any person engaged in witchcraft. More barons were named as commissioners. The Fowlis affair had sparked a local witch-hunt. The naming of witches by ministers is the first clear reference to the involvement of the church as an institution and indicative of its subordinate role in their prosecution in this particular case. There is no record that any of those sought in the second commission were brought to justice nor that the witch-hunt led to further trials. If all other guilty parties had been convicted by 1578 it would not have been necessary for Lady Fowlis to insert into her Suspension of the 1589 Commission the names of those who were not then being pursued but whom she believed might still be at risk. It could not be to protect her brother and father, both still alive; they had been absolved by the point-of-death declarations of William MacGillivrey and Gradoche Malcolmson.[98]

Was Coinneach Odhar one of the names? The fact that he was identified as leader suggests that he held considerable powers within the witchcraft community and was recognised in this capacity by his pursuers. The name Odhar can be translated into English as dun coloured or sallow skinned. It has been suggested because of this that he was a gypsy.[99]

97 NAS: Ref.: GD 93/92. ERS Vol. XX, p. 525. The fugitive's name is rendered 'Kenneth *alias* Kennoch Owir, principal or leader of the art of magic,' in McInnes, *Calendar of Writs of Munro of Foulis*, No 92.

98 Adam, *Fearn*, pp. 180 and 150.

99 E. Sutherland, *Ravens and Black Rains; the Story of Highland Second Sight* (London, 1985), p. 248.

Gypsies, after all, had been consulted on the use of poisons. However, the translation is more fully rendered as brownish-grey or as an unhealthy pale or yellowish colour. It could be that Coinneach was not a well man and this was revealed by a complexion so distinctive that it warranted a particular appellation. Odhar is more than a name; it is a description. Rather than being a nomadic gypsy the leader of witches may have had a secure base from which to conduct his affairs.

In fact, the name of Coinneach Odhar appears in other legal documents of the time. On 3 March 1576, Margret Waus, wife of John Ross, provost of Inverness, brought a complaint in the burgh court against John Fraser, alias Stout, alleging that for the past seven years he had colluded with her servant to defraud her.[100] Her servant also plied a trade as a chapman, buying and selling animal skins including marten, weasel, beaver and otter, in the vicinity of Inverness. The trade in skins 'sold to strangers at huge and excessive prices' was so lucrative that much of it was illegal.[101] When Waus had hired her servant for a ten year term in November 1568, she had advanced him forty two merks to fund his trading on the understanding that any skins brought into Inverness were to be given to her, she being a free burgess and entitled to transact business within the burgh bounds while he, a servant, was not. The name of this chapman/servant was Kennocht Owyr, or Owir. Waus alleged that Stout knew that Kennocht was her servant and owed her money but despite this had an arrangement to meet him 'in all mercattis adjacent to this burcht, sic as Sant Boniface fair, Pardoun fair, Bryde daye, Mertemess, Munrois fair, wyth the rest of vther small mercattis adjacent to this towne' where he bought skins from him.[102] Stout denied the charges, although he agreed that he had bought skins from a dealer who was in Kennocht's

100 *Inverness Burgh Records* Vol. VIII, 1574–1576, transcribed 1900. f422. Original f347. *Records of Inverness* Vol. I. (Aberdeen, 1911), p. 247.

101 R. Hollinshead, *Scottish Chronicles: A Complete History and description of Scotland* (Arbroath, 1805) Vol. I, p. 9.

102 *Inverness Burgh Records*, transcribed f423. Original f348. *Records of Inverness*, p. 247.

company. The complaint was dismissed. No charges appear to have been brought against Kennocht Owyr.

Buying and selling animal skins and failing to repay a loan have nothing whatever to do with witchcraft. What the records show, however, is that there was a Kennocht Owyr living on the borders of legality in the same place and at the same time as Coinneach Odhar was named as leader of the Easter Ross witches. Saint Boniface Fair took place in Fortrose each year from 16 to 18 March; Pardoun fair took place at Whitsun from 15 to 17 May, also in Fortrose; Bryde Day (or Logiebride Fair) took place at Logie Wester, near Contin, on 1 February; Mertemess took place at St Martin's (the present day Resolis) in the Black Isle on 10 November and Munrois (Munro's) fair took place at Culrain from 20 to 22 June.[103] These were just some of the fairs attended by Kennocht Owyr, all within Easter Ross and the Black Isle. Fairs took place regularly, in every hamlet and parish, some weekly, some monthly and some annually. Fairs enabled people to move around the area, to buy and sell, to meet their friends and other traders or to be entertained. What better way for witches to meet, and to pass on information? There is, in short, a distinct possibility that Kennocht Owyr, chapman/servant to Margret Waus, and the Keanoch Owir of the witchcraft commissions were one and the same.

Conclusion

The Fowlis trials show that witchcraft was endemic in late sixteenth century Easter Ross. The records also suggest that until the Munro family came under threat there is little evidence that local church or civil authority took an active part it trying to curb the practice. When Robert Mor

103 J. D. Marwick, *List of Markets and Fairs Now and Formerly Held in Scotland* (Glasgow, 1890). N. Macrae, *The Romance of a Royal Burgh* (Wakefield, 1974), pp. 253, 280 and 283. A. Ross, *The Folklore of the Scottish Highlands* (London, 1976), pp. 125–126.

Munro of Fowlis sought to prosecute those conspiring against his family, he turned to central state authority rather than the church which does not appear to have played any significant role in bringing the witches to trail. The witches may have been poor but they included tradesmen and women of all ages and social class. They were not the stereotypical Scottish witch – an old poor woman who lived alone. They lived within the community in a loosely knit network and their skills, for good or evil, were called upon by all sections of society. Indeed, they appear to have been a community in themselves – with signs by which they could recognise each other and safe houses where they could meet in secret. King James VI's intervention in the trial of Lady Fowlis in 1589 provided him with first hand knowledge of witchcraft practices and he appears to have pursued the only member of the Fowlis family who had, up until then, caused harm. The devil's pact was known to at least one witch by that year and the idea does not appear to have been imposed upon her by educated persecutors. Only after the risk to the king's own life posed by the North Berwick Witches, does the devil's pact feature as a central plank in royal policy towards witchcraft with the implication that the notion was borrowed from witches and then used against them. Not only does the data have implications for our understanding of who witches were and what they believed, it shows that 'elite' and 'popular' culture were inter-mixed and related and renders redundant any clear cut distinction between the two.

Several features of the Fowlis affair have their parallels in the legend of the Brahan Seer. The involvement of a powerful woman with evil intent is at the heart of the Fowlis affair. She is from the leading house of the area in her time and is of sufficiently high social status to have escaped the full severity of the law. Such a woman is also central to the Brahan Seer legend. More specifically, the Chanonry of Fortrose where nine of the witches were burnt is where the Coinneach Odhar of the Brahan Seer legend is reputed to have met a similar fate. The witnesses to the public spectacle of the Fowlis executions were drawn, as were the witches themselves, from different towns and hamlets throughout the region. The signatories to Balnagowan's protestation of innocence included men from Dornoch in Sutherlandshire, Inverness and Ardersier near Nairn.[104] News of the burnings would have spread throughout the region. Witches had reason to remember the severity of the judicial process. The salutary effect could be seen in the fear of Hector's associates a decade later. The burnings at Chanonry would not be easily forgotten.

Likewise, the magical stones, which enabled Hector Munro to recover from his illness, were among the few props that appear to have worked successfully. The use of witches' stones, usually small holed pebbles, was relatively widespread and examples have been found all over Scotland.[105] They were generally used to ward off the threat of evil spirits to humans and livestock. Their use by Marion to provide enchanted water is unusual. The fact that the King demanded to see the stones while at Chanonry and that they were taken all the way to Aberdeen and there left with the Justice-Clerk may have added to their significance. The use of a single magical stone, for an equally unusual purpose, is an important feature of the Brahan Seer legend.

The use of poison is an integral part of the Fowlis affair and in some versions of the Brahan Seer legend it plays a significant role. At least one person died at the hands of Lady Fowlis. Twelve years after the event, according to the dittay, people were still able to point out where Marie, Lady Fowlis's nurse, made her fatal error. The spot became a noted landmark; the grass where the poison spilt was so contaminated that animals would not graze there.[106] Other victims, including some of high social status, never fully recovered. They continued to live in the community and their presence ensured that the use of poison was not easily forgotten. Lady Balnagown was still an invalid when Lady Fowlis came to trial in 1590.[107] The intervention of the king and the reopening of the case against Lady Fowlis gave the people a reminder of the events that had led to the judicial burnings at Chanonry.

104 Adam, *Fearn*, pp. 135–136.

105 R. W. Reid, *Illustrated Catalogue of the Anthropological Museum, Marischal College, University of Aberdeen* (Aberdeen University Press, Aberdeen 1912), p. 10.

106 Pitcairn, *Trials*, p. 194.

107 Lady Balnagown died 6 October 1602, Adam, *Fearn*, p. 167.

Finally, there is the name of Keanoch Owir. If, as leader of the witches during the Fowlis affair, Keanoch Owir was responsible for their conduct, then he deserves to be remembered as somebody who had an influence on King James's early perception of witches and their craft. The events and *dramatis personae* have parallels in the Brahan Seer legend and suggest a context for the legend's genesis. The connection between Lady Isabella Mackenzie of Seaforth and witchcraft, an essential part of the Brahan Seer legend, is examined in the next chapter.

CHAPTER 3

Witchcraft Trials in Restoration Scotland: Rational Reluctance and Corrupt Exploitation

Introduction

During the course of the seventeenth century the Seaforth Mackenzies, from their seat at Brahan Castle, supplanted the Munros of Fowlis as the dominant family in Easter Ross. According to the Brahan Seer legend, Coinneach Odhar was burnt to death for witchcraft on the orders of Isabella, Countess of Seaforth some time in the latter half of that century. The Countess's actions were precipitated by the seer's insolent response after she had consulted him about her husband's absence in Paris. The burning of the Brahan Seer was carried out, according to legend, with the co-operation of the church. The previous chapter shows that Coinneach Odhar was a real person who lived and engaged in witchcraft a hundred years earlier and suggests that he is the historical figure on whom the legend is based. This chapter attempts to substantiate this claim by considering whether it would have been possible for the Countess to summarily execute a Coinneach Odhar (as the legend has it) without recourse to due process of law. In so doing it also examines the shift in attitudes towards witchcraft among educated elites between 1597, the year King James VI's *Daemonologie* appeared in print, and the 1660s. It suggests that by the Restoration developments in attitudes among those in power, as well as the workings of the legal process, would have meant that Isabella could not have put a seer to death as the legend relates.

The prosecution of witches in the Fowlis affair had been instigated by local lairds, and as far as can be gauged from the evidence, without any meaningful involvement by the church. While central state control had been exercised by the king in person – he had instructed the pursuit of the principal defendant – it had been left to local lairds to try and sentence the witches. In the sixty years that followed much had changed in the perception of witchcraft among those whose job it was to administer justice. Taking King James VI's examination of the North Berwick witches in 1589–90 as her starting point, Christine Larner expresses the view that witch-hunting was a top-down process emanating from central authority with social control (especially of women) as the motivating purpose.[1] This view has been challenged by more recent writers who favour a bottom-up model with prosecutions emanating from within communities and with social control being just one of a myriad range of different reasons why witches were pursued. These reasons, according to Robin Briggs, were dependent on local circumstances and on local individuals.[2] Brian Levack argues that members of local elites usually took the lead in pursuing and prosecuting witches and that central authority acted as a restraining influence.[3]

Julian Goodare points out that top-down and bottom-up models should not be seen as mutually exclusive. Instead, he argues that local church rather than civil authority was invariably the instigator of prosecutions and that Kirk sessions and the Privy Council always acted in 'harmonious co-operation' to stamp out witchcraft with the latter having ultimate control.[4] This bilateral interpretation cannot be sustained when seventeenth century witchcraft cases in and around Easter Ross are closely examined. These fell into two distinct phases – those which occurred during the national witch-hunt of 1661–62, when numerous witches

1 C. Larner, *Witchcraft and Religion* (Oxford, 1984), p. 26. J. Goodare (ed.), *The Scottish Witch-Hunt in Context* (Manchester, 2002), pp. 1, 2 and 123.

2 R. Briggs, 'Many Reasons Why: Witchcraft and the Problem of Multiple Explanation' in J. Barry, M. Hester and G. Roberts (eds), *Witchcraft in Early Modern Europe* (Cambridge, 1996), pp. 49–63.

3 B. Levack, 'State-Building and Witch-hunting in Early Modern Europe' in Barry, Hester & Roberts (eds), *Witchcraft in Early Modern Europe*, pp. 96–115. pp. 102–103.

4 J. Goodare (ed.), *The Scottish Witch-Hunt in Context* (Manchester, 2002), p. 134.

were apprehended and some executed, and the relatively few cases which occurred in the years thereafter. Local authorities included lairds and lawyers as well as members of the Kirk and this meant that tensions could, and did, arise between churchmen and law officers at local level. This was also true at national level. Parliament, or the Privy Council acting for the Crown, and the General Assembly of the Church of Scotland did not always act in harmony in the pursuit of witches, nor did local Kirk sessions always pursue witches with the severity demanded by the General Assembly.

This chapter argues that where witch-hunts did occur they were precipitated at local level and were usually instigated with the co-operation of the church. While central state authority acted (as Levack suggests) as a restraining influence local lairds and church sessions were also capable of taking a moderate view of popular magical practices. This argument is based on an examination of state papers, church records from the presbyteries and Kirk sessions of Inverness and Dingwall and the diaries and chronicles of neighbours and contemporaries of the Seaforths who had first hand experience of witchcraft examinations and trials. A member of the Seaforth family, Sir George Mackenzie of Rosehaugh, Lord Advocate, wrote extensively of his experiences of witchcraft trials and provides the views of a learned man of his time. These documents illustrate two models of elite involvement in witchcraft trials following the Restoration; a rational reluctance to prosecute witches on the one hand and corrupt exploitation on the other. Mackenzie's writings place him very much in the former bracket. The framework of the legal system under which witchcraft cases were heard and the social environment which precipitated the hunt of 1661–62 and the years thereafter illustrate what was required by law in bringing a case to trial and the safeguards in place to avoid miscarriages of justice. An arbitrary execution such as that ascribed to Countess Isabella was not possible in law, although an examination of specific cases from in and around Easter Ross during the 1661–62 hunts shows that despite theoretical safeguards, abuses did occur. It indicates that the employment of prickers secured confessions; and that an admission of the devil's pact was central to securing convictions. Such an admission is notably absent from the Brahan Seer legend, suggesting that the seer's death at the hands of Isabella did not occur during the national hunt of 1661–62. The involvement of members of the Mackenzie family with witchcraft, the restraining influences from central authority and a moderate response to witchcraft from local church officers make it even less likely to have occurred in the years following.

Witchcraft: legal process and social environment

The legal process of bringing a witch to trial in seventeenth century Scotland involved several steps, failure at each one of which could have brought proceedings to a halt. The first step was to allege that a crime had been committed and to identify the accused.[5] This was very often instigated by the church, either by local Kirk session or the more senior presbytery session, after hearing the complaint of a parishioner. A witch was usually arrested and interrogated by church officers and local magistrates and a confession obtained, often under duress. The examiners applied to the criminal court for a trial; supporting their application with depositions from witnesses and the accused's confession. Law officers then decided if there were prima facie grounds for a trial. If there were, the trial took place. If found guilty, sentence was pronounced and the convicted witch was executed.[6] Since King James VI's examination of the North Berwick witches, and the publication of his *Daemonologie*, a pact with the devil had become a central tenet of belief in witchcraft among churchmen and state officials. Proof of the devil's pact, allied to malice, was what ultimately secured convictions.[7]

5 Ibid., p. 123.

6 Ibid., p. 124 and Levack, 'State-Building,' p. 102.

7 R. Pitcairn (ed.), *Ancient Criminal Trials in Scotland*, Vol. III (Edinburgh, 1833), p. 602. B. Levack, 'The Great Scottish Witch-hunt of 1661–1662' *The Journal of British Studies*, Vol. XX (1980–81), pp. 90–108. p. 108. C. Larner, *Witchcraft and Religion* (Oxford, 1984), p. 32.

Witchcraft cases were tried in the superior courts. These took place in the Central Criminal Courts of Justiciary in Edinburgh or at Justiciary Aires, where justice-deputes from the central courts presided over circuit courts in the provinces. Alternatively, commissions could be granted by Parliament or the Privy Council enabling local elites – including lairds, magistrates and church officers – to prosecute and sentence witches.[8] Certain procedures should have ensured that witches received a fair trial under these commissions. In 1644, and again in 1649, the Commissioners of the General Assembly of the Church of Scotland had petitioned parliament to suggest that lawyers and physicians join ministers in examining witches.[9] This is not to suggest that leniency was being contemplated but rather that the church authorities wanted consistency between church and state in the apprehension and trial of witches. The assembly also instructed their presbyteries in 1649 that when they sought commissions for trying and punishing witches only the ablest and most conscientious men should judge them.[10] Parliament approved these measures although the Privy Council was to continue to grant commissions 'according to custome' and to rely on the wisdom and impartiality of local authorities. [11]

During the Interregnum, between 1652 and 1660, Scotland was ruled by an English government. Robert Baillie records in 1655 that there is a '[w]ant of justice, for we have no Barron-Courts: our sheriffs have little skill, for common being English sojours; our Lords of Session, a few English, unexperienced [sic] with our law, and who, this twelve moneth, hes done little or nought.'[12] The English commissioners had gone to London on parliamentary business in the summer of 1654 and were absent for over

8 Levack, 'State-Building,' p. 102.

9 *Acts of the General Assembly of the Church of Scotland* (Edinburgh, 1843), pp. 44 and 216.

10 A. F. Mitchell and J. Christie (eds), *The Records of the Commissions of the General Assembly of the Church of Scotland, 1646–1647*, Vol. II (Edinburgh, 1892), pp. 240 and 329.

11 APS Vol. VI pt. I, p. 197.

12 R. Baillie, *The Letters and Journals of Robert Baillie 1637–1662* (Edinburgh, 1841) Vol. III, p. 288. The diarist John Nicholl makes the same point. A *Diary of Public Transactions and Other Occurrences ...* (Edinburgh, 1885), p. 155.

a year. Apart from this obvious shortcoming, they were trying to deliver a comprehensive legal system without co-operation from Scottish law officers of every grade. Lairds like Alexander Brodie of Brodie remained loyal to the king. They were concerned about how they were perceived by their peers and most of all were mistrustful of the motives of the English governors. From early 1653 Brodie resisted several attempts, some from Oliver Cromwell, to get him to act as a Justice of the Peace. He finally succumbed to pressure and held his first court in Elgin on 20 October 1655 but consistently refused to take the Oath of Allegiance which would have meant swearing loyalty to a Sovereign other than the king.[13] Many of the advocates and clergy refused to co-operate for the same reason.[14] The reintroduction of the traditional Scottish legal system after a decade of unfamiliar English procedures was a contributory factor in the 1661–62 witch-hunts.[15] Once initial localised hunts beginning in the Lothians had become known, with prickers travelling round the country confirming pacts with the devil, witch-hunts gathered momentum as neighbours settled old and recent grievances. In several cases the accused had been a witch for some years but not charged 'throw the confusion of the tymes.'[16] An old witch in Bute was brought to account for events which had taken place 'before the great Snaw about 28 yeires syne.'[17]

13 A. & J. Brodie, *The Diaries of the Lairds of Brodie 1652–1685* (Spalding Club, Aberdeen, 1863, reprint of part printed 1740), pp. 176, 178, 183 and 188.

14 P. Thomas (ed.), *Mercurius Politicus: The English Revolution III: Newsletters During the Civil War, Newsbook 5, 1652–53* (London, 1971), pp. 92–93. See also C. H. Firth, *Scotland and the Commonwealth: Letters and Papers Relating to the Military Government of Scotland, 1651–53* (Edinburgh, 1895), pp. 390–40.

15 Levack, 'The Great Scottish Witch-hunt,' p. 108.

16 J. N. R. MacPhail (ed.), *Highland Papers* Vol. III (Edinburgh, 1920). Cases in Bute, 1662, some delations going back over 20 years. See especially pp. 14 and 18 for the case of Margrat NcWilliam. R. Burns Begg records several old cases, one from 40 years earlier, in 'Notice of Trials for Witchcraft at Crook of Devon, Kinross-shire, in 1662' in *Proceedings of the Society of Antiquaries of Scotland,* Vol. 22, 1888, p. 211–241. pp. 222, 223, 226, 228 and 231.

17 MacPhail, *Highland Papers* Vol. III, p. 18.

One reason advanced for the 1661–62 witch-hunts was the apparent leniency shown by English commissioners in witchcraft cases.[18] William Clarke, Secretary to the English Army Commander in Scotland, described them at their work in Edinburgh in 1652. They spent a day reading commissions, called forward sheriffs from the several southern counties, and fined those who did not appear, an indication of the lack of support from Scottish law officers. Then:

> three days have been spent, in the tryall and fining of severall persons for adultery, incest and fornication, for which theyre were above 60 persons brought before the Judges in a day; and it is observable that such is the malice of these people, that most of them were accused for facts done divers years since, and the chief proof against them was their own confession before the Kirk … But that which is most observable is, that some were brought before them for witches … there were six of them in all, four whereof dyed of the torture.[19]

The witches had been hung up by the thumbs and had lighted candles applied to various parts of their body. The Judges demanded an investigation of the ministers and others responsible for sanctioning such treatment. The parliamentarian Bulstrode Whitelock recorded in October, 1652, 'Letters [received] that sixty persons, men and women, were accused before the commissioners … at the last circuit for witches, but they found so much malice, and so little proof against them, that none were condemned.'[20] Whitelock's misrepresentation of Clarke's letter has been used by scholars to inflate the number of cases of witchcraft in Scotland and given rise to the perception that the English commissioners were more lenient than their Scottish counterparts because they were

18 Levack, 'The Great Scottish Witch-hunt,' pp. 91 and 93.

19 Clarke was writing to William Lenthhall, Speaker to the Parliament at Westminster. His letter is dated from Edinburgh, 23 October 1652. C. H. Firth, *Scotland and the Commonwealth,* pp. 367–368. *Mercurius Politicus* Vol. 6, pp. 9–10. See also J. Maidment (ed.), *The Spottiswoode Miscellany* (Edinburgh, 1845), pp. 90–91.

20 Bulstrode Whitelock, *Memorials of the English Affairs* (Oxford, 1853) Vol. III, p. 458.

thought to have dismissed such a large number of cases at one sitting.[21] The English Commissioners condemnation of torture has also been used to show them acting leniently. However, in 1649 the Scottish Committee of Estates, despite being on a war footing, had passed an act against the use of torture in witchcraft cases but defeat by Cromwell had prevented this from being implemented.[22]

Robert Baillie's rather ambiguous assertion in 1659 that '[t]here is much witcherie up and down our land; though the English be but too spareing to try it, yet some they execute,' has been used to support the argument for English leniency but it would appear that the English tried, impartially and according to the evidence, whatever crimes came before them.[23] Edward Mosely, among the first to be appointed in 1652, was still assiduously going about his work in early April, 1659, when he and another English commissioner presided over several days at a trial in Dumfries in which they condemned to death nine out of ten women, the survivor being reprieved by a not proven verdict and banished from the parish.[24] There is no suggestion here of leniency. The absence of witchcraft cases brought before the courts must be attributed to other causes. This trial took place a few short weeks before the legal system broke down at cessation of the commonwealth and prior to the restoration of Charles II. Between 6 May 1959 and August 1660, when the Committee of Estates was temporarily charged with attending to legal matters, and until such time as a Scottish Parliament sat on 1 January 1661, the legal system was at a virtual standstill.[25]

21 Levack, 'The Great Scottish Witch-hunt,' p. 92. C. Larner, *A Source Book of Scottish Witchcraft* (Glasgow, 1977), pp. 50–53. See also G. F. Black, *A Calendar of Cases of Witchcraft in Scotland 1510–1727* (New York, 1938), p. 63.

22 APS Vol. VI, pt. II, p 538 Act 370.

23 Baillie, *Letters* Vol. III, p. 436. Cited by Levack, 'The Great Scottish Witch-hunt,' p. 93.

24 J. Maxwell Wood, *Witchcraft and Superstitious Records in South East District of Scotland* (Wakefield, 1975), pp. 112–113.

25 APS Vol. VI (ii) p. 892b. Baillie, *Letters*, p. 430. Levack, 'The Great Scottish Witch-hunt,' pp. 93–94.

Few witches were brought before the English judges. It is possible that fewer cases of all crimes were brought before them. Reaction to the English governors was very likely the same for most common people as it was for lairds like Brodie, namely an underlying mistrust of a foreign occupation which manifested itself in keeping a safe distance. Despite this, legislation enacted during the Commonwealth had made the bringing of witchcraft cases more accessible, at least in principle. The jurisdiction of Justices of the Peace had been widened in 1655 to bring it more into line with England.[26] It was now easier to bring a number of different cases before the lower courts thereby freeing up the superior courts where witchcraft cases were heard.[27] When King Charles II restored the Scottish Parliament in 1661 it re-constituted legal responsibilities implemented by the English and JPs continued to hear cases against fornication, adultery, swearing and blasphemy.[28] Although laws against such crimes had been matters for the civil authorities since the time of King James VI, they had been dealt with by a superior court with the need for more complex legal procedures.[29] To expedite and simplify matters the church had come to regard these as falling within its jurisdiction. The church had a monetary incentive to enforce the 1567 law against fornication. It had been amended in 1649; increased fines imposed on both men and women were to be paid to the Kirk session, 'to be imployed be thame upon pious uses.'[30] By placing such crimes under the jurisdiction of JPs the civil authorities were reclaiming authority usurped by the church.

Witches could, however, still be tried locally by commissions obtained from Parliament or, more usually, from the Privy Council. At the height of the 1661–62 hunts these were accompanied by instructions on how to

26 APS Vol. VI (ii), pp. 832–836.

27 APS Vol. IV, p. 539.

28 APS Vol. VII, pp. 306–313, at Edinburgh 9 July 1661.

29 APS Vol. II, pp. 485, 539: Vol. III, pp. 25, 210, 212, 213: Vol. VI. (i), p. 184: Vol. VI (ii), p. 596.

30 APS Vol. III, p. 25, Vol. III, p. 210 and Vol. VI (ii), p. 152

proceed so that the trial took the same legal form as a Justiciary Aire.[31] An assize of fifteen honest men had to be summoned by written and signed warrant from those named in the commission and it was they, and not the commissioners, who decided a person's innocence or guilt. A dempster, who pronounced the sentence, had to be appointed and sworn. A procurator fiscal had to be chosen and sworn. He was to record the swearing of the jurors, the confessions of the witches, the verdict and the sentence. He was to submit the charges and the list of jurors into the hands of the clerk to the court who was to keep the records of proceedings. He was to read out the commission after which the court must be fenced; formally declared in progress in the King's name and not to be interrupted. The accused was (or were) to be brought in. The names of the jurors were to be called in her presence, the dittay read out and the accused asked to confirm the charges. She was then to be asked if she had any objections to members of the assize. Only if no objections were raised was the assize to be sworn and the trial allowed to proceed. After hearing the evidence the assize was to retire to a secure room to consider its verdict and to choose a chancellor who was to declare their verdict on return to court. The commissioners were then to pronounce the verdict in a prescribed manner. Sentence was mandatory, the instructions made no provision for leniency. If found guilty witches were to be 'strangled to a stake and their body burnt to ashes, and their moveable goods to belong to His Majesty.'[32]

Such commissions were the most susceptible to abuse. They were often only a formality and the Privy Council did not grant them unless an accused's guilt had already been established from the evidence submitted. Commissions were very often obtained in the name of the pursuer who was then able to try the case in person and nominate his own assize, or jury.[33] Cases of illegal incarceration and torture did occur and the Privy Council issued its first recorded commission expressly forbidding such

31 Wm. Mackay, 'The Strathglass Witches of 1662' in TGSI Vol. IX, pp. 113–121. p. 116, document dated 12 June 1662.

32 Ibid., p. 116.

33 Goodare, *The Scottish Witch-Hunt*, p. 133.

treatment on 7 November 1661.[34] The minister of Rhynd in Perthshire, and several (named) accomplices, was ordered to appear before the Council for illegally proceeding against persons charged with witchcraft.[35] The Privy Council issuing a proclamation against such abuses on 10 April 1662, having been 'certainlie informed that a great many persons in severall parts of the kingdom' had been seized and thrown into gaol where they had been 'pricked, tortured and abused' as suspected witches by persons who had no authority to treat them in such manner. The Council was concerned that 'many innocents may suffer' from those 'who either caryes envy towards them or are covetous after their meanes.'[36] The Council did not entirely ban the use of torture; it was retained as a measure which could be authorised in special circumstances. Commissions issued from the date of the proclamation carried instructions forbidding the use of torture.

In the years immediately after the hunts of 1661–62 fewer and fewer case of witchcraft came before the civil authorities, and guilty verdicts, particularly in the central criminal courts, diminished from lack of credible evidence.[37] The church's position was, in contrast, reactionary. As late as 1707 the General Assembly was asking presbyteries to reflect on some uniform way to censure ecclesiastically 'such as should be convicted of witchcraft or charming and their consulters who escape civil punishment.'[38] Even this was a respite for witches, as the ultimate sanction of the church was not death by burning but excommunication. The varied range of punishments meted out by presbyteries included fines,

34 RPC 3rd series Vol. I, p. 73.

35 Ibid., p. 188.

36 Ibid., p. 198.

37 W. G. Scott-Moncrieff (ed.), *The Records of the Proceedings of the Justiciary Court 1661–1699* Vols. I and II (Edinburgh, 1905). These cite several instances of trials, including those held during the years of the national hunt, where witches were set free for various reasons.

38 *Acts of the General Assembly 1690–1713* Edinburgh, 30 January 1699, session 10, overture iii, recommendation that former acts of G/A concerning witchcraft should be revived & 1707 for above, npn.

banishments and public repentance, generally more moderate responses than that demanded by the Assembly.

Witchcraft accusations were held in abeyance during the Interregnum due primarily to a reluctance across all levels of society to have dealings with English law officers. The Restoration, with the reintroduction of a familiar Scottish legal system, laid the foundation for venting a lot of pent-up spleen. Conditions were right for someone like Countess Isabella to bring a charge of witchcraft. When witches were apprehended in and around Easter Ross during the national hunt of 1661–62 what most concerned their examiners was finding evidence of the devil's presence without which a witchcraft accusation was unlikely to succeed. While there were opportunities for abuse – torture and pricking were used to extract confessions – accusations of witchcraft needed the active support of the church and prosecutions depended on evidence of a pact with the devil. The Brahan Seer of legend was not accused of having a pact with the devil, a necessary condition of successful prosecution, suggesting that Isabella did not burn any witch during the national hunt. This is evident from an examination of the pursuit of witches in the region during 1661–62 as seen through the eyes of Isabella's contemporaries.

The pursuit of witches in and around Easter Ross, 1661–62

The national witch-hunt of 1661–62 was the last of several which had swept across the nation since King James VI's crisis with the North Berwick witches of 1590–91. Others occurred in 1597, 1628–30 and 1649.[39] No definitive reasons can explain why any of the witch-hunts erupted. It has been asserted that for a hunt to get underway 'both central and local authorities had to panic.'[40] The term 'panic' suggests an irrational

39 Goodare, *The Scottish Witch-hunt*, p. 136.

40 Ibid., p. 137.

response. Witch-hunts took place in Easter Ross and the Black Isle and in the neighbouring counties of Inverness-shire and Moray during 1661–62. While there is evidence from these cases that there was some degree of panic at local level, evidence also suggests that, in the main, both local and central authorities responded in a rational manner to events as they were presented to them and according to their world-view. This rationality manifested itself as a reluctance to prosecute witches by some of their examiners and corrupt exploitation for personal gain by others.

One laird with first hand experience of examining witches was Alexander Brodie of Brodie who lived in Moray, a short ferry ride across the firth from Chanonry on the Black Isle. He had moved in the highest circles of government prior to the Interregnum.[41] He maintained diaries which provide insights into the beliefs and actions of those who had to administer justice in witchcraft cases during the years following the Restoration of Charles II and on the beliefs and actions of the witches themselves. Brodie's diaries, though not complete, run from 1652 until his death in 1680.

Brodie was attending court in London in March, 1662, when he 'heard from Scotland that ther was a great discoueri of witchcraft in the parish of Dyk; and in my land, they had purposd euel against my son and his wyfe.'[42] This coincided with the first stirrings in nearby Auldearn against the celebrated Isobel Goudie and her colleagues, whose colourful confessions were obtained before a commission which included Mr Harry Forbes, minister of Auldearn, over several weeks in April and May 1662.[43] While in Edinburgh in June on his return north, Brodie obtained and read the depositions of 'Park's witches.'[44] John Hay of Park, a near neighbour of Brodie, was one of several lairds granted a commission by the Privy Council on 7 May 1662, to try Isobel Elder and Isabel Simson from Dyke.[45] Although Brodie dismissed their confessions as 'the devil's

41 APS Vol. VI, p. 461.
42 Brodie, *Diaries*, p. 246, entry dated 24 March 1662.
43 Pitcairn, *Trials*, Vol. III, pp. 602–618.
44 Brodie, *Diaries*, p. 259.
45 RPC 3rd series Vol. I, p. 206.

deluding of silly wretches,' these two women were to be pursued for over a year.[46]

In April 1663, Elder and Simson escaped from custody. Brodie, who was due to examine them, dithered over their pursuit, thinking their escape was an act of God. When the witches were recaptured he prayed that they would be 'absolu and find noe caus of death.'[47] Brodie was not alone in not wishing to be responsible for killing them. A week after their recapture a meeting was called to hear their testimony. Two of the commissioners, Robert Innes of Moortoun and John Hay of Park, declined to attend. The witches became obstinate and denied what they had confessed. Brodie asked God to provide the judges with understanding, to free them from prejudice and error, and 'to open the harts and mouths of thes poor wretches.'[48] Despite these religious entreaties Brodie recorded that 'it troubled me that ani constraint should hau bein usd to them; that they should hau bein beaten.' Elder and Simson had been beaten contrary to law. The commission granted to try them was the first issued by the Privy Council after its proclamation of 10 April 1662 expressly forbidding the use of torture in witchcraft cases.[49] The commission instructed that, if found guilty, it must be 'upon voluntar confessions without any maner of tortur or other indirect meanes' and at the time of their confession 'they were of right judgment, noways distracted or under any earnest desyre to dy.'[50] Only then, and if they reiterated their confession in court, were they to be found guilty and the death sentence imposed upon them.

At a subsequent meeting of the commissioners at Forres on 23 April 1663, Brodie not only submitted himself to God's guidance but also suggested that they should write to the Bishop of Moray for advice. There is no evidence that the Bishop's advice was forthcoming. Brodie also noted with some annoyance that another of the commissioners, Alexander

46 Brodie, *Diaries*, p. 259.

47 Ibid., p. 293.

48 Ibid., p. 294.

49 RPC 3rd series Vol. I, p. 198.

50 RPC 3rd series Vol. I, p. 206. See also p. 243, for case of Janet Breadheid.

Dunbar of Grange, had failed to appear.[51] At a further meeting six days later, Brodie records that 'Ther was litl don, because ther was not a quorum of the commissioners. Moortoun declind, euen efter he promisd; which mad our meiting uneffectual.'[52]

The trial of Elder and Simson took place on 1 May 1663. The gravity of the occasion, and what it meant to pass sentence of death, was much in Brodie's mind as proceedings began. His fellow commissioners shared his apprehension. They had no idea what awaited them, so they committed themselves to God's work 'that it may be to His glori, the bearing doun of sin, terrour of others, and the comfort of thes that ar imployed in it.'[53] Despite their protestations of innocence 'the poor creaturs wer found guilti.' Although Alexander Dunbar of Grange was against the death sentence the witches were condemned to die. The Baillie of Forres was instructed to take care of them and provide for their execution, 'which did soe irritat, that ther was noe peace.' Brodie 'desird not to be lookd on as the pursuer of thes poor creaturs.' He does not record what prompted the accusations of witchcraft, only that '[t]he witneses agreid clearli and fullie' to the charges, nor does he state from which sector of the community they emanated. Park accompanied Brodie back to his home but despite entreaties he refused to stay the night. The following day Brodie requested Mr Forbes to provide succour to the witches and to see if they would confess their sins. On the afternoon of 4 May 1663, Isobel Elder and Isabel Simson were burnt at Forres. They 'died obstinat,' refusing to confess their guilt.[54]

Brodie and his fellow commissioners had been involved in several earlier trials or examinations in the area including those of Isobel Goudie and Janet Breadheid, whose confessions had been provided allegedly without 'compulsitouris.'[55] Included in the evidence against Goudie was that

51 Brodie, *Diaries*, p. 294.

52 Ibid., p. 296.

53 Ibid.

54 Ibid.

55 Ibid., pp. 259, 273 and 274 and for depositions of Goudie see Pitcairn, *Trials*, pp. 602–603, and for Janet Breadheid's deposition, p. 616.

John Hay of Park had lost male children in infancy and that witchcraft had been confessed as the cause. Goudie and her colleagues had been accused of malefice against Mr Harry Forbes and of using his church in Auldearn for their nocturnal gatherings.[56] Crops, ale and livestock had been destroyed and confessions made to murder.[57] The devil as master and sexual partner featured prominently in their testimonies. What sealed their fate was 'particularlie SATHAN, Renunciation of Baptism, with diverse malefices.'[58] This judgement appeared as an endorsement by the justice-depute, Alexander Colville, on the second of Isobel Goudie's four confessions. He returned the commission, passing it for trial with a note reading, 'Tak cair of this peaper. See the Justice deputis judgement of it. Show this to the Commissioneris.'[59]

Sentencing of witches was not taken lightly and certainly in the case of Brodie and his colleagues not without considerable heart searching. This did not prevent them being complicit with the beating of the witches, nor did it prevent them passing sentence as the law required. Their competence to try such complicated cases is another matter although Brodie did seek advice where he could find it. During his early involvement in the examination of Elder and Simson he held a lengthy conversation with Alexander Colville, a staunch Presbyterian from Blair in Fife, and like Brodie a former commissioner of the Church of Scotland's General Assembly. He had presided over his first witchcraft trial in 1629 and had been one of three justice-deputes sent to try the spate of cases in the Lothians which sparked off the 1661–62 witch-hunt.[60]

Responding to Brodie's interest Colville told him that the mark by which prickers identified witches was not infallible 'because phisicians think by natural means the flesh may be deadned and feeling taken

56 Pitcairn, *Trials*, pp. 603 and 605.

57 Ibid., pp. 611 and 612.

58 Ibid., p. 610.

59 Ibid.

60 RPC 2nd series Vol. 3, pp. 2, 3 and 4, and for other early cases of Colville, pp. 290, 334, 345 and 619. RPC 3rd series Vol. I, pp. 11, 12 and 17.

away.'[61] He said that witches could not really transport themselves nor change into the shape of a familiar other than in their imaginations. He added that a deposition that a person had been seen by one individual in a particular place was not sufficient evidence without corroboration. It may be that transportation and shape changing formed part of the charges against Elder and Simson, hence Brodie's interest. The discussion about prickers suggests that this may have been how their confessions were obtained. In any event Brodie was armed with wisdom regarding fallibilities in evidence before the case came to trial. Despite his scepticism about witchcraft practices, Colville would continue to apprehend and burn witches.[62] He offered Brodie a place on one of his commissions; Brodie declined.[63] Brodie applied the law despite his feelings. His fellow commissioners had their own misgivings. They were operating within a framework in which both church and state provided authority for their actions. Thus doubly sanctioned, they carried out their duties. Others had no compunction about using the law for their own ends, as Alexander Chisholm of Cromer's abuse of tenants accused of witchcraft attests.

A contemporary of Brodie, the Rev. James Fraser of Wardlaw, witnessed the persecution of Chisholm's tenants at first hand. His single paragraph, dated 1 March 1662, is mostly concerned with the activities of a pricker, one Paterson, 'who had run over the kingdom for triall off witches' and who had been responsible for the deaths of two persons in Elgin, two in Forres and 'one Margret Duff [sic, should be Isabel Duff], a rank witch, burn [sic] in Inverness.'[64] The dating suggests that the two witches Fraser refers to at Forres were Elder and Simson, burnt there on 4 May 1663. They were originally brought to trial under a warrant dated 7 May 1662; their examination by a pricker would have taken place before this. From Inverness, Paterson came to Fraser's own parish of Wardlaw, near Beauly, where he examined nineteen people, fifteen of whom (all named) became

61 Brodie, *Diaries*, pp. 260 and 264. The conversation took place on Sunday, 22 June 1662.

62 Ibid., p. 264.

63 Ibid., p. 260.

64 Fraser, *Chronicles*, p. 446.

famous as the Strathglass Witches. A sixteenth Strathglass witch, Hector McLean, was in the Tollbooth in Inverness on theft charges.[65]

On 26 June 1662, the same day as the commission was issued for trial of the Strathglass witches, three other commissions were issued against a total of thirteen (named) witches in the Beauly area. Chisholm of Cromer sat on the commission which executed Isabel Duff.[66] The account of the Strathglass Witches is relatively well documented for an event of the time and shows that people in power were capable of abusing the law to achieve their own ends, even if that entailed death for those found guilty.[67] For many years a colony of Macleans had lived as law abiding tenants on Chisholm's lands in Strathglass, to the south-west of Beauly. In early 1662 a number of them were accused of witchcraft and put under the questioning of Chisholm by the ministers and elders of the parishes of Kilmorack and Kiltarlity in the Presbytery of Inverness in which they lived.[68] They were taken forcibly to James Fraser's church at Wardlaw where Paterson cut off their hair, bundled it all together and hid it in a stone dyke. Fraser provides no explanation for this action.[69] Fourteen women and one man were then stripped naked, had their bodies rubbed all over by Paterson, and were pricked with a brass pin. Chisholm applied successfully to the Privy Council for a commission to try them. The application named him, his brother and two cousins as commissioners.[70] The commission was accompanied by instructions on how to proceed at the trial.[71]

The Strathglass witches were saved by the intervention of Sir Rory Maclean of Duart, chief of the name, to whom the husband of one of the accused women appealed for help. His petition to the Privy Council contends that Chisholm wanted the Macleans, who had been his 'kynd-

65 RPC 3rd series Vol. I, pp. 233–234.
66 RPC 3rd series Vol. I, pp. 233–234 and 237. Mackay, 'The Strathglass Witches,' p. 115.
67 Mackay, 'The Strathglass Witches,' pp. 113–121.
68 The Records of the Presbytery of Inverness are not extant for this period.
69 Fraser, *Chronicles,* p. 446.
70 Mackay, 'The Strathglass Witches,' p. 115. RPC 3rd series Vol. I, p. 237.
71 Mackay, 'The Strathglass Witches,' p. 116.

lie tenants these 2 or 300 years bypast,' removed from their land and had resorted to accusations of witchcraft because he could not expel them by legal means.[72] It was alleged that the women, in addition to being generally maltreated, were tortured by being kept awake, by being hung up by their thumbs and having the soles of their feet burnt at the fire. One woman lost her mind and another died as a result of this cruelty. The Privy Council withdrew the commission and ordered Chisholm to appear in person at Edinburgh, together with the accused. Chisholm and his allies from the Kirk denied that they had used torture and pleaded that transporting all those involved would put them to great expense.[73]

The case was referred to a justice-depute who instructed that the prisoners be brought for examination to the gaol in Inverness. There, on 6 October 1662, John Neilson, a notary public, declared in the presence of (named) witnesses, that he had examined the women for signs of torture but had found none. He also asked them if they had signs of torture, but they could show none. He did not ask if they *had* been tortured; injuries would have healed and their hair would have grown in the several months which had elapsed since the women were forcibly removed from their homes. Chisholm waited at the door of the prison vault; his presence is unlikely to have had a neutral influence on events.[74] When Brodie learnt that none of the witches at Inverness were condemned he records his disquiet that 'if God prevent not, will be of veri ill example.'[75] There is no record that the tenants returned to their homes where they would have been under the discipline of 'the ministers and other gentlemen' of their parishes. Neither the ministers nor their parishioners were strangers to each other. William Fraser had been minister of Kiltarlity since 1624, his son, Donald, minister of Kilmorack since 1649.[76]

72 RPC 3rd series Vol. I, p. 237.

73 Ibid., p. 243.

74 Mackay, 'The Strathglass Witches,' pp. 118–120.

75 Brodie, *Diaries*, p. 276. The entry is dated 8 October 1662, two days after Neilson's examination of the witches.

76 H. Scott, *Fasti Ecclesiae Scoticanae: the Succession of Ministers in the Parish Churches of Scotland* (Edinburgh, 1870), pp. 263, 265, 298, 303.

James Fraser does not condemn the accusations nor does he question witchcraft as such – his criticism is directed towards pricking and its attendant maltreatment as a means of discovery. Referring to the practice generally, he observes that 'Itt is sure some witches were discovered, but many honest men and women were blotted and broak by this trick.'[77] Concerning those examined at Wardlaw, he writes that 'Severall of these dyed in prison, never brought to confession.'[78] This compares with one death reported by Maclean of Duart in his petition to the Privy Council.[79] Fraser may be right; Paterson examined four witches brought by the chamberlain of Ferrintosh near Dingwall, in addition to those from Strathglass. When Paterson, who earned a great deal of money and had two servants, was later found out to be a woman, Fraser had an additional reason from condemning this 'vile varlet imposture.'[80] Prickers were becoming exposed as charlatans by the time Fraser witnessed the actions of Paterson, and medical explanations were being offered to account for the devil's mark. John Hay, a messenger in nearby Tain, complained to the Privy Council in May, 1662, that due to the 'boundless furie of some malitious enemies' he had been shaved over all his body and pricked 'to the great effusion of his blood' by one John Dick.[81] He wanted his tormentor arrested and imprisoned. Hay, a public servant, knew how to have his rights upheld. The sheriffs, their deputies, magistrates and justices of Inverness, Tain and Dornoch were instructed to apprehend Dick and send him to gaol in Edinburgh there to await the Council's further deliberations.[82] They were instructed to proclaim Hay's good name from the market cross at Tain.[83]

77 Fraser, *Chronicles*, p. 446.

78 Ibid.

79 RPC 3rd series Vol. 1, p. 237.

80 Fraser, *Chronicles*, p. 447.

81 RPC 3rd series Vol. I, pp. 210 and 251–252, and see also imprisonment at this time of pricker John Kincaid in Tranent, pp. 210 and 224.

82 RPC 3rd series Vol. I, p. 210.

83 Ibid., p. 252.

The employment of professional prickers was one of the driving forces behind the 1661–62 national witch-hunts. Confirming the involvement of the devil through the discovery of the devil's mark was the underlying motivation for witchcraft prosecutions at this time. Lairds such as Brodie displayed a rational reluctance to participate in examinations and collude in torture. Legal constraints were put in place to stop unlawful detention and torture. Prickers were exposed as fraudulent and imprisoned. Lairds such as Chisholm of Cromer were not averse to exploiting existing beliefs and practices to their own corrupt ends. Notwithstanding the cruelty shown towards the Strathglass witches the records show the extent to which persons had to adhere to a prescribed legal process which militated against them acting in an arbitrary and unlawful manner such as that ascribed to Countess Isabella in burning the Brahan Seer. The national hunt precipitated a culture of rational reluctance to prosecute witches rather than one of corrupt exploitation. This is evident by the diminution in witchcraft trials in the years following, suggesting that she is unlikely to have had a Seer put to death during this period.

Countess Isabella, the Mackenzie family and witchcraft

Kenneth Mackenzie, 3rd Earl of Seaforth, fought against Cromwell's forces in the Highlands until harsh winter conditions forced him to seek terms from General Monck in January 1655.[84] He was imprisoned in the 'sconce' at Inverness but released on bail several times depending on the prevailing political climate.[85] Rev. James Fraser of Wardlaw, a former student colleague of Mackenzie at the University of Aberdeen, recorded in 1660

84 C. H. Firth (ed.), *Scotland and the Protectorate: Letters and Papers Relating to the Military Government of Scotland from January 1654 to June 1659* (Edinburgh, 1899), p. 225.

85 F. D. Dow, *Cromwellian Scotland* (Edinburgh, 1979) pp. 193 and 247. Brodie, *Diaries*, p. 190. APS Vol. VI. Pt II, p. 906.

that the prisoners had been set free and while a fellow prisoner, Glengary, went abroad and then to the Court in London, 'The Earle of Seaforth keeps home, and is matcht with a kinswoman of his own, a daughter of the Laird Tarbuts; after all mens hops of him debases himselfe mean sprited to marry below himselfe, getting neither beuty, parts, portion, relation.'[86] Fraser did not approve of Seaforth's marriage to Isabella. She does not appear to have been popular; Brodie of Brodie was certainly glad when she passed his house and did not visit.[87] Local historian, Robert Bain, variously describes her as 'masterful, the evil genius par excellence' and 'disreputable' although his dislike appears to be based on her alleged treatment of the Brahan Seer rather than on historical evidence.[88]

After the restoration of Charles II, members of the Mackenzie family held high office and were certainly associated with witchcraft at this time. George Mackenzie of Rosehaugh, first cousin to Isabella's husband, was a justice-depute from July, 1661 until resigning in December, 1664. At the beginning of his legal career he had been sent with the more experienced Alexander Colville to try the Lothian cases which sparked off the 1661–62 witch-hunts.[89] He was appointed Lord Advocate in 1677.[90] Isabella's brother, Sir George Mackenzie (later Viscount Tarbat and the Earl of Cromarty), was variously one of the College of Senators, a Privy Councillor, Secretary of State for Scotland and Justice-General.[91] He, together with other family members, was granted a commission in May 1662 to try three (named) women at Scatwell in Easter Ross. This commission was issued on the same day as that to try Elder and Simson. In August he was granted a commission to try two (named) women

86 Fraser, *Chronicles*, p. 421.

87 Brodie, *Diaries*, p. 364.

88 R. Bain, *History of the Ancient Province of Ross* (Dingwall, 1899), pp. 215 and 230.

89 RPC 3rd series Vol. 1, pp. 11 and 12.

90 Ibid., p. 470. RPC 3rd series Vol. V, pp. 232–233. And see also R. Chambers, *A Biographical Dictionary of Eminent Scotsmen* (Edinburgh, 1860) Half volume V, pp. 50–53.

91 RPC 3rd series Vol. I, pp. 184 and 216. And see also Chambers, *Biographical Dictionary* Half volume V, pp. 49–50.

in Cromarty in the Black Isle.[92] Although the outcome of these cases is not recorded it is possible that some of these witches were among those examined by Paterson at Wardlaw or identified by one of the other prickers doing their rounds at this time. Isabella's husband, Earl Kenneth, held a number of baronies. He was appointed Sheriff of Ross for life in 1662 and appointed to the Privy Council in 1674.[93] In terms of kin in positions of legal power Isabella was very well placed should she ever have had recourse to law. If she knew anything at all of how it worked, she would have known she was committing a crime had she burnt the Brahan Seer as legend dictates.

According to legend, the Countess burnt the Seer with the co-operation of the church while the earl was absent in Paris. There is as yet no historical evidence that Seaforth ever visited Paris though such a trip could have been accomplished relatively easily and pass unrecorded. The Countess could have been left in charge of her husband's affairs while he was away. Rosalind Marshall provides several examples of legal documents from this time drawn up by men of comparable social class who had to be out of the country for varying periods and who left their affairs in the hands of their spouses.[94] The wives were variously authorised to uplift rents, grant leases, act as factor and generally run the entirety of the estate.[95] Countess Isabella could have exercised similar authority. Would this enable her to order the execution of the Brahan Seer, apparently on a whim? By comparison, almost a hundred years earlier at a time and place more remote from law and order, it is recorded from the Isles that Mairghread Macleod, wife of Domhnall Gorm Mór MacDonald of Sleat had the chief's poet exiled for his rudeness towards her.[96]

92 RPC 3rd series Vol. I, pp. 207 and 248.

93 Ibid., p. 224. RPC 3rd series Vol. IV, p. 381. APS Vol. VIII, p. 384.

94 R. K. Marshall, *Women in Scotland 1660–1780* (Edinburgh, 1979) and more fully in her later work *Virgins and Viragos, a History of Women in Scotland from 1080 to 1980* (London, 1983). *Virgins and Viragos*, p 71.

95 Marshall, *Virgins and Viragos,* pp. 144–145 and *Women in Scotland*, p. 39.

96 D. U. Stiùbhart, 'Women and Gender in Early Modern Western Gàidhealtachd' in E. Ewan and M. M. Meikle (eds), *Women in Scotland c1100–1750* (East Linton, 1999), p. 237.

The Seaforth family had particularly close and long standing links with the church at Chanonry of Fortrose which contains the family mausoleum. It had formerly been the cathedral but converted to a church some time after 1572 when the lead had been stripped from the roof to be replaced by thatch.[97] The building was in a constant state of disrepair and the family started to attend the parish church in Dingwall, Seaforth being constituted an elder on 2 August 1674, and the earliest year for which Kirk session records are extant.[98] After the witch-hunt of 1661–62 very few cases of witchcraft appeared before the presbytery sessions and when they did, ministers and elders showed a marked leniency towards those witches who were believed to have caused no physical harm.[99] In September 1668, the presbytery of Dingwall spoke to Countess Isabella, rather than the earl, urging that her chamberlain make four (named) stubborn offenders, including a Kenneth McKenzie, who lived on her land, yield obedience to the church following some unspecified wrongdoing.[100]

The presbytery of Dingwall appears to have had a relaxed attitude to witchcraft; charmers were sharply rebuked by the moderator and required to repent their sins in public while dressed in sackcloth. This sentence was passed on a handful of witches from 1649 until 1690.[101] However, the internal quarrels of the Church engulfed the Dingwall presbytery with particular bitterness. Reforming ministers supported the Solemn League and Covenant of 1643 which called for the preservation of the reformed religion. Discord was such that no presbytery meetings were held between 13 April 1658 and 19 May 1663.[102] This lack of local control may have been shared by the neighbouring presbytery of Inverness and

97 C. G. MacDowall, *The Chanonry of Ross: An Account of Fortrose and Rosemarkie and the Cathedral Kirk of Ross* (Inverness, 1963), pp. 59 and 69.

98 N. Macrae, *The Romance of a Royal Burgh; Dingwall's Story of a Thousand Years* (Wakefield, 1974), p. 317.

99 MacDowall, *The Chanonry of Ross*. Wm. Mackay (ed.), *Inverness and Dingwall Presbytery Records, 1643–1688* (Edinburgh, 1896), pp. xxxvi–xlii. A. Mitchell (ed.), *Inverness Kirk Session Records 1661–1800* (Inverness, 1902), p. 44.

100 Mackay, *Dingwall Presbytery Records*, p. 321.

101 Ibid., pp. 181, 156, 196, 240, 325, 327, 329, 333, 334 and 344.

102 Ibid., pp. 296–300.

contributed to the rash of witch-hunts in the area during 1661–62 which were exploited by Chisholm of Cromer.[103]

Surviving church records indicate that witchcraft practices continued in the area and that punishments were usually less than severe. A tantalising reference suggests that members of the Seaforth family may have engaged in witchcraft. Brodie records in his diary for 7 February 1679, 'Rori Mcenzi, the E. of Seaforth's brother, din'd heir. He told me the buisines of the supposd witchcraft about Redcastel, and cleared himself and his wyf and al his of it …'[104] Isabella's husband, Kenneth Mackenzie, had died at Chanonry a few weeks earlier. Rory was his youngest brother. He appears to have volunteered the story and his apparently understated denial of his family's involvement suggests that they shared the church's moderate attitude towards magical practices.

Redcastle, in the Black Isle, was a Mackenzie stronghold and was at the centre of a later witchcraft case more fully reported and commented upon. This case provides further evidence against Countess Isabella's arbitrary execution of the Brahan Seer. In July 1699, twelve (named) persons, nine women and three men were examined on charges of witchcraft and the records indicate that others were involved.[105] Chief suspect was a tenant of Redcastle's, John Glass of Spittal whose wife, mother and father-in-law, 'a person always suspected of witchcraft' were among the accused.[106] The charges stemmed from a dispute between Glass and his parish Kirk of Kilernan.[107] Among other indiscretions he had expressed his belief that Catholicism was the best of all religions. The Episcopalian minister, John Mackenzie, and the Kirk session ordered him to stand

103 Ibid., pp. 300–301.

104 Brodie, *Diaries*, pp. 409 and 407.

105 R. Chambers, *Domestic Annals of Scotland* Vol. III (Edinburgh, 1861), pp. 216–217. J. Maidment (ed.), 'Representation by Sherif-Depute of Ross to the Commissioners of the Privy Council Anent the Witches of Kilernan' in *Reliquie Scoticae: Scottish Remains in Prose and Verse* (Edinburgh, 1828), pp. 1–4.

106 NAS, *Book of Adjournal Series D*, DI/66 process D/No. 3. And Larner, *Source Book*, p. 280. (JC3/1 case 673)

107 Maidment, 'Representation.'

in sackcloth and to pay a mulct to the poor. Glass declared that somebody would pay dearly for his treatment. Shortly thereafter the minister died of a fever. A local warlock, Donald Moir, confessed that Glass had employed him to get rid of the minister and that he, with others, had made effigies, helped by the devil in the shape of a black man.[108] Moir was found hanged in his cell while awaiting trial. Glass, whose sons were absent from their house on the night Moir died, allegedly threatened to shoot the minister, presumably Mackenzie's replacement, if he suggested that Glass was responsible. Glass thought he would fare badly if placed before a local assize and submitted a Bill of Advocation to the Lords of Justiciary, requiring that his case be heard before a superior court.

A Representation to have this overturned was submitted to the Privy Council by the Sheriff-Depute of Ross and his fellow law officers. Their blunt message was that Glass would not escape punishment if examined before a local commission. They desired nothing more 'But the Glory of God, the safety of our Country, and the exhoneration of our consciences, by a well grounded Zeal against the Enemies of Heaven and Earth, who are numerous and distinctly known in these parts.'[109] The district was in a state of alarm, they reported, while the wrongdoers awaited trial. The mystery of two deaths had to be resolved; witchcraft was the only possible explanation and had to be punished.

The Privy Council instructed a committee to look into the matter. Two of the women confessed their involvement in witchcraft and the judges recommended that they be given '*some arbitrary punishment*' (emphasis added).[110] The other accused were also to be given some arbitrary punishment. This appears to be the first case of witches found guilty of plying their craft for which the death penalty was not prescribed by the Privy Council.[111] John Glass and a (named) female accomplice were ordered to be released for want of evidence. Further, the local commissioners had to notify the committee of any sentence before it was carried

108 Ibid., p. 2.
109 Ibid., pp. 3 and 4.
110 Chambers, *Domestic Annals* Vol. III, pp. 216–217.
111 Ibid., p. 217.

out. They released Glass as directed but thought fit to fine and banish him. When they reported this to the committee their verdict was overturned. In 1700, with the case concluded, Rorie Mackenzie, younger, of Redcastle, who had stood cautioner for Glass, successfully petitioned the Privy Council to have the bond of caution removed.[112]

These events occurred over twenty years after the 3rd Earl of Seaforth's death but the Rev. James Fraser, of Alness in Easter Ross, writing about witchcraft to Robert Wodrow on 18 April 1727, considered the Redcastle case 'the most remarkable that has been of that kind in this country.'[113] Fraser is dealing with events within living memory and his description would seem to rule out the public spectacle of any witch being burnt at Chanonry during this time – the fate, according to legend, of the Brahan Seer.

While the Redcastle case may have been among the first where the Privy Council directed a sentence for witchcraft other than the death penalty, there is clear evidence that their lordships' concern with the harshness of punishment was no new phenomenon. Disquiet with the legal system with regard to witchcraft had long been expressed by Isabella's kinsman, Sir George Mackenzie of Rosehaugh, Lord Advocate, and the most important of the Mackenzie family involved in witchcraft in a judicial capacity. His examination of the Lothian cases early in his career provided him with insights into the kinds of charges brought, the types of persons making charges, and the types of persons charges were being brought against. While acknowledging that some ecclesiastical laws were not civil laws and vice versa, Mackenzie did not think the two could be separated in the case of witchcraft. The Devil was very much a force to be reckoned with; the religious beliefs and laws of the land reflected this. He considered witchcraft 'the greatest of crimes' and since it included 'the grossest of heresies ... and treasons against God' and was attended by 'other horrid crimes' such as murder and poisoning it should be punished 'by the

112 NAS, *Book of Adjournal Series D*, DI/66 process D/No3. Larner, *Source Book*, p. 280. (JC3/1 case 673)

113 C. K. Sharpe, *A Historical Account of the belief in Witchcraft in Scotland* (London, 1884), p. 181.

most ignominious of deaths.'[114] However, its very horridness required the most rigorous examination of evidence and Mackenzie condemned 'next to the Witches themselves, those cruel and too forward Judges, who burn persons by thousands as guilty of this Crime.'[115] Mackenzie did not deny the existence of witches, though he thought them 'not numerous.'[116]

Mackenzie drew up a list of observations which he hoped would persuade judges to be cautious in their consideration of witchcraft trials. It was a very mysterious crime, he thought, and it was dangerous that the most ignorant persons who were normally accused, 'and oft-times Women,' should be tried for something they did not understand.[117] The accusers were 'Masters, or Neighbours who had their Children dead, and are engaged by grief to suspect these poor creatures.'[118] Mackenzie recommended that physicians consider the effects of fear and melancholy on the imaginations of men who had been kept imprisoned and deprived of proper food and sleep. They will, he suggested, lose their reason. Most prisoners were tortured and all their confessions extracted by this means. Witnesses and jurors were afraid that if witches were released back into the community they would exact revenge 'and I have observed that scarce ever any who were accused before a Countrey Assize of neighbours, did escape that Tryal.'[119] Equally disturbingly, witches had told him privately that they preferred death to the prospect of living a life where they would forever be at the mercy of their less charitable neighbours.

According to Mackenzie, claims that witches could change into animals and transport themselves through solid objects 'and a thousand other ridiculous things ... *which all Divines conclude impossible*' (emphasis

114 G. Mackenzie, *The Laws and Customs of Scotland in Matters Criminal* (Edinburgh, 1678), p. 85.

115 Mackenzie, *The Laws and Customs*, p. 85.

116 G. Mackenzie, *Pleadings in Some Remarkable Cases Before the Supreme Courts of Scotland Since the Year, 1661* (Edinburgh, 1673), p. 185.

117 Mackenzie, *The Laws and Customs*, p. 86.

118 Ibid., p. 87.

119 Ibid., p. 88.

added), were nothing more then the product of over fertile imaginations.[120] Mackenzie dismissed the devil's mark as a naturally insensitive spot on the body; the trade of pricker he derided as a 'horrid cheat.'[121] Natural causes should always be considered the most likely explanation when a person died after having been threatened, unless a pact with the devil had been proved or confessed.[122] Mackenzie's rationality could extend only so far. He argued that where a person died after it was clearly proved that there was malice against her and clay or wax images had been used and a confession admitted, then witches may be found guilty.

In addition to their fears and prejudices, Mackenzie observed that men were not sufficiently familiar with the complexities of such a crime to be competent to try it and when confessions were sent to the Privy Council it was entirely reliant on documentary evidence to determine whether or not to grant a commission. Mackenzie acknowledged that it was customary for local gentry to hold witches prisoner until such time as they thought fit to send them to Justices of the Peace or to magistrates but this was unlawful unless good evidence could be produced against them. Mackenzie accepted as good evidence the confessions of other witches or the evil reputation of the accused but he did suggest that Kirk Sessions, which normally made the initial enquiries, should proceed with caution when taking depositions in such cases.[123] Mackenzie's observations were not published until 1678 but the records of the Judiciary Courts show that he and his fellow justices-depute were exercising restraint from 1661 onwards.[124] There is no guarantee that Countess Isabella shared Rosehaugh's views, but she is unlikely to have been unaware of them and she could not have acted on her own. It seems inconceivable that in a culture of rational reluctance to prosecute witches Countess Isabella arbitrarily executed the Brahan Seer for a slight to her dignity.

120 Ibid., p. 87.

121 Ibid., p. 91.

122 Mackenzie, *Pleadings*, p. 196. *The Laws and Customs*, pp. 92–93.

123 Mackenzie, *The Laws and Customs*, p. 102.

124 Scott-Moncrieff, *The Records of the Proceedings of the Justiciary Court*, passim. J. Lauder, *Fountainhall's Historic Notes* (Edinburgh, 1848), p. 163.

Conclusion

Since the events of the Fowlis affair a near century earlier, many changes had taken place with regard to witchcraft in the attitudes of those in power and in the workings of the legal process. By the Restoration, the church was invariably the instigator of prosecutions at local level and while central authority acted as a restraining influence, local authority – both church and civil – could and did take a moderate view of popular magical practices. This was not because elite thinkers shared a belief in these practices but evidence of their disengagement from this aspect of popular culture. Many of the popular witchcraft beliefs and practices were treated by churchmen and lawyers with scepticism or ridicule. Witchcraft as a crime punishable by death was maintained, not in respect to what witches necessarily believed but by their prosecutors' conception of a pact with the devil allied to malice. One of the driving forces behind the national hunt of 1661–62 was the employment of professional prickers whose job it was to forcibly extract confessions. When the hunt abated, due in part to a realisation on the part of rational thinkers that prickers were cheats, a more restrained approach to witch prosecutions prevailed. Sceptics looked first at natural rather than supernatural causes to explain otherwise inexplicable events and the fear of witchcraft, which depended on mystery for success, diminished. This is evident both at national level, through the records of the courts, and in and around Easter Ross through the records of the various presbyteries in the area. A culture of rational reluctance to prosecute witches is evident from the diaries of Brodie of Brodie and the observations of the learned Mackenzie of Rosehaugh.

While the actions of Chisholm of Cromer provide evidence of corrupting the system, safeguards were in place and the evidence against Countess Isabella having had the Brahan Seer put to death is strong. She would have been guilty of murder had she not followed legal procedures which, while open to abuses, were quickly amended to curb them. The Brahan Seer was not accused of having a pact with the devil. It is unlikely that he would have been condemned to death without it during the national hunt of 1661–62. The Seer was guilty of no more than insulting behaviour so it is unlikely that he would have been condemned to death in the years following. When the phenomenon of second sight is examined the evidence becomes even more persuasive against there being a contemporary of Isabella who suffered the fate of the Brahan Seer of legend.

CHAPTER 4

Enlightenment and Elite Interest in Second Sight

Introduction

The previous chapter suggested that Countess Isabella of Seaforth could not have had the Brahan Seer put to death as a witch by burning in the years following the Restoration. The evidence against her executing the seer is even more compelling from an examination of second sight. In the present schema second sight has replaced witchcraft as the predominant idiom through which 'non-rational' or 'popular' beliefs are understood by 'elites' because it was a kind of 'private' or 'secret' strand of thought within an ostensibly rational Enlightenment culture and because it is the basis for the Romantic invention of the legend of the Brahan Seer. Second sight came under the scrutiny of the scientific community during the last quarter of the seventeenth century and continued to attract intellectual interest intermittently thereafter. Some of the earliest enquiries into second sight were directed towards the very geographical region in which the Brahan Seer was supposed to have lived and to contemporaries of Isabella who knew her. The Countess's brother, George Mackenzie, Lord Tarbat, made the first recorded enquiries and it was he who provided Robert Boyle with information which galvanised London intellectuals into a scientific examination of the phenomenon. No evidence exists to suggest that a person with a reputation as is now ascribed to the Brahan Seer flourished at this time, nor is mention made of any seer being put to death for practising his art. People with second sight were not considered to be witches and were not prosecuted as such. The Seaforths were, if anything, sympathetic towards the phenomenon and the family not without its reported adepts. Any contact with a Brahan Seer figure would have been recorded.

The Seaforths participated in a shared 'culture' in which second sight was important. According to Michael Hunter, enquirers such as Boyle, John Aubrey, Edward Lhuyd, Samuel Pepys and others examined second sight in late seventeenth-century Scotland because, as men of their age, they believed in both a natural and a supernatural world.[1] They were trying to confirm the supernatural by scientific means. They were not, according to Patrick Curry, trying to draw a line between magic and reason 'but through magic, dividing it into acceptable and unacceptable sorts.'[2] They distanced themselves from the beliefs and superstitions involved in witchcraft. Boyle was a member of the Royal Society, founded in 1660 to promote an empirical approach to the environment. Members engaged in rigorous and systematic observation of 'matters of fact.'[3] It was no longer sufficient to accept previously held convictions without putting them under scrutiny. Individuals were questioning the position of institutional authority across all domains as new discoveries challenged political, religious and scientific orthodoxy. Interest in second sight was both scientific and religious. Believed to be God given, it could confirm the most fundamental Christian belief that there was an afterlife. Further, if science could confirm that there were people gifted with prophetic powers as described in the Bible this would, in turn, confirm the validity of the Good Book.

Second sight came to the fore of scientific enquiry due in part to the uncertainties of the times. A proliferation of predictions and prophecies from political and religious circles were disseminated through pamphlets and almanacs which had become widely available during the Interregnum. The official monopoly of the Company of Stationers, who controlled the

1 M. Hunter, *The Occult Laboratory: Magic Science and Second Sight in Late 17th Century Scotland* (Woodbridge, Suffolk, 2001), pp. 1–28. M. Hunter, *Robert Boyle (1627–91): Scrupulosity and Science* (Woodbridge, Suffolk, 2002), passim. Michael Hunter has consolidated many of the relevant texts from this period and this chapter is particularly indebted to his work.

2 P. Curry, *Prophecy and Power: Astrology in Early Modern England* (Cambridge, 1989), p. 39.

3 Hunter, *Occult Laboratory*, p. 4.

content of such publications, had been terminated in 1649 and a large amount of printed material was produced to satisfy a general interest in astrology.[4] This took different forms. High astrology, the study of the current movements of the heavenly bodies and their implications for planet earth and human life, disappeared in the face of scientific empiricism. Judicial astrology, the making of predictions for individuals based on a horoscope, could be considered a middle way between high astrology and a popular or 'profane' astrology. This was 'based on popular religion and folk wisdom' according to supporters, or upon 'superstition and ignorance,' according to critics.[5] Curry has drawn on the work of Peter Burke to suggest that the rise of a newly emergent middle class polarised belief in astrology between elite and popular cultures. The middle class was part of the elites who saw it as their duty to reform and improve popular values and beliefs. They facilitated this quest by separating themselves from a common culture to which they had once belonged.[6] This was exemplified by belief in prophecy. 'Only the prophecies of the Bible continued to be taken seriously by the learned.'[7]

This chapter challenges this position, suggesting instead that enquiries into second sight reveal a continued interconnection between elite and popular culture. The key distinction is not between elite and popular belief but between public and private interest. Interest in popular prophecy cannot be treated as purely the culture of the uneducated, seeking assurances for future happiness. Some of the elites tried to ascertain if major events could be predicted, although their enquiries were both discreet and private. Their discretion, according to Hunter, who examined the case of Robert Boyle, was founded more on social rather than intellectual grounds.[8] Boyle was reluctant to publish a collection of 'Strange

4 Curry, *Prophecy and Power*, pp. 19–20, 118, 138 and 95–105. A. Geneva, *Astrology and the Seventeenth Century Mind: William Lilly and the Language of the Stars* (Manchester, 1995), pp. 272 and 282.

5 Curry, *Prophecy and Power*, p. 138.

6 Ibid., p. 153.

7 P. Burke, *Popular Culture in Early Modern Europe* (London, 1974), p. 274.

8 Hunter, *Scrupulosity and Science*, pp. 223–244.

Reports' on supernatural phenomena because he did not wish to damage his reputation by appearing to involve himself in matters inappropriate for one of his aristocratic station.[9] Nor did Boyle wish to appear unduly credulous; a charge levelled at John Aubrey who published his *Miscellanies* in 1696; a book full of accounts of the supernatural, including prophecies, apparitions and second sight.[10] Such accounts were questionable in the prevailing scientific climate. To avoid ridicule, discretion had to be exercised between the public utterances and private beliefs of the enquirers. The examination of second sight by Boyle and his immediate successors was short-lived due in part to scepticism from freethinkers, of both a scientific and religious persuasion. This metropolitan culture of scepticism was articulated in the coffee houses, theatres and the published periodicals of the time.[11] The exposure of fraud in the case of Janet Douglas in Edinburgh in 1677, the mercenary actions of the second sighted seer, Duncan Campbell, in early eighteenth century London, and the impossibility of rigorous scientific examination, all contributed to the demise of second sight as an appropriate topic for public scientific study.

Interest in second sight was re-stimulated in the mid-eighteenth century following the Jacobite rebellion but was confined to a small number of enquirers. Henry Baker's correspondence on the subject remains unpublished while the Rev. Donald Macleod's subscription list was meagre. Baker's interest was scientific; he had written treatises on the use of the microscope so the notion of seeing objects not visible to the naked eye was not alien to him.[12] However, his correspondence does show that some members of the Royal Society retained a private belief in popular prophecy.[13] Macleod's interest was religious, he was trying to counter freethinkers who questioned religious orthodoxy and looked to the phenomenon

9 Ibid., p. 236.

10 J. Aubrey, *Miscellanies upon Various Subjects* (London, 1784)

11 Hunter, *Scrupulosity and Science*, p. 236.

12 H. Baker, *The Microscope Made Easy, etc* (London, 1743) and *Employment for the Microscope* (London, 1753).

13 Henry Baker Correspondence, the John Rylands Library, Manchester, *English Ms 19*, Vols. 3, 4 and 5.

of second sight as confirming the existence of disembodied spirits.[14] John Wesley, founder of the Methodists and who railed against the 1736 repeal of the Witchcraft Act on the grounds that witchcraft was proscribed by scripture, sought out instances of apparitions and second sight as proof of a spirit world.[15] Dr Samuel Johnson's interest was intensely personal. The thought that his great intellect came to nothing when his body drew its last breath filled him with dread. He would have welcomed any evidence that his soul, or spirit, continued beyond his material existence. However, his need for evidence beyond the mere anecdotal ensured that his analytical mind was never provided with the verification it craved.[16] The scepticism of his literary friends certainly influenced James Boswell's public utterances on second sight while a general disinterest and scepticism is evident from Baker and Macleod's enquiries.

Travellers who passed through the Highlands generally reported incidents of second sight in a critical manner. Most accounts consigned the phenomenon to the past and dismissed it as some curious example of the remnants of some bygone superstition. The fact that travellers did report it and that people provided accounts confirmed that second sight continued to form part of popular culture. Scottish second sight had peculiar cultural manifestations, such as seeing the arrival of impending visitors, the wearing of a shroud denoting impending death or seeing a funeral cortege.[17] It became recognised as a peculiarly Scottish, indeed Highland, phenomenon. A. J. L. Busst has drawn attention to the influence of travellers in Scotland, such as Dr Johnson, on European writers,

14 T. Insulanus (Donald MacLeod), *A Treatise on the Second Sight, Dreams and Apparitions: With Several Instances Sufficiently Attested* (Edinburgh, 1763).

15 J. Wesley, *The Works of the Rev. John* Wesley 17 Vols. (London, 1809–1813) Vol. 4, p. 448, Vol. 5, p. 190, Vol. 13, pp. 210, 211 and 244.

16 B. Redford (ed.), *The Letters of Samuel Johnson* 5 Vols. (Oxford, 1992) Vol. II, pp. 75 and 79 for Johnson's anxieties. And see C. E. Pierce, *The Religious Life of Samuel Johnson* (London, 1983).

17 M. Martin, *A Description of the Western Islands of Scotland Circa 1695* (London, 1703) pp. 300–335. Insulanus, *A Treatise*, passim.

travellers and scientists.[18] Although travellers to the region were mostly of a sceptical bent regarding second sight, perhaps the most notable visitor, Johnson, kept an open mind. His account in particular helped widen interest across Europe and helped lay the foundation for the Romantic perception of the Highlands which gave rise to the legend of the Brahan Seer. This awareness also ensured that when animal magnetism (mesmerism) came to the fore at the close of the eighteenth century second sight again came under scientific scrutiny. Animal magnetism caused a stir across all social classes because of the claims made for it. Apart from its healing attributes practitioners claimed to be able to mesmerise clients into a state where they could see into the future. Soon clairvoyants, as they were called, were claiming that they could make prophetic pronouncements by self-inducing their mesmeric state and by the mid-nineteenth century demonstrations became a popular attraction in public theatres and private salons. As interest in clairvoyance rose it attracted detractors as well as supporters and came under scrutiny from the medical profession. Second sight became subsumed within clairvoyance and scientific explanations were provided to account for it. Interest in second sight as a purely Scottish phenomenon declined partly for the above reason and partly because, according to Busst, 'both its credibility and its practice were dying out in Scotland.'[19] This chapter argues that the decline was not confined to a particular class, neither was it terminal.

Enquiries into second sight among contemporaries of Countess Isabella show that second sight was perceived differently to witchcraft and not punished under witchcraft laws. The Mackenzies believed in second sight and recorded instances but made no mention of a Brahan Seer figure. The enquirers' difficulty in obtaining credible testimony was exacerbated by the conflicting descriptions of second sight and seers emanating from the region. Scepticism directed towards something which could not be proved as a matter of fact led to tensions between the private and public spheres of elite interest rather than between elite and popular culture. By

18 A. J. L. Busst, 'Scottish Second Sight: The Rise and Fall of a European Myth' *European Romantic Review* Vol. 5, part 2 (1995), pp. 149–177.

19 Ibid., p. 168.

the mid-eighteenth century, events surrounding the Jacobite Rising of 1745 triggered a renewed interest in second sight as a prophetic medium.

Early enquiries into second sight

If Countess Isabella had been involved with the burning of a seer, her acquaintance James Fraser, minister of Wardlaw, who chronicled the minutiae of his age and who witnessed the maltreatment of the Strathglass witches, seems a likely candidate for knowing about and recording it. Equally relevantly, if a seer did live in the neighbourhood who had the gift of second sight to the degree claimed for the Brahan Seer then, whether or not he came to a violent end at the hands of Lady Isabella, Fraser would seem well placed to record that seer's pronouncements. He reports no such individual. He does, however, record a conversation in 1643 between Donald Glasshach, a man who 'could forsee anything that happened about the place,' and Lady Katherine Fraser who had refused all entreaties to marry an unpleasant widower, Sir John Sinclair of Dunbeath.[20] The relationship between Glasshach, 'a common servant about the house' and Lady Katherine, a single young woman, contrasts with that between the powerful Isabella and the Brahan Seer. Glasshach 'accosted' Lady Katherine, berating her in Gaelic for her wilfulness. He told her to marry Dunbeath who would make her wealthy and leave her happy. Events proved him right.

When the Highlands as a geographical region came under scrutiny from the metropolitan scientific community towards the end of the seventeenth century, Fraser was one of the ministers canvassed by enquirers for his local knowledge.[21] John Aubrey's enquiry into second sight was helped by a questionnaire drawn up by James Garden, professor of theol-

20 J. Fraser, *Chronicles of the Frasers (The Wardlaw Manuscript)*, pp. 284–285.

21 Hunter, *Occult Laboratory*, p. 205. He was contacted by the Welsh academic Edward Lhuyd by letter dated 18 December 1699.

ogy at King's College, Aberdeen. One of Garden's correspondents, writing in 1694, was a 'minister living near Inverness.'[22] While there is no direct evidence to confirm that this was Fraser, Garden's minister recounts the Glasshach story in near identical terms to Fraser's *Chronicles*.[23] He also tells of a young man in the parish of Wardlaw being brought before the session on a charge of witchcraft and confessing to having second sight. He does not record the outcome. If, as seems likely, Garden's correspondent was Fraser, then the story of 'Mistriss Kate' appears to be the best example of second sight in his experience and it refers to events of fifty years earlier. One of Garden's colleagues from King's College who grew up in Easter Ross returned to the area and enquired into second sight at Garden's request. Of the two inconsequential accounts he could remember from the 'many instances' he heard, nothing related to Garden suggests that a local seer was so well known that he could carry the epithet the Brahan Seer.[24] Garden was discreet in not naming his sources; he professed to know nothing himself of second sight and wrote Aubrey desiring his name be kept out of any publication.[25] He was clearly willing to assist the enquiry in a private rather than a public capacity and although he gave no reason for his reserve he perhaps thought he would attract ridicule. If so, he was to be proved right.

Isabella's brother, George Mackenzie, Lord Tarbat, likewise took an active interest in second sight. It was because of this that he was invited, on the afternoon of Thursday, 3 October 1678, to the Pall Mall home of Robert Boyle. Boyle later recorded the interview during which Tarbat advised him that he had overcome initial scepticism after being witness to two incidents which had taken place in 1653 and 1652 respectively.[26] At Boyle's request Tarbat wrote him a letter recounting the two events.

22 Hunter, *Occult Laboratory*, p. 145. C. A. Gordon (ed.), 'Professor James Garden's Letters to John Aubrey, 1692–5', *Miscellany of the 3rd Spalding Club*, Vol. 3 (Aberdeen, 1960), pp. 6–56.

23 Hunter, *Occult Laboratory*, p. 145. Fraser, *Chronicles*, pp. 284–285.

24 Hunter, *Occult Laboratory*, p. 144.

25 Ibid., p. 155.

26 Ibid., pp. 51–53, 90–94 and 165–169.

Although undated it is thought to have been written in 1680.[27] Tarbat appears to be the first person to look into second sight beyond the mere gathering of instances. He laid down some generalities as to its properties. He told Boyle that while many Highlanders had second sight, it was more prevalent among the Islanders; that men, women and children had it indiscriminately; it was not hereditary – people could acquire the faculty in childhood or adulthood and had no knowledge of how it arose. Most who had it deemed it something they would rather not have and visions lasted only so long as the seer did not blink, so only the fearless tried to hold their gaze.

Tarbat declined to impart second-hand accounts, preferring instead 'to put myselfe than my friends on the hazard of being laughed at for Incredible Relationes.'[28] In his letter to Boyle, Tarbat recounts a tale not mentioned at their meeting; of having been introduced to a 'notable Seer' from the Islands and questioning him as to the love prospects of a young lady present. The seer described the man who would marry, and die before, her. 'This was in the year 1655 … tho there was noe thought of their marriage till two years thereafter.'[29] The seer and nobility appear comfortable in each other's company. Tarbat confirmed the identity of the husband-to-be when he met the seer with the man in 1657. 'This was som few moneths before their marriadge and the man is since dead, and the Lady still alive.' Tarbat's delicacy forbids him from naming the lady but the circumstances fit the period of marriage between Countess Isabella and Earl Kenneth. The earl died in December 1678, after Tarbat's interview with Boyle but before his letter. If the lady is Isabella, it suggests this to be her most noteworthy involvement with a seer known to her brother. If Isabella had been instrumental in burning a seer Tarbat could have told the tale without divulging her name. The seer's fate alone would have been worthy of note. Tarbat makes no mention of such an incident, suggesting that it did not happen. The family's belief in second sight may have been occasioned by Isabella's husband, Earl Kenneth, who 'was com-

27 Ibid., p. 91.

28 Ibid.

29 Ibid., pp. 92–93.

monly reported' among the ruling elites in Scotland to have the second sight which he neither affirmed nor denied when the Secretary of State, the Duke of Lauderdale, 'raillys' him about foretelling a storm.[30] These Mackenzie anecdotes illustrate the tension between the public culture of scepticism and the private beliefs of educated elites with regard to second sight as opposed to a distinct cleavage between elite and popular culture. The family's sympathetic attitude to second sight appears to rule out an arbitrary execution.

Another reason for thinking that Countess Isabella could not have had the Brahan Seer burned for a witch is that second sight was not illegal and the distinction between it and witchcraft practices which were illegal (until 1736) had been made in court. Further, the distinction between witchcraft and second sight had been made in the minds of divines. When the Privy Council called upon Sir John Lauder of Fountainhall in 1677 to examine the dumb teenager, Janet Douglas, his concern was to ascertain if she had used witchcraft to identify witches responsible for the death of a West Country laird. Some five or six people had been burnt on her evidence and others imprisoned on unrelated charges since her arrival in Edinburgh. Fountainhall could find no evidence of witchcraft and the Privy Council ordered Douglas to be banished from the realm as a cheat and impostor. Second sight was only one of several hypotheses advanced to explain her faculty. Her examiners would not convict her of witchcraft without evidence of a pact with the devil.[31] Second sight evaded any taint of usurping God's work by being involuntary and so was treated with sympathy rather than condemned like other forms of voluntary divination. George Mackenzie of Rosehaugh argued that any form of divination was prohibited by law but remarked that 'these forbidden practices may sometimes be excused by ignorance, or if it can be cleared by circumstances, that the user designed nothing but an innocent jest or recreation.'[32] Many notable figures examined Janet Douglas. An

30 Ibid., pp. 174, 179 and 180, letter dated 19 June 1700.

31 J. Lauder, *Fountainhall's Historical Notes* Vol. I (Edinburgh, 1848), p. 144.

32 G. Mackenzie, *The Laws and Customs of Scotland in Matters Criminal* (Edinburgh, 1678), p. 96.

account by George Hickes, chaplain to the Duke of Lauderdale, was sent to Samuel Pepys. He gathered information on second sight and details of the Douglas case circulated in London.[33]

The Rev. Robert Kirk produced an account of second sight in 1692.[34] Although not published until 1815, several manuscript copies passed among those interested in the phenomenon. Kirk's account was based on his research into Perthshire fairy lore in which those with second sight see fairy 'co-walkers' who attend the living. He thought the acquisition of second sight hereditary, generally passing from father to son. There were few women seers 'and their predictions not so certan [sic].'[35] An acquired skill enabled seers to differentiate between signs from good and bad spirits. Part of Kirk's treatise is devoted to defending second sight from a charge of witchcraft which he does by noting the absence of the devil's mark, and despite describing how men could be inducted into its mysteries in an initiation ceremony, by noting the involuntary nature of its acquisition.[36] By invoking earlier scholars and the Bible, second sight, unlike witchcraft, was shown to be 'not unsuitable to reason nor the Holy Scriptures.'[37] Kirk concluded that seers would prefer to be rid of their faculty because of the horrors it exposed.

Travellers throughout this period reported popular belief in, and instances of second sight. Among the earliest was the Englishman, Thomas Kirk, told by a gentleman believer at Dornoch, in 1677, of 'a sort of people ... that had foresight of things to come ... they believed their ancestors

33 Hunter, *Occult Laboratory*, pp. 174–178. J. R. Tanner (ed.), *Correspondence of Samuel Pepys 1679–1700* (London, 1926), pp. 370–375.

34 Edinburgh University Library, Ms. Laing III, 551 'The Secret Commonwealth or a Treatise Displaying the Chief Curiosities Among the People of Scotland as They are in Use to this Day' Transcribed by C. Campbell. S. Sanderson (ed.), *The Secret Commonwealth of Elves, Fauns and Fairies and a Short Treatise of Charms and Spels* (Cambridge, 1976). Hunter, *Occult Laboratory*, pp. 77–106.

35 Hunter, *Occult Laboratory*, pp. 88 and 94.

36 Ibid., pp. 86, 102 and 103.

37 Ibid., pp. 86 and 98.

had been witches and got the boon of the devil ...'[38] Since 'they would gladly be quit of this faculty' their belief in its origin suggests both a form of punishment and a warning against engaging in witchcraft.[39] Martin Martin's recording of numerous instances from the Western Isles probably created the most interest among the scientific community in London.[40] Men, women and children had second sight and so did domestic animals, especially horses. Second sight did not descend through families and its acquisition was only known after the fulfilment of a prophecy. Martin notes the innocence of its acquisition, it could not be transferred in any way, '[n]either is it acquir'd by any previous Compact.'[41] The Seers, although 'generally illiterate' are 'well-meaning People' of good character who do not profit from their power. He would not be the last to record its decline, it 'was much more common twenty Years ago than at present; for one in ten do not see it now, that saw it then.'[42]

Confirming that second sight was free from witchcraft was the prime consideration of the divine Robert Wodrow, when he sent a questionnaire to John Maclean, on Mull. Wodrow was especially eager to hear from the Rev. John Beaton who had provided Edward Lhuyd with information on second sight in 1699.[43] Maclean, replying in April 1702, volunteered neither information nor opinion of his own. He wrote on behalf of Beaton, who 'cannot say much, but what experience has made common. It was frequent here some few years ago, and not yet altogether extinguished; and he affirms that it readily went from father to son, but not of the best livers. He refers you to Mr Frazer anent it ...'[44] Beaton is referring Wodrow to the Rev. John Fraser whose treatise on second sight was published

38 P. Hume Brown (ed.), *Tours in Scotland 1677 and 1681: Thomas Kirk and Ralph Thoresby* (Edinburgh, 1892), pp. 34–35.

39 Ibid., p. 35.

40 M. Martin, *A Description of the Western Islands of Scotland* (London, 1703), pp. 300–335.

41 Ibid., p. 301.

42 Ibid., pp. 301, 306, 309 and 312.

43 Hunter, *Occult Laboratory*, p. 25.

44 Ibid., p. 209 and L. W. Sharp (ed.), *Early Letters of Robert Wodrow 1698–1709* (Edinburgh, 1937), pp. 159–162.

posthumously in 1707.[45] Fraser died in August 1702 but had replied to Wodrow earlier in the year, 'you may fully persuade yourself that severall persons hes it, *that it is free of paction* yea, and are found to be pious and hes abundant sense, neither is it propagated from father to son' (emphasis added).[46] In these few brief words Fraser reassures Wodrow of the absence of witchcraft but contradicts Beaton's description on the question of heredity and on the character of the seers. In his treatise Fraser drew heavily on biblical references to explain both the antiquity and legality of second sight.

The initial enquiry into second sight was short-lived: by the end of the seventeenth century Boyle and Aubrey were dead and several of the remaining enquirers were in their twilight years. Only Aubrey in his *Miscellanies* (1696) and John Beaumont in his *Treatise* (1705) added substantially to Martin Martin's detailed account of second sight published in 1703.[47] The *Treatise* was essentially a reworking of what had gone before, recycling Tarbat's letter to Boyle and Garden's letters to Aubrey. Although neither correspondent was identified in print their names were known, indicating that they and second sight were topics of private discussion in elite circles.[48] The freethinker John Toland thought Garden 'altogether as credulous as Dr Martin,' an observation he jotted in the margin of his copy of Martin's book.[49] Even Lord Tarbat's intellect was said to be limited.[50] Toland was sceptical of second sight, expressing his contempt for the triviality of some instances described by Martin and

45 J. Fraser, *Deuteroscopia: A Brief Discourse Concerning the Second Sight* (Edinburgh, 1707). Hunter, *Occult Laboratory*, pp. 187–204.

46 Hunter, *Occult Laboratory*, pp. 212–213.

47 Martin, *Description of the Western Islands of Scotland*, pp. 300–335.

48 J. Beaumont, *An Historical, Physiological and Theological Treatise on Spirits, Apparitions, Witchcrafts, and Other Magical Practices* … (London, 1705), p. 84.

49 Toland's Marginalia in Martin's *Description of the Western Islands of Scotland*: British Library Ref: c. 45.c.1 p 300. The marginalia are entered throughout the book but are especially concentrated on the chapter on second sight. Toland's friend, Lord Molesworth, wrote several notes of his own. Toland distinguished between the two by adding their respective initials (note on flyleaf).

50 Ibid., p. 326.

providing natural explanations for others. He believed that a detailed comparative study of the natural world and the human condition of the times was sufficient for any author to make predictions as to future events and only their fulfilment made them meaningful.[51] As for superstitions, he argued, these are beliefs inculcated into people to keep them in ignorance, and trying to find evidence by natural means in support of such beliefs is futile.[52] Toland's main target in his pursuit of superstition was the Catholic Church. Toland's friend, Lord Molesworth, added his own scathing remarks. 'I knew this poor ignorant Martin, and one day exposed him so much to the ridicule of very good company (whither he was brought to dine) upon the account of the second sight which he pretended to maintain, that he never afterwards durst appear again in that company. The Royal Society were much to blame to admit such a person among them ...'[53] Molesworth wondered why 'these imposters, with Duncan Campbell at the head of them, are not whipped, publickly out of all communityes, or more secretly punished.'[54] The fact that Martin was admitted to the Royal Society and that he and others were prepared to examine second sight is an indication that there was no sharp division between elite and popular culture. The division here is between sections of the elite.

One attribute generally reported of second-sighted seers is that they sought no profit or gain from their faculty. The exploits of Duncan Campbell in the first quarter of the eighteenth century challenged this conception. Not much is known of him in his early years. Campbell arrived in London in 1694 at the age of fourteen and earned his living from second sight. According to his biography, published in 1720, he was patronised by large numbers of people across all social classes including

51 S. H. Daniel, *John Toland His Methods, Manners and Mind* (Montreal, 1984), pp. 88–89. P. McGuinness, A. Harrison and R. Kearney (eds), *John Toland's Christianity Not Mysterious: Texts, Associated Works and Critical Essays* (Dublin, 1997 (1696)).

52 Daniel, *John Toland*, p. 99.

53 Toland, Marginalia, pp. 303–304. Hunter, *Occult Laboratory*, p. 31.

54 Toland, Marginalia, p. 300.

Queen Anne.[55] The first published record of him was in the *Tatler* of Thursday, 12 May 1709, when Richard Steele notes, 'A Gentleman here this evening was giving me an Account of a dumb Fortune-teller who outdoes Mr Partridge, my self, or the Unborn-Doctor, for predictions.'[56] Campbell was deaf and dumb and though he claimed his second sight was not dependent upon these sensory deficiencies many thought they were a hoax and contrived numerous ploys in an attempt to unmask him.[57] Campbell's knowledge of second sight seems to have been derived from printed works. He claimed Highland and Lapland descent, both of which were probably spurious.[58] In an article in the *Spectator* of Wednesday, 3 September 1712, Steele again satirises the credulity of those who consult Campbell but his public attacks are more circumspect than those of Joseph Addison whose barbed wit in the same publication is aimed more directly at Campbell.[59] Campbell communicated by finger touch and wrote his answers down. His unorthodox methods added to the general air of mistrust among sceptics. Since he was the only second sighted person many people knew, any shortcomings in his character or doubts about his prophetic abilities would have influenced their perception of second sight and seers in general. *A New General Dictionary*, which first appeared in 1735, five years after Campbell's death, defined second sight as 'a *pretended* inspiration ... a privilege that many inhabitants of the western islands ... are said to be endowed with ... (emphasis added).' However, it

55 G. A. Aitken (ed.), Romances and Narratives by Daniel Defoe series, Vol. IV, *The History of the Life and Adventures of Mr Duncan Campbell* (London, 1895), p x. See also R. M. Baine, *Daniel Defoe and the Supernatural* (Athens, USA, 1968), pp. 143 et seq. One of the central arguments of Baine's book is that the biography of Campbell was not written by Defoe but by William Bond, pp. 147 et seq.

56 D. F. Bond (ed.), *The Tatler No. 14*. The Unborn-Doctor was a quack.

57 D. Campbell, *Secret Memoirs of the Late Mr. Duncan Campbel [sic] the Famous Deaf and Dumb Gentleman Written by Himself Who Ordered They Should be Publish'd After His Decease* (London, 1720), p. 228.

58 R. M. Baine, *Daniel Defoe and the Supernatural*, p. 149–150.

59 D. F. Bond (ed.) *The Spectator* 5 Vols. Steele's article is under the pseudonym of Dulcibella Thankley, No. 474. Addison, no. 323 under the name of Clarinda, no. 505 under the name of Titus Trophonius and no. 560.

continued through several editions to observe that 'Mr Campbell, the famous impostor of that nation lately resident in London, hath destroyed the whole credit of that pretension.'[60]

In *The Free-Holder* of 23 March 1716, Addison satirises a Highland seer by the name of Second Sighted Sawney whose 'mother but narrowly escaped being burnt for a witch.'[61] The purpose of the article was to mock Jacobite supporters. The character of Isaac Bickerstaffe, invented by Jonathan Swift, adopted by Steele and then Daniel Defoe, was used mercilessly to debunk any pretended prophecies, especially those of the most noted almanac producer and astrologer of the time, John Partridge. Swift had predicted Partridge's death in a pamphlet '*Predictions for the Year 1708, etc …*' and then given an account of its fulfilment. Partridge had responded in print that he was alive and well, only for Bickerstaffe to claim he was an impostor. The general public and wits alike were kept amused by the rivalry.[62] When Defoe assumed the name of 'Isaac Bickerstaffe, Elder, having the 2d sight' it was for the more serious reason of advocating peace in the country.[63] Defoe relied on the credulity of his readers and used deception to get his message across. *The British Visions; Being Twelve Prophecies for the Year, 1711* was first printed in the north before being reprinted in London. This gave Defoe time to insert some notable events occurring early in the year and then claiming success for the accuracy of his prophecy. Defoe changed his persona for subsequent editions, the pamphlet issued in 1712 was called *Highland Visions,* and the predictions were by a *Second Sighted Highlander*, the title he used until the last edition for 1715 wherein the failed Jacobite rebellion is roundly condemned.[64]

60 T. Dyche and W. Pardon (eds), *A New General Dictionary* 10th edition (London, 1760). See also Baine, *Daniel Defoe and the Supernatural*, pp. 159 and 215.

61 J. Addison, *The Free-Holder* No. 27 (1716).

62 H. R. Montgomery (ed.), *Memoirs of the Life and Writings of Sir Richard Steele* (Edinburgh, 1865), pp. 138–144.

63 D. Defoe, *The British Visions; or, Isaac Bickerstaff, Senr: Being Twelve Prophecies for the Year, 1711* (1711), p. 4. The copy in Special Collections of Aberdeen University bears a cover ascribing authorship first to Sir Richard Steele and then to Jonathan Swift.

64 Baine, *Daniel Defoe and the Supernatural*, pp. 118–128.

For the time being scepticism had triumphed over belief for educated metropolitan elites and those who took an interest in second sight did so in a private rather than a public capacity. Their continued interest is evident from their enquiries during later events of national and religious importance.

Travellers' tales: gathering scepticism and religious demands

A renewed interest in second sight in the middle of the eighteenth century appears to be partly the last flickering of the enquiry precipitated by Lord Tarbat's meeting with Robert Boyle. For some enquirers a publicly voiced scepticism contrasted with a private need to seek confirmation of deeply held religious beliefs, particularly with regard to evidence for an afterlife. The possibility of predicting momentous events exercised the minds of others. When Henry Baker, writer, scientist and son-in-law to Daniel Defoe, began writing to the Rev. Archibald Blair it was to commiserate the death of Blair's brother.[65] Having gained Blair's confidence, Baker asked in a letter dated 4 November 1746 if he knew anything of second sight, setting out the historical credentials of the phenomenon from the time of Plutarch, and referring to instances in scripture. Baker was writing on behalf of friends but was coy about identifying those with whom he was to share the fruits of his enquiry. He asked a series of question on the properties of second sight and seers. His eighth and final question was, 'Did any of these second-sighted people foresee and foretell the miseries that have lately befallen your poor unhappy country?'[66] When Blair replied with a lengthy account of the opinions of the ancients, Baker

65 *Henry Baker Correspondence*: English MS 19, Vol. 2, nos. 197, 215; the John Rylands University Library of Manchester. Baine, *Daniel Defoe and the Supernatural*, p. 93.

66 *Baker Correspondence*, Vol. 2, no. 281.

brought him back to the matter in hand by reiterating this question.[67] The immediate events of the failed '45 Jacobite rebellion had clearly initiated the enquiry.

Blair did his best to satisfy Baker, supplying him with several inconsequential accounts including two involving contemporary members of the Seaforth family.[68] New accounts were so hard to come by that Blair referred Baker to Martin's and Fraser's published works, going so far as to obtain and send a copy of the latter which Baker had not seen. Baker had read Martin's account and thought little of it because it did not satisfy his need for well-attested matters of fact.[69] He suggested that Fraser's book would be of little use having previously been advised by one of Blair's correspondents that Martin's was the better of the two. When Baker did receive the book he noted politely that it was 'highly acceptable, and seems written with Good sense and great Modesty.'[70] Neither Blair nor a friend of his was able to provide evidence to suggest that the events of the Jacobite rebellion had been the subject of second sighted prophecy.[71] Yet, precisely because of the turmoil, John Ramsay of Ochtertyre had noted that 'in the year 1745 the Isle of Skye swarmed with prophets.'[72] Blair relayed a story concerning Duncan Forbes of Culloden, the late Lord President, only to find that Baker had heard it directly from Forbes 'with some few other particulars having been well acquainted with him.'[73] A person's social relationship clearly had a bearing on the extent of information imparted. When Blair was unable to obtain details of the gift from a second sighted man in Caithness who preferred to 'keep it secret' and when Lord Drummuir 'thought it not

67 Ibid., Vol. 2, no. 291, Blair to Baker, 4 December 1746. Vol. 3, no. 29, Baker to Blair, 31 January 1747.

68 Ibid., Vol. 3, nos. 355, 29 October 1748 and 356b.

69 Ibid., Vol. 3, no 162, 27 October 1747.

70 Ibid., Vol. 4, no 67, 10 February 1749.

71 Ibid., Vol. 3, no 110, letter from John Cumming to Blair, 20 June 1747.

72 A. Allardyce (ed.), *Scotland and Scotsmen in the Eighteenth Century* Vol. II (Edinburgh, 1888), p. 468.

73 *Baker Correspondence,* Vol. 4, no 67, 10 February 1749.

advisable' to answer questions regarding an instance to which he had been witness, Blair advised Baker that he had no more information to give. The exchange of letters had lasted over three years.[74]

The reticence shown by the seer and a member of the nobility was matched by Baker's friends. Only by what appears to be an unintentional slip does he reveal them to be 'some curious people of the Royal Society.'[75] Over a year passed before Blair asked what was the Society's opinion on second sight. Baker replied, 'as a Society we never give our Opinion of any doubtfull Matter, as that would lead us into Endless disputes, and divert our Enquiries into Nature by Experiments, into wrangling and useless Debates. Neither could this Subject be brought before us as a Society not coming within the Design of our Institution.'[76] Baker himself seemed sceptical in public. While editor of the *Universal Spectator* in 1732, he had published an essay highly critical of a woman's claim to have seen an apparition.[77] The boundaries between science, religion and the supernatural were not definitive though a phenomenon such as second sight was considered worthy of investigation only in a private capacity.

A similar contrast between public scepticism and private curiosity was shown by Sir Richard Steele who encouraged Donald Macleod, minister of Hamer, in Skye, to investigate instances of second sight to prove the existence of spirits. Writing under the name Theophilus Insulanus, Macleod attacked all atheists, deists and freethinkers who cast doubt on the immortality of the soul.[78] His enquiry lay dormant for many years, having been instigated at Steele's request during a debate on the topic with 'wise and learned gentlemen.'[79] Steele's private enquiry for well-authenticated instances of second sight seems at odds with his public attacks in the *Spectator* and *Tatler* but may explain his circumspection

74 Ibid., Vol. 4, no. 134, Blair's last letter dated 15 August 1749.

75 Ibid., Vol. 3, no. 119, 15 August 1747. Baker mentions them again in his letter of 27 October 1747, Vol. 3, no. 162.

76 Ibid., Vol. 4, no. 67, 10 February 1749. Hunter, *Scrupulosity*, p. 244.

77 Baine, *Daniel Defoe and the Supernatural*, p. 93.

78 Insulanus, *A Treatise.*

79 Ibid., pp. 1 and 107.

therein. Steele had been in Edinburgh several times during the period 1717 to 1721 when he had worked as a Commissioner for the Forfeited Estates. He was a strong supporter of the Society for the Promotion of Christian Knowledge and very likely its Scottish equivalent, so may have met Macleod in this capacity.[80] Steele died in 1729; there is no reference to Macleod in his published correspondence.[81]

Macleod graduated from King's College, Aberdeen, in 1715 but was not appointed to his first charge, Contin, in Easter Ross, until 1720.[82] He may have undertaken his enquiry and begun collecting oral accounts some time during this period. He drew on historical and biblical references to overcome the 'stale objection' that second sight was 'only seen by mean, silly illiterate people.'[83] Most of the over one hundred instances are undated; several were provided in response to a postal enquiry to clergymen colleagues and factors in December 1756. Macleod does not explain why it took him so long to pursue his enquiry. One noted seer in Glenelg refused to meet Macleod's envoy, his minister having 'blamed, or rather threatened him last year, for unseasonably publishing some of his predictions.'[84] To his credit, Macleod added to his treatise letters from several of his correspondents, some of whom provided warm support 'amidst the sneers and ill-nature of parsons and factors,' and some of whom were downright hostile to an undertaking 'likely to be perverted for superstitious ends.'[85] The book was published by subscription, Macleod sending lists to his fellow ministers. Rev. Morrison from Uig in Lewis put

80 R. Blanchard, *The Correspondence of Richard Steele* (Oxford, 1941), p 126. Blanchard, 'Richard Steele and the Secretary of the SPCK,' in C. Camden (ed.), *Restoration and Eighteenth Century Literature* (Chicago, 1963), pp. 287–295.

81 Blanchard, *The Correspondence of Steele*. Montgomery, *Memoirs of the Life of Steele*.

82 H. Scott (ed.), *Fasti Ecclesiae Scoticanae* Vol. III (Edinburgh, 1870), p. 293.

83 Insulanus, *Treatise*, p. 84.

84 Ibid., p. 120.

85 Ibid., pp. 117, 122, 137 and 169.

his name down for one copy; 'there are none but myself in my parish to use the book.'[86] One hundred copies were printed in 1763.[87]

James Beattie, professor of moral philosophy and logic at Marischall College, Aberdeen, read Insulanus's treatise. He accused the author of 'extreme credulity' and dismissed most of the accounts as 'trifling and ridiculous.'[88] Beattie supplied several natural reasons why instances of second sight were reported from the region, all based on the melancholy landscape. Long distances travelled in solitude and in inclement weather were bound to raise apprehensions; through tiredness or hunger a state of wakefulness could often be misunderstood, dreams being misconstrued as reality. The notion that God provides a marginalised people with a prophetic faculty which serves no purpose must be dismissed as absurd. The advancement of knowledge and industry saw a proportionate reduction in belief so that 'none but ignorant people pretend to be gifted in this way.'[89]

Others among the intellectual elites were no so ready to dismiss the phenomenon out of hand, however. Two eminent writers who provided Scottish second sight with an intellectual stimulus were Doctor Samuel Johnson and Mr James Boswell. Johnson's interest stemmed from his terror of annihilation. He could not believe that at the end of conscious life there was simply nothing and he sought any source of information which might confirm that death was not final.[90] Accounts of second sight which referred to approaching death held particular significance for him. His constant fear of death and a desire for proof to confirm his belief in the immortality of the soul were to remain with him throughout his

86 Ibid., p. 170.

87 Hunter, *Occult Laboratory*, p. 40.

88 J. Beattie, 'An Essay on Poetry and Music as They Affect the Mind; Written 1762' in *Essays* (Edinburgh, 1776). Beattie's observations on second sight are contained in a lengthy footnote, pp. 480–482.

89 Beattie, 'An Essay on Poetry, pp. 480–481.

90 Redford, *The Letters of Samuel Johnson* Vol. II, pp. 75 and 79 for Johnson's anxieties. And see Pierce, *The Religious Life of Samuel Johnson*.

life.[91] Yet, his scepticism was such that he required more than anecdotal testimony to confirm his belief. It was at least in part for this reason that Johnson and Boswell set out on their *Tour to the Hebrides* in August 1773.[92] They took with them Boswell's copy of Martin's *A Description of the Western Islands of Scotland,* a copy of which Johnson had been given, and which he had read avidly, as a boy. They used the book as a guide and were able on numerous occasions to enquire into second sight, hearing many stories presented with differing degrees of evidence and clarity.[93] Neither traveller thought the tales, with one exception, worth recording, but it seems they heard enough of them for Johnson to explain the high incidence of accounts referring to death. 'Death, which is considered as the greatest evil, happens to all. That they should often see death is to be expected; because death is an event frequent and important.'[94]

Johnson, like Martin, reported second sight as being a phenomenon more prevalent in the past. He notes that according to many Lowland Scots 'its reality is no longer supposed, but by the grossest people.'[95] On the other hand 'islanders of all degrees, whether of rank or understanding, universally admit it, except the Ministers, who universally deny it, and are suspected to deny it, in consequence of a system, against conviction.' Johnson reported that Rev. Martin Macpherson, a native of Barra, had told him frankly that he had come to Skye 'with a resolution not to believe it.' Another minister, the Rev. Donald MacQueen, of Kilmuir, Skye, said that he did not believe in second sight because he had not come across 'any well attested instances; and if he should, he should impute

91 G. B. Hill and L. F. Powell, *Boswell's Life of Johnson* Vol. III. pp. 295–296 and also p. 153 when discussing the death of Hume. See also Vol. IV, p. 374 and Vol. V, p. 180.

92 Hill and Powell, *Boswell's Life of Johnson* Vol. V, p. 13 et seq.

93 Ibid., p. 13, n 3. Samuel Johnson, J. Fleeman (ed.), *A Journey to the Western Isles of Scotland* (Oxford, 1985), pp. 57–58. James Boswell, R. W. Chapman (ed.), *Journal of a Tour to the Hebrides with Samuel Johnson* (London, 1951), p. 263.

94 Johnson, *A Journey*, pp. 89–90.

95 Ibid., p. 90.

them to chance.'[96] Boswell voiced his opinion that the clergy wanted to appear more enlightened than the rest of their flock and took the view that MacQueen was prejudiced against second sight.[97] He was certainly determined to stamp out superstitions. The practice of using witchcraft charms to obtain milk from their neighbours' cows had been widespread among the women when he had arrived in his parish in 1740. MacQueen had eradicated the belief by inviting the women to take as much milk as they wanted from his cows, provided they did not touch the animals.[98]

Johnson makes specific reference to the properties of second sight, how the events described are particular to local events within the culture in which they are uttered and how they serve no practical purpose.[99] He may have had in mind the account received from Lachlan McQuarrie of Ulva when he wrote this. McQuarrie had gone to Edinburgh with a manservant. An old woman remaining in the house had predicted that her master would return next day in the company of two gentlemen and with the servant dressed in a new uniform of red and green. These events transpired as predicted, McQuarrie having bought his servant's uniform on the spur of the moment so that the old woman could have had no prior knowledge of his intentions.[100] Boswell passes no opinion as to his belief or otherwise in the authenticity of this story neither does he record that Johnson had any opinion either way. This is the only account of second sight recorded by either traveller. According to Johnson's observations people with second sight made no effort to gain materially from their faculty. Seers did not flaunt it and nobody pretended to have it when they did not. As for being peculiar to the Hebrides, he opines that second sight 'is nowhere totally unknown' before concluding, 'I never could advance my curiosity to conviction; but came away at last only

96 Hill and Powell, *Boswell's Life of Johnson* Vol. V, pp. 163–164, and Boswell, *Journal of a Tour*, p. 266.

97 Boswell, *Journal of a Tour*, pp. 311–312.

98 Hill & Powell, *Boswell's Life of Johnson* Vol. V, p. 522, and Boswell, *Journal of a Tour*, p. 266.

99 Johnson, *A Journey*, p. 90.

100 Boswell, *Journal of a Tour*, pp. 376–377.

willing to believe.'[101] Evidence strong enough to convince Johnson never materialised. His enquiry into second sight provided no incontrovertible evidence for life after death.

While Johnson's position on second sight remained consistent, Boswell's belief, which at one time had been very strong, weakened after his return. Indeed, the erosion in his belief may have begun before their tour ended. During the last week of October 1773, they were dining, in company, with the Duke and Duchess of Argyle at Inverary Castle, when Boswell was somewhat discomfited by the Duchess's coldness towards him. At one point 'I said something of my belief in second sight. The Duchess said, "I fancy you will be a *Methodist*"' (original emphasis), the only words she directed towards Boswell during the entire evening.[102] The Rev. John Wesley, founder of the Methodists, believed in apparitions because he thought them evidence for an afterlife and he had examined several reported sightings by women at first hand. His interest in second sight stemmed from the same source. During a hectic period of preaching up and down the country, Wesley asked a native of Skye if he knew of any man with second sight. When his informant replied that he had known 'more than one or two' Wesley demanded to know how he could tell they were not faking. The Islander described instances which later enquiry showed to have been correct in every respect. This was Wesley's only specific mention of second sight. Enquirers like Wesley found it difficult to get information on second sight, his informant said, because those who have it 'count it a great misfortune, and it is thought a scandal to their family.'[103] People in the Highlands valued their place in the community. Social pressure seemed to be exerted against a public acknowledgement of second sight even among those who professed to have the faculty.

101 Johnson, *A Journey*, p. 91.

102 Ibid., p. 358 and Boswell, *Journal of a Tour*, p. 402. F. A. Pottle and C. H. Bennett (eds), *Boswell's Journal of a Tour to the Hebrides with S. M. LL. D* (London, 1936), p. 355.

103 Wesley, *The Works* Vol. 4, pp. 218–219, his journal for Sunday, 19 August 1764. The conversation took place in London.

Some fifteen months after their return to London, Boswell and Dr Johnson met at the Turk's Head, Gerrard Street, for the regular Friday evening meeting of their Literary Club when they dined in the company of about a dozen friends. Before Johnson's arrival the group was discussing his newly published '*Journey to the Western Isles*' and of his leaving the Hebrides 'willing to believe the second sight.'[104] This position, according to Boswell, attracted 'some' ridicule. Boswell's effort to defend Johnson, by pointing out that he was never entirely convinced without proof, ended in humiliation. He declared, 'I *do* believe (original emphasis). The evidence is enough for me, though not for his great mind. What will not fill a quart bottle will fill a pint bottle. I am filled with belief.' The dramatist, George Colman's response brought discussion on the matter to an abrupt end. 'Are you?' he asked. 'Then cork it up.'[105]

The reaction of his friends and the rebuff he had suffered at the hands of the Duchess of Argyle may have influenced Boswell's change of heart regarding belief in second sight. When, in 1785, twelve years after the tour, he published his own account, he acknowledged that he had 'returned from the Hebrides with a considerable degree of faith in the many stories of that kind which I heard ... but, since that time, my belief in those stories has been much weakened, by reflecting on the careless inaccuracy of narrative in common matters, from which we may certainly conclude that there may be the same in what is more extraordinary.'[106] Boswell's publicly stated belief in second sight became similar to the Doctor's. Only proof of matters of fact would elevate it from the superstitious to the scientific, even if, like electricity or magnetism, it was not understood.

Travellers who enquired into second sight often found a diminution of belief within Highland communities and a reticence to provide instances from seers and neighbours alike. This suggests that within these communities a tension existed between private belief and public expression similar to the tension that existed among educated elites. While touring Scotland in 1807, the naturalist Sir John Carr wondered if any

104 Hill and Powell, *Boswell's Life of Johnson* Vol. II, p. 318.

105 Ibid.

106 Boswell, *Journal of a Tour*, p. 424.

'old crazy or crafty' people had second sight and 'whether mental imbecility continued to prolong the folly of its delusion.'[107] Despite his stated contempt, Carr made repeated investigations, blaming Dr Johnson for providing 'an indirect sanction' to a belief in second sight. He writes that Johnson 'avowed that he believed in the *evidence* of second sight; and therefore he must have believed in second sight itself' (original emphasis).[108] Carr's misinterpretation of the doctor's position provided him with the intellectual protection he needed to brush off any ridicule which came his way. He 'more than once excited a look of contempt' when asking about second sight, and concluded that 'I do not believe that there is a Scotchman, in the least degree enlightened, who now believes that such a faculty ever existed in his country.'[109]

A contemporary traveller, the geologist John Macculloch, reported that on arrival in St Kilda none of the islanders even pretended to have had foreknowledge of his coming. He discussed various superstitions with the inhabitants before concluding that second sight, like witchcraft, 'has become a subject of ridicule; and, in matters of this nature, ridicule is death.'[110] This ridicule must have come from within the community but whether instilled by native inhabitants or the efforts of the island's minister is not known. St Kilda supported a particularly isolated and close-knit community, the influence of a strong-minded individual, especially one in a position of authority, would have carried considerable weight. When the Rev. E. D. Clarke had visited the island a decade earlier, he reported that superstitions were so rife, 'It were futile to enumerate all the silly chimeras with which credulity has filled the imaginations of a people so little enlightened.'[111] He singled out second sight as worthy of particular

107 J. Carr, *Caledonian Sketches or a Tour through Scotland in 1807* (London, 1809), p. 456.

108 Ibid.

109 Ibid., p. 459.

110 J. Macculloch, *A Description of the Western Isles of Scotland* Vol. II (London, 1824), pp. 32–33.

111 E. D. Clarke, *The Life and Remains of the Rev. Edward Daniel Clarke* (London, 1824), p. 277.

mention. Clarke tried, without success, to convince the island's credulous minister, otherwise 'a declared enemy of general superstition' that the arrival of boats expected at intervals contingent upon the vagaries of the weather was easily explained. The minister's credulity was not, however, founded on such first hand accounts but on 'some marvellous tales' he had heard from the island of Pabbay.[112]

Writing of second sight in Skye, in 1834, J. G. Dalyell observed that 'although not entirely extinct, the same credulity which fostered its subsistence has been long on the wane.'[113] None of Dalyell's correspondents provided first hand accounts. Instead, they reported cases from witnesses who were known to them and in whom they placed implicit trust. In an era of scientific endeavour where the verifiability of empirical data was crucial to the acceptance of evidence, such testimony, Dalyell implied, was worthless. Such accounts suggest that belief in second sight waned as people became less credulous. However, they do not show so much a tension between elite and popular culture but rather between private belief and public disclosure within different sectors of society. One of Sir Walter Scott's many friends and admirers, Mrs Anne Grant of Laggan, reported the case of a 'devout' minister (possibly her husband) who had cleared all thoughts of superstitions from his mind except a sneaking regard 'for one darling idol,' namely second sight.[114] Mrs Grant believed in second sight and she wrote to Scott with an 'authentic instance.'[115] She also told him that she had not revealed her true beliefs in her *Essays on the Superstitions of the Highlanders of Scotland* for fear of having her

112 Ibid., p. 279.

113 J. G. Dalyell, *The Darker Superstitions of Scotland Founded on a Series of Annual Journeys* ... (Edinburgh, 1834), p. 468.

114 A. M. Grant, writing as 'By the author of "Letters from the Mountains,"' *Essays on the Superstitions of the Highlanders of Scotland* 2 Vols. (London, 1811) Vol. I, p. 257.

115 J. P. Grant (ed.), *Memoir and Correspondence of Mrs Grant of Laggan* 3 Vols. (London, 1844), Vol. II, p. 76. C.O. Parsons, *Witchcraft and Demonology in Scott's Fiction* (Edinburgh and London, 1964), p. 10n/11n. Citing a letter, April 1827, Walpole Collection NLS.

children hurt by the ridicule she felt such an admission would attract. She took it for granted that Scott was a believer.[116]

Sir Walter Scott is never far from the centre of the story of the Brahan Seer legend, not merely because of his fame and influence as a Romantic writer but because he was close to the Seaforth family at the time the prophecy regarding their demise was coming to fulfilment. Unlike Dr Johnson's interest in second sight, which, prompted by his religious beliefs, remained constant, Scott's belief, in common with his belief in apparitions, seems to have changed over the years from credulity to scepticism, a change that he regretted. Scott's biographer, J. G. Lockhart, found two notebooks entitled 'Walter Scott, 1792' (when Scott was twenty-one). These contained snippets of interest including 'Notes on the Second Sight, with extracts from Aubr[e]y and Glanville.'[117] Although Scott's own thoughts are not recorded, it cannot be doubted that that he had a lifelong interest in second sight. This does not mean, of course, that *he* believed in second sight, only that he took an interest in those who did.

When 'past middle life' he sailed in a yacht round the mainland and the Hebrides in the autumn of 1814, Scott and his party stopped off at Dunvegan in Skye. He noted in his journal 'we learn that most of the Highland superstitions, even that of second sight are still in force.'[118] Scott's use of the word 'even' and his singling out of second sight suggest that of all the superstitions, whatever they were, that a belief in second sight should *still* exist was the one he found the most surprising. Scott himself knew that his susceptibility to the marvellous had declined in direct proportion to an increase in rational scepticism as he grew older and the burdens of bereavement, debt and ill health began to take their toll. Although he wrote *Letters on Demonology* at the request of Lockhart to '[lend] a blow to explode old and worn out follies,' in the final chapter

116 Grant, *Memoir and Correspondence of Mrs Grant* Vol. III, pp. 186–187. Parsons, *Witchcraft and Demonology in Scott's Fiction*, p. 11n. Citing a letter, May 1828, Walpole Collection NLS. W. Scott, H. T. C. Grierson (ed.), *The Letters of Sir Walter Scott*, 12 Vols. Vol. 12, p. 166.

117 J. G. Lockhart, *Memoirs of the Life of Sir Walter Scott, Bart* Vol. I, pp. 200/201.

118 Lockhart, Vol. III p. 228. 23 August 1814, while at Dunvegan and Scott, *Letters on Demonology and Witchcraft* p. 395.

he reasoned 'that tales of ghosts and demonology are out of date at forty years and upwards; that it is only in the morning of life that this feeling of superstition "comes o'er us like a summer cloud", affecting us with fear ...'[119] He goes on to record that he would have provided a livelier and more interesting account of demonology and witchcraft had he written about them when he was much younger.

Scientific explanations and the popularity of animal magnetism

Despite scepticism and a reported diminution in belief, second sight continued to attract intellectual attention in the early years of the nineteenth century. Thanks to the accounts of travellers such as Martin and Johnson it became widely known on the continent where it became subsumed within the phenomenon of clairvoyance – a derivative of animal magnetism – and subjected to scientific scrutiny.[120] New scientific discoveries and a change in attitude from the rational enlightenment which had dominated earlier enquiries to a philosophical Romanticism, which preferred intuition to reason and imagination to common sense, began to influence what was considered suitable subjects of enquiry. In Scotland, Sir Walter Scott requested his friend, the scientist David Brewster, to examine strange phenomenon and to publish his findings. Although Brewster makes no direct reference to second sight the bulk of his enquiry is taken up with spectral illusions. He provides medical explanations, such as fevers or stress for some illusions, and atmospheric explanations for others.[121] One

119 Scott, *The Letters of Sir Walter Scott*, ed. Grierson Vol XI, p. 301 in a letter to Lady Louisa Stuart, 31 October 1830 and Scott, *Letters on Demonology* p. 398.

120 Busst, 'Scottish Second Sight,' pp. 149–177.

121 D. Brewster, *Letters on Natural Magic Addressed to Sir Walter Scott, Bart* (London, 1832). None of the cases examined by Brewster occurred in Scotland; Germany, Cumberland and the English Channel coast being among the locations.

of several medical doctors whom Scott consulted on such topics in his later years was John Abercrombie who asserted that dreams explain some accounts of second sight while others are explained by spectral illusions which are thought to be real.[122] These are caused by a combination of unusual lighting and mental distraction through illness, grief or tiredness. By using 'a well regulated mind' where imagination is tempered by reason, 'the two extremes of credibility and scepticism' can be avoided and the appearance of apparitions explained using an understanding of how minds acquire facts.[123]

Another nineteenth-century medical practitioner who tried to explain the appearance of apparitions was Samuel Hibbert. His central hypothesis was that 'apparitions are nothing more than ideas, or the recollected images of the mind, which have been rendered as vivid as actual impressions.'[124] After providing medical reasons for numerous cases, including nervous irritation, hysterical temperament or exaggerated religious devotion, he dismissed second sight as superstitious imagery.[125] Hibbert argued that belief in second sight would have disappeared by the start of the eighteenth century if it had not been deliberately harnessed to counter the scepticism of freethinkers by staunch religionists such as Wesley and Aubrey. They used the prophetic nature of second sight as proof of an afterlife over and above the evidence contained in the scriptures. The truths contained in the Bible were enough for Hibbert.[126]

When 'animal magnetism' appeared on the medical scene in 1780s Paris, supporters extolled its virtues in whole or in part. Detractors likewise spoke out against it with differing degrees of emphasis.[127] The term

122 J. Abercrombie, *Inquiries Concerning the Intellectual Powers and the Investigation of Truth* (London, 1846), p. 228.

123 Ibid., p 351.

124 S. Hibbert, *Sketches of the Philosophy of Apparitions* (Edinburgh, 1825), p. 61.

125 Ibid., pp. 133 and 212–221.

126 Ibid., p. 215.

127 H. Mackenzie, *The Lounger, a Periodical Paper Published in Edinburgh*. Vol. III, pp. 300–311, Saturday, 23 December 1786, and H. Mackenzie, *The Works of Henry Mackenzie* Vol. VII (Edinburgh, 1808), pp. 4–19. Carr, *Caledonian Sketches*, pp. 458–459.

'animal magnetism' was coined by Franz Anton Mesmer (1734–1815) who hypothesised that the motion of planets affected the fluids in the human body in a way analogous to the moon's effect on the ebb and flow of the oceans.[128] His treatment consisted of applying magnets to various parts of the body to create an 'artificial tide' with which to regulate the physical and mental condition of his patients.[129] Mesmer thought that everything in the universe is connected by a fluid which, in turn, is connected to our internal sense organs so that it does not matter from which direction, in either time or space, a stimulus comes.[130] He claimed to have discovered a 'critical sleep' in which people were able to bring other times into the present. He continued, 'all that which "has been," has left some sort of trace; similarly, that which "will be" is already determined by the totality of causes which must bring it about; this has led to the idea that within the universe everything is present, and that the past and the future are nothing but different references which parts of this universe have towards each other.'[131]

Despite such claims there is no evidence that Mesmer conducted experiments on this 'critical sleep' during his active life. It was left to a disciple, the Marquis de Puysegur, to disseminate on the somnambulistic effects of animal magnetism, its highest manifestation being spontaneously induced clairvoyance, or prevision – the ability to see people and events distant in time and place from the seer. Clairvoyance attracted the attention of doctors, scientists and academics, as well as the interest of the public at large. Clairvoyants performed in salons, theatres, at public gatherings and private sittings, in the very homes of their rapt audiences. They were a particular favourite of the middling classes.[132] The example of a clairvoyant providing a tolerably accurate description of the far off

128 F. A. Mesmer (trs. by G. Bloch), *Mesmerism; a Translation of the Original Scientific and Medical Writings of F. A. Mesmer* (Los Altos, CA, 1980).

129 Ibid., pp. 26 and 48.

130 Ibid., p. 110, in his essay, 'On His Discoveries', first published in 1799.

131 Ibid., p. 122.

132 A. Winter, *Mesmerised: Powers of Mind in Victorian Britain* (London, 1998), pp. 143–146. E. Lee, *Report Upon the Phenomena of Clairvoyance or Lucid*

residence of an enquirer is typical of the question and answer exchanges in many accounts of the time.[133]

The activities of practitioners stirred up so much controversy that the French Royal Academy of Sciences commissioned a report from their medical section, some of whose members subjected themselves to experimentation in order to obtain first hand experience.[134] Their report, submitted in June 1831, concluded that somnambulism certainly exists 'when it gives rise to new faculties which have been designated by the names of *clairvoyance, intuition,* and internal *prevision*' (original emphases).[135] The report stopped short of endorsing universal prevision and also pointed out that somnambulism and its effects could be faked, with obvious potential for deception.

Alexander Wood claimed that most cases of clairvoyance were based on deception and in those few instances where deception had not been proved it was easier to posit the theory that the fraudsters had simply evaded detection.[136] Wood cites the work of Dr John Forbes to support his argument. Forbes had examined several clairvoyants at first hand. Over a number of trials the results ranged from complete failure to varying degrees of inconclusivity. Although Forbes concluded that all the demonstrations he had witnessed had been feigned he did not, unlike Wood,

---

Somnambulism to the President of the Parisian Medical Society (London, 1843), pp. 22–23.

133 See Wm. Gregory *Letters to a Candid Inquirer on Animal Magnetism* (London, 1851) for his sessions with a clairvoyant from Shetland, pp. 146–148 and his cases p. 432 et seq. E. Lee, *Animal Magnetism* (London, 1843), p. 79.

134 J. C. Colquhoun, *Report on the Experiments on Animal Magnetism made by a Committee of the Medical Section of the French Royal Academy of Sciences, 21 & 28 June 1831* (Edinburgh, 1833), pp. 88–89.

135 Colquhoun, Conclusions of the *Report,* pp. 192–201, this reference p. 194. Note: the term *clairvoyance* was reserved in the report for the heightened awareness of a person's own mental and bodily state. Other writers use the term to describe the state which extends beyond the self, and it is in this context that the term has been used throughout this book.

136 A. Wood, *What is Mesmerism; an Attempt to Explain its Phenomena* (Edinburgh, 1851), p. 4.

dismiss the possibility of clairvoyance existing. Adopting a Johnsonian position, he professed himself 'ready to believe [it] on obtaining sufficient proof of [its] reality.'[137]

Dr William Gregory, Professor of Chemistry at the University of Edinburgh, was sufficiently impressed by the testimony of friends, like-minded colleagues and correspondents to declare, in 1851, that 'all the phenomena without exception have been observed ... as occurring spontaneously without any artificial process, even clairvoyance, that stumbling block to the sceptic.'[138] He suggested that by studying clairvoyance, the curious could understand the appearance of apparitions in divination, magic and witchcraft, all of which could be explained by animal magnetism. Gregory explained Highland second sight using the principles of animal magnetism. An 'extreme voluntary reverie' may produce a 'conscious lucid state' in which the seer is on the border of ordinary consciousness and a dreamlike state similar to magnetic sleep when a seer sees real, not illusive, objects with an internal vision which is not understood. He cites the fulfilment of the Seaforth prophecy as the crowning example of Highland second sight.[139] Gregory saw the last Lord Seaforth when he was an old man and suffering from the afflictions which are an integral part of the prophecy regarding his family's downfall, although he does not say if he saw him in a professional capacity. His account, however, owes much to the written words of Sir Walter Scott's biographer, J. G. Lockhart, and he does not positively state that he had heard any such prophecy while Seaforth was still alive.[140] The timing of Gregory's endorsement of second sight coincided with a stimulus which was to propel a derivative of animal magnetism into another domain of popular culture.

In the same year, Dr J. H. Bennett drew attention to a mania sweeping across all Scotland, from the salons of Edinburgh society, through

137 J. Forbes, *Illustrations of Modern Mesmerism From Personal Investigation* (London, 1845), p. x.

138 Gregory, *Letters*, pp. 17–18, 302 and 158.

139 Ibid., pp. 276 et seq.

140 J. G. Lockhart, *Life of Scott, Memoirs of Sir Walter Scott* Vol. II (London, 1914), p. 501.

the halls of Edinburgh University students to the academic portals of the Royal Medical Society. The cause was a Dr Darling and a Mr Day who gave lectures and demonstrations to huge popular acclaim wherever they went. One of the tenets of animal magnetism was that manifestations were accomplished by 'transference of the senses' from magnetiser to patient.[141] Bennett's experiments had convinced him that this was impossible and what were being transferred were suggestive ideas.[142] What Bennett is describing, and what Darling and Day were demonstrating, was hypnotism. This achieved a status of its own, initially as a means of enabling surgeons to perform operations without the need for anaesthetic and later as a music hall entertainment where the subjects became the apparently unthinking extension of the hypnotist's will. The medical world discovered the use of ether, followed by chloroform, as a means of anaesthetising patients prior to operations and the psychic world turned its attention to spiritualism. Animal magnetism drifted into a backwater in medical history. Second sight, through its association with clairvoyance, remained on the margins of science and featured in the literary fiction of Romantics such as Scott.

Conclusion

The scientific focus of the early enquiry into second sight was centred in London where it occupied relatively few men, most of whom knew each other and most of whom were in the late years of their active working lives. Their reluctance to be seen to be publicly engaged with a topic considered unsuitable by many of their social peers meant that those who did look into second sight did so in a private, rather than a public, capacity. Opponents of second sight were blessed with erudition and

141 J. H. Bennett, *The Mesmeric Mania of 1851* (Edinburgh, 1851), p. 21.

142 Bennett, *Mania*, pp. 13, 17 and 20.

the means to express their scepticism through their books, plays and periodicals. Second sight, based largely on anecdotal evidence, failed to respond to strict empirical scrutiny. It also failed to provide confirmation of religious prophecy. This latter failure was partly entailed by the first but even when that objection could be overcome and witnesses of unimpeachable character swore to the veracity of prophetic events these were few in number and generally related to inconsequential events such as the arrival of an impending visitor. The vast majority of cases could be explained by alternative means. Among these alternative means, of course, were deception and delusion.

Second sight came under scrutiny from a variety of sources, ranging from the scientific to the philosophical, and natural, physiological and psychological causes were presented to explain it. Its roots in superstition and as a former source of wonderment were replaced by a new age of wonderment based on scientific discovery, and where the sources of wonder were tangible. Not only were there amazing feats of mechanical and civil engineering there were wonderful feats of ingenuity whose sole aim was to entertain. Exploration alone produced new marvels in the realms of botany, anthropology, zoology and geology. Although second sight was disseminated to a wider audience under the guise of clairvoyance, it was not forgotten as a peculiarly Scottish phenomenon. Despite scepticism from educated elites and from within Highland communities, it continued to be believed in at a popular level and by those among the elites whose private curiosity had sustained intellectual interest through the Age of Reason. The accounts of travellers stimulated interest across the continent and helped influence the Romantic literature of the nineteenth century. It was in this context that the legend of the Brahan Seer was created. As for Lady Isabella, a sympathetic, but discreet belief in second sight among the different social classes of her community would appear to preclude her from having had a seer burnt as a witch. The scientific enquiry initiated by her brother did not identify a person who could be described as the Brahan Seer. However, the name of Coinneach Odhar had not been forgotten and continued to circulate in oral tradition.

CHAPTER 5

Coinneach Odhar in Oral Tradition

Introduction

The name of Coinneach Odhar, first encountered in historical records of the sixteenth century, re-emerged in the literature of the eighteenth and nineteenth centuries when historians, memoirists and folklorists turned their attention to the material of oral tradition. This included the folktales, local histories and social practices of the past. Paul Thompson points out that throughout Europe the oral medium was once the only way of passing on all knowledge, from history to craft skills, until superseded by the written word during the Enlightenment when science demanded empirical veracity and documentary evidence.[1] This chapter is concerned with the dissemination of a legend and not the transmission of historical accuracy. Were it confined to the latter the case has already been made that oral stories are misleading about the burning of Coinneach Odhar at Chanonry by the vengeful Countess of Seaforth. Not all oral narratives are based on truth or fact. Beliefs, religious or secular, need not depend on truth or fact. Even in accounts of personal experiences, '[s]tories may have more symbolic value rather than be credible versions of the past.'[2] Any symbolic value contained in a recounting of the past influences the presentation of any tale at any time and gives rise to the inclusion, or omission, of features which have meaning for both narrator and audience.

Memory plays an important role in oral tradition. Jack Goody observes that 'since there is no fixed text from which to correct, variation

1 P. Thompson, *The Voice of the Past: Oral History* (Oxford, 1978), p. 18.

2 Ibid., p. 46.

is constantly creeping in, partly due to forgetting, partly due perhaps to unconscious attempts at improvement, adjustment, creation.'[3] He suggests that 'it is dangerous to speak of a collective memory in oral culture,' as memories are retained by individuals who are 'always susceptible to selective forgetting and remembering.'[4] Where memory is the only authority, tradition is being continually reinvented. However, communities do have a communal history which is as important as a personal history for an individual; the difference is that all members of a community can see it, refer to it and criticise it. Shared values and beliefs ensure that only that which is acceptable to the community will be communicated. This chapter explores how people in different parts of the Highlands and Islands used tales surrounding Coinneach Odhar to explain different unfolding events that were of significance to them. Only the advent of literature stabilised the narratives so that written texts, rather than the spoken word, became the authoritative versions of events. In contrast to oral tradition, which only enters into the historical record when, long after its origin, someone decides to write it down, events are usually fixed in time and place by being written down when, or soon after, they happen.

The Highlands of Scotland had a distinctive and particularly strong oral tradition founded on an ancient Gaelic past when a professional body of poets, trained in their art, was employed to create, and narrate from memory, verses describing important events in the lives of powerful men and their families. By the eighteenth century these educated poets were superseded by the more informal storytellers and poets of the *ceilidh* house (*taigh céilidh*).[5] When the folklorists of the nineteenth century sought out the oral traditions of the Highlands they did so, according to Malcolm Chapman, because they were seen to be 'disappearing before science,

3 J. Goody, *The Power of the Written Tradition* (London, 2000), p. 40.

4 Ibid., pp. 43–44.

5 D. S. Thomson, 'The Gaelic Oral Tradition,' *The Proceedings of the Scottish Anthropological and Folklore Society* Vol. V. No 1 (1954), pp. 1–17. M. Newton, *A Handbook of the Scottish Gaelic World* (Dublin, 2000), p. 81.

rationality, and modernity.'[6] Folklore itself was raised to a science which used classifications of folk-tale types in a theoretical framework. It was seen in a positive or negative light, being either the follies and superstitions of pre-scientific reason or the authentic, unaffected and vibrant accounts of the past.[7] This latter notion predominated among nineteenth-century Highland collectors seeking to preserve cultural artefacts in a pure state. An exception to this general rule was Hugh Miller, who, while 'accurately conveying the tenor of local tradition did so with considerable input of his own.'[8] Miller's input is no different from that of an oral story teller, excepting that his literary contributions helped fix traditional narratives in printed texts. However, a predominately literate society does not cease to be an oral society. Traditions may be transmitted in either medium, or as a mix between the two. 'Only comparatively recently,' notes Penny Fielding, 'has the old authority of "folklore" been replaced by a less discrete "popular culture" in which speech and writing interact.'[9] Literary sources act as points of reference. When different versions of tradition are committed to paper criticisms and comparisons arise.

Eric R. Cregeen and a team from the School of Scottish Studies spent several years of field research on the Hebridean island of Tiree, looking into the oral tradition of the indigenous people.[10] Tiree was chosen partly because it changed hands in the seventeenth century and the social upheavals of that time brought the people together in protest so that the notion of clanship persisted longer there than elsewhere. Tiree also had unrivalled documentary sources and when these were compared with oral

6 M. Chapman, *The Gaelic Vision in Scottish Culture* (London, 1978), pp. 118 and 124.

7 R. Bauman, 'Folklore,' in R. Bauman (ed.), *Folklore, Cultural Performances and Popular Entertainments* (London, 1992), p. 31.

8 D. Alston, 'The Fallen Meteor: Hugh Miller and Local Tradition,' in M. Shortland (ed.), *Hugh Miller and the Controversies of Victorian Science* (Oxford, 1996), pp. 206–229. p. 217.

9 P. Fielding, *Writing and Orality: Nationality, Culture, and Nineteenth-Century Scottish Fiction* (Oxford, 1996), p. 3.

10 E. R. Cregeen, 'Oral Tradition and History in a Hebridean Island,' *Scottish Studies*, No. 32 (1998), pp. 12–37.

accounts told by the fireside 'it was impossible to distinguish what was historical from what was literary or folkloristic.'[11] The researchers also found that oral tradition in its various forms – whether songs or genealogies – stretched no further back than the late eighteenth century, and then only through very old people. Folklore characteristics had invaded historical accounts so that, for example, the gradual abandonment of a village due to encroaching sand had evolved into a single extraordinary event in 'the Spring before the battle of Waterloo.'[12] Some accounts believed by locals to be of historical events transpired to be based on tales of Fionn. Only when accounts turned to the experiences of near kin did the historical detail outweigh the conventions of story telling and poem. Cregeen concluded that '[t]he most valuable oral tradition in Tiree was locally and family-centred.'[13]

However, even local and family centred traditions are influenced by literary sources. In her anthropological study of a crofting community in Skye, Sharon Macdonald describes how many of the stories of the Land Wars of the 1880s had been acquired be people doing their own reading of 'popular, accessible' written sources such as newspapers rather than by being handed down through oral tradition.[14] She also found that local events were generally less well remembered than events from further afield in the Highlands. This was in part due to news content being addressed to a wider audience by the media and in part to the demise of the *ceilidh* house, where until the 1950s all mail and newspapers for the community had been delivered and where people had gathered to exchange news. Macdonald also identifies 'non-remembering' as another disrupting factor in the transmission of oral tradition. She cites the case of an octogenarian, Calum, and his wife, Peggy.[15] He would tell stories, recite poems and even sing of how 'the people' had stood up to the landowners or deceived

11 Ibid., p. 14.

12 Ibid., p. 20.

13 Ibid., pp. 31–32.

14 S. Macdonald, *Reimagining Culture: Histories, Identities and the Gaelic Renaissance* (Oxford, 1997), p. 111.

15 Ibid., pp. 112–114.

excise men looking for illicit stills. Calum was more reticent in the presence of his wife. She avoided such stories altogether, always telling ones that were personal. Her father had been a landlord whose large farm had been converted into crofts by the Land Court. Peggy had 'forgotten' this part of her history which did not sit well with the community's conception of a united people. Her neighbours, who got on well with her, were also clear that '[t]here's things that's best forgotten.'[16]

This desire to avoid divisiveness within communities is only possible if members have shared values and beliefs which act as a restraint on what is being transmitted. People will transmit what they choose to transmit in a form suited to a particular audience but then only within culturally determined norms. Political, educational, economic, cultural and religious factors limit or influence the quantity and quality of orally transmitted tradition. The personal correspondence of Sir Walter Scott and the memoirs of Elizabeth Grant of Rothiemurchus regarding the fulfilment of the prophecy predicting the decline of the Seaforth family at the beginning of the nineteenth century are exemplars of elite narratives showing belief in the content of oral tradition. James Fraser's *Wardlaw Manuscript* of the late seventeenth century provides a context for the prophecy linking Coinneach Odhar with the Seaforth family while Hugh Miller, in his *Scenes and Legends of the North of Scotland* (1835) provides the first folklorist's account of Kenneth Ore [sic] from Easter Ross. The Macleod family's *Bannatyne Ms.* (1829) provides an alternative account from the Western Isles. An active series of correspondence to, and articles in, the radical newspaper *The Highlander* in the early 1870s suggest that the name of Coinneach Odhar was known over a wide area of the north and islands and that the numerous prophecies attributed to him were taken lightly by some readers and more seriously by others.

Highland oral tradition shifted from a formal to an informal medium and declined as modernity encroached on the region. Oral accounts of Coinneach Odhar were created and passed on within that tradition. Different accounts of his *floruit* emanated from different regions within

16 Ibid., p. 114.

the Highlands and Islands and these were recorded by folklorists and conveyed by individuals through the columns of a newspaper. This 'popular, accessible' source helped fix the narrative concerning aspects of the seer's life and the acquisition of his supernatural powers. The historical events surrounding the demise of the once powerful Seaforth family were linked to a prophecy which arose to explain their decline and the name of Coinneach Odhar became associated with the prophecy. Literature and oral tradition combined to perpetuate the connection.

Highland oral tradition: gathering a declining culture

Highland oral tradition, according to Michael Newton, had roots nurtured in the old order of Irish monasteries whose influence declined some time around the twelfth century to be replaced by the patronage of powerful Gaelic chieftains.[17] They retained professional poets (*filidh*) as an important part of their retinues, requiring them to versify significant events in their lives and those of their kinsfolk. These poets practised formal conventions of verse construction and having finished a composition they passed it on to a *bard* or reciter (*reacaire*) whose job it was to perform the piece. Poems were expressed within a panegyric code where the emphasis was on presentation before a public assembly. A person was praised or satirised according to circumstance, with judgements being articulated on his character, appearance or conduct. The closeness of people to the natural world was emphasised by the use of anthropomorphic metaphor to link human qualities to natural objects.[18] A lord's retinue also included a hereditary storyteller (*seanchaidh*) whose job it was to act as a depository for all history and tradition pertaining to the clan, its territories and its neighbours. *Seanchaidhs* required prodigious

17 Newton, *A Handbook*, p. 81.

18 Ibid., pp. 93 and 98. Thomson, 'The Gaelic Oral Tradition,' pp. 2–3.

memories but as a professional class they disappeared, along with the professional poets, in the face of loosening clan bonds during the late eighteenth century.[19]

This strength of oral tradition was sustained throughout the eighteenth century and into the nineteenth century when poems continued to be collected from word of mouth rather than from written sources often long after they had been composed. Derrick Thomson demonstrates the strength of this tradition by examining poems from *The Book of The Dean Of Lismore,* compiled largely from oral dictation between 1512 and 1526, and comparing them with poems collected from oral sources in the mid eighteenth century.[20] He concludes that in many cases they were essentially the same. However, the professional class of poets had given way to amateur bards and storytellers and the focus of oral tradition had switched from the institution of the formal assembly to the informal assembly of popular tradition in the *ceilidh* house. Trained bards and *seanchaidhs,* and their descendants, would have attended many of the early *ceilidh* meetings and their methods and expertise would have provided a standard to which others could aspire. The move from aristocratic formality to popular informality brought with it a corresponding shift in the emphasis of what was sung or spoken about. The focus on the affairs of the nobility gave way to 'the everyday events and familiar personalities of the contemporary scene ... the experiences and emotions of the ordinary islanders.'[21] The *ceilidh* gatherings, the focal point of the community in the long winter nights, persisted until the middle of the twentieth century. They were, according to Newton, 'crucial in disseminating the lore and values of society from the older generations to the younger ones of both genders.'[22] Everybody took part and as well as showing respect for elders and honoured guests the gatherings required and engendered 'active minds, excellent memories, [and] faithfulness to the original version of

19 Cregeen, 'Oral Tradition,' p. 12.
20 Thomson, 'The Gaelic Oral Tradition,' p. 4.
21 Cregeen, 'Oral Tradition,' p. 17.
22 Newton, *A Handbook*, p. 101.

the 'text.'[23] Tale-telling was important but seen only as one aspect 'of an astounding range of news, songs old and new, jokes, history, anecdotes, gossip and the like, of which the tale, as a sort of cinema or high art of the day, is only a part.'[24]

The *ceilidh* house was not the only place where communities gathered. Songs accompanied many of the working practices carried out at a communal level, from shared harvesting of crops, to rowing and fishing, so that everybody, quite literally, pulled together. Perhaps most famously, the working of cloth by women, traditionally carried out in the evenings, was accompanied by waulking-songs (*òrain-luidh*) often composed by the women while they worked. The waulking-songs usually centred on relationships of a romantic nature but political comment directed towards a distant government was not unknown.[25] Economic and technological changes in working practices, and the demographic changes these entailed, coupled to the more general disruption of people from close knit communities during the clearances, adversely affected the ability of people to retain both the skill of performing and the content of orally transmitted traditions.

Among the most famous of the nineteenth century collectors who took an interest in various forms of oral narrative was John Francis Campbell of Islay, who wanted 'stories of all kinds, true stories excepted' and 'begged for the very words used by the people who told the stories, with nothing added, or omitted, or altered.'[26] Campbell wanted the folk-tales in a pristine state so that they, and the Gaelic language in which they were couched, could be compared with other tales and other languages, thus confirming his theory that in antiquity both had come from a

23 Ibid.

24 T. A. McKean, *Hebridean Song-Maker: Iain Macneacail of the Isle of Skye* (Edinburgh, 1997), p. 98.

25 Newton, *A Handbook*, pp. 131–132. McKean, *Hebridean Song-Maker*, pp. 101–103, 117 and 142. Margaret Bennett, personal communication, unpublished fieldnotes, Traditional Singing Weekend, Cullerlie, 6 June 2002.

26 J. F. Campbell, *Popular Tales of the West Highlands* (Hounslow, 1983 (1860)), pp. xiii and xiv.

common stock of Indo-European peoples. Although it was folktales rather than historical events Campbell was after, his observations – and those of the men who helped him – on the state of oral tradition, are of interest because they shed light on the forces impacting on the medium.

One of Campbell's contributors, Hector MacLean, schoolmaster in Islay, described what he found when collecting material during the summer of 1859. 'In the Islands of Barra, the recitation of tales during the long winter nights is still very common.'[27] However, conditions elsewhere were very different. 'In North Uist and Harris these tales are nearly gone.'[28] MacLean's explanation for this discrepancy encapsulates the main anxieties and changes sweeping the Highlands at the time. '[M]ost of the people in Barra and South Uist are Roman Catholics, can neither read nor write, and hardly know any English. From these circumstances it is extremely improbable that they have borrowed much from the literature of other nations.'[29] The loss of tales in the other islands he put down 'partly to reading, which in a manner supplies a substitute for them, partly to bigoted religious ideas, and partly to narrow utilitarian views.'[30]

Campbell's other main contributor, Hector Urquhart, gamekeeper at Ardkinglas, recounts (1860) how it had been common practice in his native Pool-Ewe, Ross-shire, when he was a boy, thirty or forty years earlier, for the young to gather on long winter nights to hear tales their elders had learnt from their forebears. Times change, he observed, '[t]he minister came to the village in 1830, and the schoolmaster soon followed, [they] put a stop in our village to such gatherings.'[31] Urquhart had not heard a single tale recited since then until he started collecting on Campbell's behalf. With most of the old men dead and the few survivors having lost their memories '[he] only got but a trifle to what [he] expected.'[32] Both these collectors identify external authority, personified

27 Ibid., p. iv.
28 Ibid., p. v.
29 Ibid.
30 Ibid., p. vi.
31 Ibid., p. vii.
32 Ibid.

by ministers and school teachers, actively and deliberately suppressing oral culture. Increased literacy was often linked to religious education. Schools supported by the Society in Scotland for Propagating Christian Knowledge augmented or acted as substitutes for parochial schools in many areas.[33] The extent to which these changes were implemented, welcomed, encouraged or resisted would have had a bearing on the speed of decline of all traditions in individual communities. The minister in Kincardine noted of his parishioners during the 1790s, 'they still retain a sacred regard for the clan and the family they are sprung from; but it must be allowed, that this feeling is on the decline. The tale, the song, and the dance, do not, as in the days of their fathers, gild the horrors of the winter night.'[34] Campbell identified other reasons for the loss of oral tradition. The arrival of '[r]ailways, roads, newspapers and tourists, are slowly but surely doing their accustomed work.'[35] People began to rely on other media, particularly the written word, for their entertainment and information. The first recorded newspaper in Inverness, *The Inverness Journal and Northern Advertiser* had made its appearance in 1807.[36] It was followed ten years later by the *Inverness Courier*, whose circulation covered all of the northern counties.[37] It still exists.

Another of Campbell's contributors, John Dewar, a worker from the Argyle estates, recalled listening to tales 'upwards of fifty years ago' in the Loch Lomond district.[38] Many of these tales were about cattle raids, clan battles, the weapons, manners and dress of his ancestors. Campbell himself heard many such tales throughout his life but sadly he gathered none, despite this being 'by far the most abundant popular lore.'[39] He did,

33 Newton, *A Handbook*, pp. 63 and 70. J. Sinclair, *The Statistical Account of Scotland 1791–1799: Inverness-shire, Ross and Cromarty* Vol. XVIII (Wakefield, 1981 (1791–1799)), pp. 216, 271 and 548.

34 Sinclair, *The Statistical Account* Vol. XVIII, p. 518.

35 Ibid., p xxiv.

36 J. Barron, *The Northern Highlands in the Nineteenth Century: Newspaper Index and Annals* 3 Vols. (Inverness, 1903–13), Vol. I, p. 4.

37 Ibid., p. 132.

38 Campbell, *Popular Tales*, p. li.

39 Ibid., p. xxxv.

however, describe the way in which such tales were told. 'It is' he wrote, 'a history devoid of dates, but with clear starting points.'[40] Incidents took place before, during or after some other more noteworthy event which acted as a reference point in time. Incidents took place near, at, in or on some identifiable landmark, natural or man made, which provided a reference point in place. A landmark may even have been erected to commemorate an event and thus, like many natural landmarks, have acquired a history of its own. Such popular history, declared Campbell, 'has still a great hold on the people' even though he thought it too localised to be the subject of his study.[41]

Such sentiments, and the subject matter of Campbell's enquiry, would have been anathema to Hugh Miller whose study of oral tradition preceded Campbell's by some quarter of a century. Miller regretted the loss of oral knowledge of the past and set himself the task of preserving the 'Sibyline [sic] tomes of tradition.'[42] Miller, a noted scientist and devout Christian, had no patience with old superstitions if they still had a detrimental affect on the lives of the people. He collected some 350 tales and customs from around his hometown of Cromarty on the Black Isle and analysed these into three main classes.[43] The first class contained traditional tales which recorded actual events. These had always taken place locally and at their heart was the accurate depiction of characters. Miller associated such tales with male storytellers. The second class contained tales drawn from the imagination, the very stuff of Campbell's enquiry. These Miller considered as having no great merit, being poor imitations 'of extravagant and ill-conceived originals.'[44] The third class of tales formed the greater part of his collection, those which were a complex mix of historical accuracy and locally derived invention, some supplied by Miller

40 Ibid.

41 Ibid.

42 H. Miller, *Scenes and Legends of the North of Scotland* (Edinburgh, 1994 (1835)), p. 2.

43 Miller, *Scenes and Legends*, pp. 3–5, 206 and 218. Alston, 'The Fallen Meteor', pp. 206–229. See especially p. 220.

44 Miller, *Scenes and Legends*, p. 4.

himself. Into this class, which Miller associated with female storytellers, falls the oral tradition of Coinneach Odhar which he recorded. In Miller's work can be seen the vibrancy of oral tradition with the emergence of new stories and the transference of old stories to new locations, both important facets of the Coinneach Odhar narrative.[45]

In twentieth-century Tiree, Cregeen and his team found the characteristic of oral tradition identified by Campbell, of using important events and locations as reference points in time and place. Similar characteristics are evident in the Coinneach Odhar narrative, excepting that among the important markers are notable men of their day. When lairds with particular physical characteristics co-existed, their appearance acted as an aid to memory to set events in time and place. The appearance of such men also acted as a sign to predict that certain events would occur. Attributing different physical characteristics to notable men at different times and in different places contributed towards the relocation in time and place of Coinneach Odhar in oral tradition. Only the advent of his appearance in the literature fixed his location and provided what became a definitive version of events.

Coinneach Odhar in oral tradition

The earliest reference to Coinneach Odhar in oral tradition appears, paradoxically but (as we have seen) predictably, in a literary text. When the naturalist Thomas Pennant toured Scotland in 1772 he was witness to the social upheavals which afflicted many of the Highlanders. Passing through Assynt in Sutherland he described the destitution into which many of them had sunk. 'This tract seems the residence of sloth, the people almost torpid with idleness ... but till famine pinches they will not bestir themselves ... Dispirited and driven to despair by bad management,

45 Alston, 'The Fallen Meteor,' p. 224.

crowds were now passing, emaciated with hunger, to the Eastern coast, on the report of a ship being there loaden with meal. Numbers of the miserables of this country were now emigrating ... too poor to pay, they madly sell themselves for their passage, preferring a temporary bondage in a strange land, to starving for life in their native soil.'[46]

Surveying this unhappy scene, Pennant observed that '[e]very country has had its prophets; Greece its Cassandra, Rome its Sibyls, England its Nixon, Wales its Robin Dhu and the Highlands their Kenneah Oaur [sic]. Kenneah long since predicted the migrations in these terms: "Whenever a MacCleane with long hands, a Frazier with a black spot on his face, a Macgregor with the same on his knee, and a club-footed Macleod, of Rasa, should have existed; whenever there should have been successfully three Macdonalds of the name of John, and three Mackinnons of the same christian name; oppressors would appear in the country, and the people change their own land for a strange one." The predictions, say the good wives, have been fulfilled, and not a single breach in the oracular effusions of Kenneah Oaur.'[47] Pennant does not say where he heard this prophecy: the sight of destitute Highlanders may have triggered a memory. Pennant had on a previous tour in 1769 passed through Easter Ross, visiting Brahan Castle, and earlier on his present tour had been in the Hebrides.[48] Nor does he say if he heard the prophecy at first hand from local people or if it was conveyed to him by a learned companion. He was accompanied on his travels by a Gaelic scholar, the Rev. John Stuart of Killin. He also acknowledged ministers who helped him; most notably Donald McQuin of Kilmuir, Skye, an informant of Dr Johnson, and Donald MacLeod of Glenelg, a correspondent of Theophilus Insulanus.[49] Their assistance suggests that not all ministers were the oppressors of oral culture.

46 T. Pennant, *A Tour in Scotland and Voyage to the Hebrides 1772* (Edinburgh, 1998), pp. 318–319.

47 Ibid., p. 319.

48 T. Pennant, *A Tour in Scotland 1769* (Edinburgh, 2000), pp. 106–107 and Pennant, *A Tour 1772*, pp. 90–314.

49 Pennant, *A Tour 1772*, pp. 1–3.

The popular reference to lairds with particular physical characteristics as an indicator of impending, evolving or current events was widespread. In this case the physical characteristics of one group and the genealogies of others suggests a conflation of different prophecies but these characteristics must have been evident at some time and their perceived coexistence deemed accountable for the parlous state of the country. Most of the lairds named are Hebridean by principal family territory, suggesting that area as Pennant's source. However, the inclusion of Fraser from the Beauly area and Macgregor, whose principal territories included Sutherland and Argyle suggest that the travails besetting the country were not confined to a single locality. The transfer of a laird's physical characteristics from one prophecy to another was not unknown. The black spotted Fraser is among a group of lairds with distinguishing physical characteristics whose co-existence a century earlier presaged the decline of the Fraser family.

Writing of the events of 1666, James Fraser of Wardlaw observes that 'There is an old prophesie runns concerning the Frasers, viz, that some great and fatall change will happen to fall out when every leading famely of the name shall have but one sone; and this casualty is now observed among them ...'[50] Fraser goes on to list the several leading familes of his name who were at risk before recording 'another prediction of some great alteration uppon the famelies ... when a black-kneed Seaforth, blackspotted Lord Lovat (Fraser), squinteyed Mckintosh and ... a Chisholm blind of an eye would live in one age. Those four are just now contemporary: and though much stress should not be laid uppon such prophesies, yet they ought not to be vilified or condemn.'[51]

Fraser records that he first heard of these two predictions from a very old man, Eneas Mckdonnell, in 1648 and was reminded of them at the time Hugh, Master of Lovat, was born on 28 September 1666. He recounts that one of the godmothers had seen a large black spot on the baby's upper lip and had called to the midwife 'take him from me, take him from me, he will do no good.'[52] Baby Lovat's blemish confirmed the old prediction.

50 J. Fraser, *Chronicles of the Frasers (the Wardlaw Manuscript)*, pp. 513–514.

51 Ibid.

52 Ibid., p. 466.

'Now are our feares commenct of the decay of this famely. The present lady like to be barren, and short lived; my Lord Lovat hectick; the Tutor of Lovat alrady cacochimick, and no hopes of his ofspring; Sibilla aged and will outlive him; Thomas Beuforts children droping off as they are born, and his lady too fatt and corpulent; and none extant but they two threatnes the worst.'[53] Worries about the health and wellbeing of powerful families were never far from their thoughts in an age of limited medical facilities, and political and religious uncertainties. All the lairds described in this prophecy are near neighbours from Easter Ross or thereabouts. It is couched in such terms as to be readily transferable to other times and to other places and later versions attributed to Coinneach Odhar appear to be variations of it.

What of the man credited with making Pennant's prediction? According to Hugh Miller's account Kenneth Ore [sic] was a Highlander from Ross-shire, who 'lived some time in the seventeenth century.'[54] He worked as a farm labourer for a prosperous clansman who lived somewhere near Brahan Castle and so intimidated the man's wife with his barbed wit that she decided to get rid of him. One day while he was out digging peats on a lonely moor she took him a jug of poison as part of his meal. Finding him asleep she set down the jug by his side and went home. When he woke up he found pressing upon his heart 'a beautiful smooth stone, resembling a pearl, but much larger.'[55] As he was admiring it he became aware that he could see into the future and recognise people's thoughts including the immediate intention of his mistress. He gained little benefit from his knowledge, 'for he led, it is said until extreme old age, an unsettled, unhappy kind of life – wandering from place to place, a prophet only of evil, or of little trifling events, fitted to attract notice when they occurred, merely from the circumstance of their having been foretold.'[56] Shortly before his death he threw his stone into a loch near

53 Ibid., p. 467.

54 Miller, *Scenes and Legends*, p. 156.

55 Ibid., p. 157.

56 Ibid., pp. 156–157.

Brahan where he predicted it would be found, when all his other prophecies had been fulfilled, 'by a lame humpbacked mendicant.'[57]

Miller's account of Kenneth Ore's life is the earliest of those emanating from Easter Ross. In terms of historical content the attempt at poisoning is reminiscent of what went on during the Fowlis affair. However, there is no reference in this account to witch burning; suggesting that at the time Miller was writing the seer was not thought to have died in such manner. That Ore is reputed to have lived to extreme old age and wandered from place to place is consistent with the itinerant wanderings from fair to fair and the flight from justice of the Coinneach Odhar from the sixteenth century. Many of the 'trifling' prophecies Miller attributes to Kenneth Ore encapsulate the changes which had occurred, or were taking place, in or around Ross-shire, testifying to their local origins. Miller, well versed in the history of the church and its upheavals at the time of the Commonwealth, introduces Kenneth Ore as an exemplar of superstitious seers, those with second sight, in contrast to religious seers, like the Covenanters Alexander Peden and Donald Cargill, for whom he reserves the term prophets. Other than their form of belief, there is no difference between the two. Both, he argues, come to the fore when people's attention is focused on some cataclysmic event, such as political or religious upheaval, pestilence or persecution.[58] Miller collected his tales in the 1820s and 1830s, many of them from his mother who was highly superstitious and steeped in the lore of the region. He acknowledges the superstitious elements contained in many of the tales, though as a devout Christian he tried to explain these away as relics of a bygone age. He makes no great effort to deal with the truth or otherwise of prophecies or other supernatural phenomena. When Miller comments that it would be easier to prove that events had occurred rather than that they had been predicted this does not indicate a disbelief in prophecy, just his acknowledgement of the difficulty of confirming a prediction before the event.[59]

57 Ibid., pp. 158–159.
58 Ibid., pp. 151–156.
59 Ibid., p. 158.

Another account of Coinneach Odhar collected from oral sources is contained in the nineteenth century *Bannatyne Manuscript*.[60] Although primarily a history of the Macleod family the manuscript digresses sufficiently to provide biographies of other notables in the Western Isles. Among them is Coinneach Ouir [sic], 'a famous seer and prophet' who, according to the manuscript, was a Lewis man from the district of Ness.[61] He lived some time in the final quarter of the sixteenth century which makes him contemporaneous with the Coinneach Odhar of the Fowlis affair. The manuscript extols Coinneach's prowess as a seer, '[h]e foretells the fate of kingdoms and Royal Dynasties, of clans, tribes and even families.'[62] Coinneach foretells the many changes in 'manners, dress, modes of living, architecture, husbandry and arms' which were to come to pass in the Highlands. He set down specific times when these would occur and provided contemporary events to mark their progress, predicting the loss of language and the ultimate demise of the Gaelic race. The author provides no examples of such prophecies. Instead, he interjects a note of realism, explaining all but the most trivial to natural causes and crediting Coinneach with a high degree of perception 'in tracing effects to causes or in deducing from causes to effects which they must surely and inevitable produce.'[63]

60 *The Bannatyne Ms*, The Dunvegan Castle Muniments, NAS ref: 2950/691/s5. 57/1–3. Some controversy exists as to which of two Macleods wrote the manuscript. The material from which it was compiled is credited to Sir William Macleod Bannatyne of Kames, a student of Highland history and tradition. The manuscript is undated though written on paper traced to 1829 from a watermark. It could have been written as late as 1857 when died the other possible author, Dr Bannatyne William Macleod, though the material was probably gathered long before the manuscript took shape. R. C. Macleod, *The Macleods of Dunvegan: From the Time of Leod to the End of the Seventeenth Century* (Edinburgh, 1927), pp. xi–xiv.

61 *The Bannatyne Ms*. ref: 2950/691/s5. 57/1–3; f113. Anon., 'Coinneach Odhar: The Great Island Seer and Prophet,' *The Clan MacLeod Magazine* (Edinburgh, 1947), pp. 411–413.

62 *The Bannatyne Ms*., f113.

63 Ibid., f116.

If Coinneach did have supernatural powers, they could only have been obtained by supernatural means. A legend to explain his acquisition rested on an old belief that the grave of a stranger had to be bought otherwise the soul could not rest and wandered nightly in a ghost-like state. Coinneach's mother was tending crops late one night to prevent cattle getting in among them. She sat at her spinning overlooking a graveyard, when to her alarm a woman in strange dress rose from a grave and went with obvious distress towards the shore. Coinneach's mother recovered her nerve and having protected herself with the sign of the Cross sat by the grave to await the return of the ghost. She placed her distaff over the grave so that its earthly presence prevented the ghost's re-entry. When the ghost returned Coinneach's mother demanded to know who she was before allowing her to pass. She said she was a princess from a foreign land who had been drowned at sea. Although buried, her grave had never been paid for and she had to wander each night to where she had been washed ashore. If Coinneach's mother would pay for the grave, even with a sheaf of corn, she would be greatly rewarded and 'the child now in your womb' would be the 'most wonderful man of his time.'[64]

Eternal rest was exchanged for 'a small black and beautiful pebble' which Coinneach's mother kept secret and forgot about until her son reached the age of seven. She asked the boy to call his father from his work in the fields but the boy refused. She remembered the stone and promised it as a reward if he would do her bidding. No sooner did Coinneach hold the stone than he uttered what proved to be his first prophecy. 'Mother, a large whale is on shore in the Raven's Cave!'[65] Coinneach's fame spread far and wide but when aged about fifty he angered the kinsmen of the Macleods of Lewis after prophesying the downfall of that family. They accosted him near the lake of Cingavale [sic, probably Langavat] intending to take away his stone but he threw it into the loch rather than let anybody else have it. The biography concludes that Coinneach 'died a few days afterwards and was buried at Ness where his grave is still shown.'[66]

64 Ibid., f118.
65 Ibid., f119.
66 Ibid., f120.

Among the many newspapers which appeared in Inverness in the last quarter of the nineteenth century was *The Highlander*, written in Gaelic and English. Like most of its contemporaries it had a brief life. Under the stewardship of the editor, John Murdoch, a radical who agitated for land reform, it ran from 1873 to 1882. A common feature in newspapers of the time was a Notes and Interrogation Column in which readers answered each other's questions. The correspondents to *The Highlander* seem determined to retain their anonymity; most used the convention of writing under a pseudonym or used only their initials. From the outset it appears that Murdoch and his correspondents indulged in some sport with the name and reputation of Coinneach Odhar. The very first edition, dated 16 May 1873, contained a question from *An Taoitear Sàileach* (A teacher from Salen, on Mull) 'Most Highlanders have heard of *Coinneach Odhar,* the Brahan "prophet." Has his life ever been written? If so, where is it to be had?'[67] This is the first printed reference to Coinneach Odhar which attaches the appellation 'Brahan "prophet"' to his name. Why the writer thought it necessary to put the latter word in inverted commas can only be surmised; perhaps he means 'so-called' and is distancing himself from admitting such a claim for Coinneach's divinatory abilities. The Teacher had to wait five weeks for his reply when C. F. wrote that 'notes of Coinneach Odhar's life have been taken by several. Donald MacLeod, the Skye Bard (now deceased) wrote his life, and it was to be published; but, through some misfortune, it was not. I, however, believe that Macleod's MSS are still extant and I have no doubt, if the *Taoitear Sàileach* searched well, but he would trace them out.'[68] C. F. then relates that Coinneach obtained his powers of divination while cutting peat and being instructed by a voice to search in a fairy mound for several round stones. C. F. places Coinneach Odhar in Easter Ross. His version is similar to the one provided by Hugh Miller and may have been influenced by that account.

67 *The Highlander* Vol. I, No. I, p. 11.

68 Ibid., No. 6, p. 3.

Yet, the legend seems to have retained considerable vigour in Island oral tradition because a correspondent to *The Highlander* replying in Gaelic to C. F.'s account provides a version identical in all important particulars to the *Bannatyne Ms* and 'commonly related far and wide in the Long Island.'[69] The term Long Island may be deliberately vague. It can mean either the island of Lewis and Harris or the whole archipelago – Lewis to Barra. In this version Coinneach's acquisition of his supernatural powers has been relocated from the Ness district in the north of Lewis to Baile na Cille in the district of Uig on the west coast of the island. During the nightly vigil the occupants of all the graves depart and soon return except Gràdhach, daughter of the King of Norway, who has farthest to travel. She gives Coinneach's mother directions where to find the magical stone near a stretch of beach still called Gràdhach's pool to this day. The site of the seer's grave could still be pointed out in Uig. The correspondent offers several prophecies attributed to Coinneach Odhar, some of them in verse, relating to battles at Alt na Torcan in Lewis and Aird nan Ceann in Benbecula, the removal of houses in Uig and Ness and the woes that would visit the parish of Lochs.[70] When Alexander Mackenzie's account first appeared in book form in 1877 he used the Uig version culled from the pages of *The Highlander* to provide a birthplace for the Brahan Seer.[71] No version of the *Bannatyne Ms* account appeared in print until the early twentieth century by which time the belief current in Stornoway was that Coinneach was a Uig man.[72] Once oral tradition is fixed in print it becomes the definitive version of where and how the seer acquired his powers. The account disseminated through the columns of *The Highlander* and later by Alexander Mackenzie, has prompted one scholar to provide a historical explanation for its genesis.

A historical Coinneach Odhar flourished in the sixteenth century and no evidence has been found from an examination of witchcraft and

69 Ibid., Vol. I, No. 11, 26 July 1873, p. 3.

70 Ibid.

71 A. Mackenzie, *The Prophecies of the Brahan Seer; Coinneach Odhar Fiosaiche* (Inverness, 1877), pp. 27–28.

72 Anon., 'Coinneach Odhar,' The Clan MacLeod Magazine, 1947, p. 411.

second sight to show that a person answering his description existed in the seventeenth century. One conclusion to be drawn is that the Easter Ross version of oral tradition has been dislocated in time. A hypothesis to explain how the story has been dislocated in place has been presented by William Matheson. The Mackenzies wrested Lewis from the MacLeods in the early seventeenth century and when Murdo Mackenzie of the Davochmoluag family from Easter Ross, chamberlain of Lewis, died there in 1643 his son George became tacksman of Baile na Cille. George's mother was Florence, daughter of George Munro of Kaitwell in Easter Ross and closely related to the Munros of Fowlis.[73] She, Matheson suggests, would have been well versed in the events of the Fowlis affair and may have spent her remaining years with her son at Baile na Cille where tales of the family's home district would have been recounted round the hearth, subsequently becoming relocated to the place of their telling. References to Lady Fowlis, the numerous burnings at Fortrose and other key elements of the affair with which Matheson says Florence would have been so familiar have been dropped or forgotten. Only the principal character in the drama, Coinneach Odhar, has remained identifiable, subsequently believed by the inhabitants of Uig to have lived and died among them.

However, there is an alternative possibility for the appearance of Coinneach Odhar in the oral traditions of the Western Isles; namely, that Coinneach Odhar was in Lewis, in person, having fled there from the witch hunt in Easter Ross. He had good reason to flee, by the time of the second warrant for his arrest many of his accomplices in witchcraft had already been burnt for their involvement in the plot of Lady Fowlis. Secondly, he had made an enemy of another powerful women, Margaret Wauss, the wife of the provost of Inverness, by his illegal involvement in the skin trade. Coinneach Odhar could very well have survived in the Western Isles where the skin trade flourished and where he would have been far from the clutches of the law. As the principal enchanter of his

73 Wm. Matheson, 'The Historical Coinneach Odhar and Some Prophecies Attributed to Him,' TGSI Vol. 46 (1968), pp. 66–88, pp. 73–74.

now destroyed group of witches he appears to have employed a form of divination in his repertoire. This divinatory skill he took with him to Lewis where he continued to practice while suppressing any reference to his past which could link him to the Fowlis affair and to the warrant for his arrest. For several reasons this hypothesis seems more plausible than Matheson's, despite the ingenuity of his detective work. It accounts for that part of the *Bannatyne Ms* which describes Coinneach Odhar living into old age. It accounts for the location of his grave which was still being pointed out at the time the *Ms* was written. It accounts for the lack of references to witchcraft and the burnings at Chanonry.

Narratives get distorted through telling, events in oral tradition get dislocated in both place and time, the content of the story is modified to suit the purposes of teller and audience. At least one reader of *The Highlander* was aware of, and appeared to be familiar with, the different accounts of Coinneach Odhar which existed in oral tradition. In the twentieth edition of the newspaper Coinneach Dubh asks if Coinneach Odhar died a natural death, and the name of the place where he died.[74] Perhaps mindful that over two months had passed since the last reference to Coinneach Odhar, his near namesake requests an early answer. Two weeks later he received thirty-two lines of Gaelic verse from N. M. who began by considering the various ways Coinneach Odhar was thought to have died. He could dismiss violent ends such as being burned, drowned, hanged or crucified because: '[He] knew an old man from Rome/ That was acquainted with an old Smith/ That saw him on his deathbed/ And by that time he had become deaf ...'[75] Coinneach was gripping tightly his 'black stone of prophecy,' until, having squeezed out all its powers, he threw it into Loch Lomhair where it would never be found until the loch was drained. Coinneach Odhar died 'Late on a Wednesday Afternoon/ When the sun was setting/ Around the year 1700' and lies at rest 'Near the brae of Allt an t-Sabhail.'[76] Like Hugh Miller, N. M. places the seer's existence in the latter half of the seventeenth century and shares with

74 *The Highlander* Vol. 1 No. 20, p. 3.

75 Ibid., No. 22, p. 3.

76 Ibid.

Miller's account the seer disposing of his stone in a loch. N. M. provides an amusing version of events but suggests that if Coinneach Dubh 'ever goes/ Over to the sheilings of Strathpeffer/ They'll readily show him there/ Where Coinneach Odhar died.'[77] The editor introduces N. M.'s verses as concerning 'the famous seer of Brahan' and the reference to Strathpeffer seems to imply this locality as his sphere of influence. However, the poet may deliberately be suggesting different locations, Allt an t-Sabhail (stream of the barn) is sufficiently commonplace as to refer to anywhere. Loch Lomhair appears to be a fiction, or perhaps the name is simply a misprint; there is a Loch Lomhain in the Uig district of Lewis.

Matheson's hypothesis may explain a version from a particular locality which prevailed through being fixed in print. However, neither Lewis nor the Easter Ross versions of the legend surrounding Coinneach Odhar are the only ones to exist in oral tradition. Alasdair Alpin Macgregor provides a version from Skye very similar in content to the Lewis version, citing Frances Tolmie, the folklorist, as his source.[78] This legend is set in pre-Christian times and narrated very much in the manner of a folktale. In the dead of night Coinneach's mother waylays the Ghost of Til, son of the king of Norway. He has to answer three questions before he is permitted to re-enter his grave. The final question concerns the fate of his interlocutor who is told she will bear a son with the gift of prophecy. Coinneach is described as a native of South Uist who, having gone blind in extreme old age, stumbles into a bog and drowns. The legend provides an explanation for a place name, PoolTiel, on the western coast of Skye where the prince's body was washed ashore. According to Macgregor, Tolmie had originally collected the legend from a Uist sailor who had heard it as a child. There is a tiny hamlet near PoolTiel called Uig, providing at least one association with its Lewis namesake. In contradiction to Macgregor's account, Matheson, who was brought up in North Uist,

77 Ibid.

78 A. A. Macgregor, *Over the Sea to Skye* (London, 1926), pp. 115–120 and in his *The Peat Fire Flame: Folk-tales and Traditions of the Highlands and Islands* (Edinburgh, 1937), pp. 253–255.

observes that although Coinneach Odhar's name is known there, 'I would not say that he figures largely in Uist tradition.'[79]

John G. Campbell, minister of Tiree in the Inner Hebrides from 1861 to 1891, gathered material entirely from oral sources from throughout the Highlands and Islands. Although not published until 1900 his account contains much that was collected prior to 1860.[80] He relates that the name of Coineach Odhar [sic], who 'is hardly known in Argyll-shire,' found his stone in a raven's nest.[81] Campbell also relates that Coinneach threw his stone into a loch, 'where it lies still,' rather than surrender it to pursuers. Although Campbell describes Coinneach as 'a native of Ross-shire' the handful of prophecies he attributes to him all relate to the Isles.[82] The name of Coinneach Odhar was known across a wide area and different accounts exist to explain his supernatural powers. These accounts seem to divide geographically between Easter Ross and the Western Isles; the latter showing an affinity with Norse legends. Within the two regions there are sufficient essential similarities in the accounts to suggest a common origin in oral tradition. The existence of notable lairds whose distinguishing features are used as a sign of contemporary events is also transferable and is suggestive of a common origin. The prophecy attributed to Coinneach Odhar, relating to the downfall of the Seaforth Mackenzies, appears to be a case where oral tradition has been harnessed to suit particular events.

79 Matheson, 'The Historical Coinneach Odhar,' p. 66.

80 J. G. Campbell, *Superstitions of the Highlands and Islands of Scotland* (Glasgow, 1900), pp. v and vii.

81 Ibid., pp. 272–273.

82 Ibid., pp. 273–274.

Coinneach Odhar and the last of the Seaforth Mackenzies

When Frances Humbertson Mackenzie, Baron Seaforth of Kintail, died aged 59 at Edinburgh, on 11 January 1815 he had been predeceased by his four sons, two of whom had died in infancy.[83] The two sons who reached young manhood died within a few months of each other. Francis John was killed in action while serving as a midshipman in the Royal Navy on 7 November 1813 when only seventeen years of age; William Frederick, Member of Parliament for the county of Ross, died at the age of twenty three on 25 August 1814.[84] Lord Seaforth had been in ill health for years, suffering 'his "little momentoes" such as headaches, attacks on his kidneys, vertigoes, etc.'[85] His teeth tormented him a great deal.[86] His death was seen by many of his friends as a blessing.[87] The end of the male line entailed the inheritance falling on Lord Seaforth's eldest daughter, Mary Frederica Elizabeth, whose misfortunes had been compounded by the recent loss of her husband, Admiral Sir Samuel Hood.[88] Lady Hood subsequently remarried and became Mrs James Stewart-Mackenzie. Apart from his other ills Seaforth was severely deaf, an impediment which plagued all three sons of his successor and which was a cause of great concern to the family.[89]

83 *Inverness Journal*, 20 January 1815, Seaforth's obituary.

84 Ibid., 2 and 9 September 1814, for obituary of William Frederick, and the Seaforth memorial tablet in Fortrose Cathedral for all.

85 Seaforth Papers: NLS Ms. 6396; f120, letter to his son 'Franchi' from Lord Seaforth, 9 November 1810.

86 Ibid., f111, letter from Charles Proby, Jnr. to his sister, Lady Seaforth, 4 May 1809.

87 Seaforth Muniments: NAS Ref GD46/15.6,6. Seaforth's death 'cannot be regretted.' Sir Vicary Gibbs, MP to Sir Samuel[blank], 16 January 1816.

88 Hood died at Madras, 24 December 1814. His obituary did not appear in the *Inverness Journal* until 16 June 1815.

89 Keith, Francis and George all suffered from deafness. Seaforth Muniments, NAS Ref. GD46/15.55, 8–11; 41, 37–39; 41, 40–43; 42, 4–5; 42.16 for concerns through summer of 1833 et seq. re George. See also GD/15.94, re Francis who travelled to

When Robert Carruthers reviewed *The Seaforth Papers*, a privately printed collection of family correspondence published in 1863, he introduced a recent history of events by observing that 'Every old Highland family has its store of traditionary and romantic beliefs.'[90] He continued his narrative, 'Centuries ago a seer of the Clan Mackenzie, known as Kenneth Oag [sic] predicted that when there should be a deaf Caberfae, the gift land of the estate would be sold, and the male line become extinct.'[91] Carruthers provides a simple version of a prophecy and is the first writer to directly link Coinneach Odhar with predicting the Seaforth family downfall. His spelling is very similar to Hugh Miller's 'Kenneth Ore.' He may have obtained the name from Miller whom he had befriended and encouraged when the latter had begun to write for the *Inverness Courier* while Carruthers was editor.[92] Among the mundane prophecies attributed to the seer by Miller is that there would be a deaf Seaforth. Such an observation is hardly profound and in view of the impediment which long afflicted the last Lord Seaforth it probably arose as a description of him. Since his three grandsons were also afflicted the condition may have been a family trait. Miller did credit Coinneach Odhar with predicting that Fortrose Cathedral would fall when full of Mackenzies. Due to the derelict nature of the building and the large numbers of Mackenzies entombed therein, this prediction requires, as Miller observes, no more than perceptiveness.[93]

Carruthers cites 'three unimpeachable Sassenach witnesses, Sir Humphry Davy, Sir Walter Scott and Mr Morritt of Rokeby,' the Member of Parliament for Northampton, whom he assures his readers 'had all

---

Berlin to consult a Dr Kramer and George, in a letter to Mrs Stewart Mackenzie from her sister, 1 June 1839.

90 R. Carruthers, 'Review of the *Seaforth Papers, Letters from 1796 to 1843*,' *North British Review* Vol. 39 1863, pp. 318–357.

91 Ibid., p. 320. The term Caberfae means Staghead and is the Seaforth family bearing.

92 *Inverness Courier*, 29 April 1829, 3 and 10 June. From 29 June 1829, Miller was a regular contributor. P. Bayne (ed.), *Life and Letters of Hugh Miller* Vol I (Edinburgh, 1871), p. 236.

93 Miller, *Scenes and Legends*, p. 158.

heard the prediction when Lord Seaforth had two sons alive both in good health.'[94] The testimony of Carruthers' witnesses reveals no endorsement of Coinneach Odhar as the source. Morritt's words are ascribed to him by a third party, J. G. Lockhart, Scott's biographer and son-in law, who writes, 'Mr Morritt can testify thus far – that he 'heard the prophecy quoted in the highlands at a time when Lord Seaforth had two sons both alive and in good health – so that it certainly was not made *après coup*.'[95] Sir Humphry Davy, scientist and inventor, who visited and socialised with the nobility of Easter Ross, clearly knew of an old prophecy connected to the Mackenzies and believed he had witnessed its fulfilment.[96] However, he attributes the prophecy to a thirteenth-century prophet. He recorded in his private notebook, 'The apparent ravings of Thomas the Rhymer, respecting the Mackenzie family, have no natural connection with the remarkable event of which I am an historical witness; no more than the rattling of the wheels of a carriage at an inn door with the death of poultry, which, however, we know is the remote cause. The chickens can as much fathom this, as we can the mysteries of our being and nature.'[97] Thomas the Rhymer, despite being a Lowland seer, was considered by many Highlanders to be their true prophet and he had particular relevance for those who supported the Jacobite cause. Only when all hopes for a Jacobite return evaporated after Charles Edward Stewart died without an heir in Rome in 1788 did Thomas's prophecies lose their currency.[98] Many prophecies formerly attributed to Thomas are now attributed to Coinneach Odhar.

94 Ibid.

95 J. G. Lockhart, *Life of Scott, Memoirs of Sir Walter Scott* Vol. II (London, 1914), p. 501n.

96 *Inverness Journal*, 6 August 1813.

97 J. Davy, *Memoirs of the life of Sir Humphry Davy* Vol. II (London, 1836), p. 72.

98 R. Black, *An Lasair: An Anthology of 18th Century Scottish verse* (Edinburgh, 2001), p. 452. R. Black, 'A Century of Coded Messages,' *West Highland Free Press* (13 February 1998), p. 19. Black, 'How Did Thomas Become the Messiah,' WHFP (30 January 1998), p. 21. Black, 'The Messiah of the Gael,' WHFP (16 January 1998), p. 19.

Sir Walter Scott was a close friend of the Seaforth family, especially of the eldest daughter on whom he kept a paternal eye.[99] In a letter to a mutual friend, written from Edinburgh several months before the death of Seaforth's last surviving son, Scott intimated that 'Poor Caberfae is here – very ill indeed and quite broken in mind and spirits ... it is piteous to see such a wreck of what were once talents of a high order.'[100] In a letter dated 23 July 1814, he expressed forthright sentiments regarding Seaforth's ill health. '[P]oor Caberfae is I fear totally comatose and the conclusion of the scene greatly to be wished for.'[101] The lingering and debilitating manner of Seaforth's illness, which his caring friends hoped would be relieved by death, was given added poignancy as his sons died around him. Speculation regarding the fate of the family would have been inevitable.

When William Frederick predeceased his father Scott wrote without elaboration, 'poor Mackenzie too is gone – the brother of our Lady Hood.'[102] Only when Seaforth finally succumbed to his illness did Scott make any reference to a prophecy. In a lengthy letter to his close friend Morritt, Scott included news of their mutual friends. 'You will have heard of poor Caberfae's death – what a pity it is he should outlive his promising young representative. His state was truly pitiable – all his fine faculties lost in paralytic imbecility and yet not sufficiently so but what he conceived and felt his deprivation as in a glass darkly ... Our friend Lady Hood will now be Caberfae herself. She has the spirit of a chieftaness in every drop of her blood but the estate is terribly embarrassed and will require great prudence in management ... I do fear the accomplishment of the prophecy that when there should be a dumb [sic] Caberfae the house was to fall.'[103]

99 H. T. C. Grierson (ed.), *Letters of Sir Walter Scott* (London, 1933–35) Vol. III, p. 29.

100 Ibid., Vol. III, pp. 393–394. To Miss Clephane, 11 December 1813.

101 Ibid., Vol. III, p. 497.

102 Ibid.

103 Ibid., Vol. IV, pp. 13–14, dated 19 January 1815.

Two days later, from his house in Castle Street, Edinburgh, Scott informed Morritt that 'I have just seen Caberfae's hearse pass. I trust they will send it by sea for on land the journey must be fearful at this season. There is something very melancholy in seeing the body pass, poorly attended and in the midst of a snow storm whitening all the sable ornaments of the Undertaker and all corresponding with the decadence and the misfortunes of the family.'[104] The dismal sight of Seaforth's final journey to join his sons in Fortrose Cathedral shows how far the fortunes of this once wealthy family had sunk. Scott described the scene in a letter to his friend Elizabeth, Marchioness of Stafford and Countess of Sutherland. 'The last days of poor Caberfae were really heaviness and sorrow … so it is a mercy that the curtain is dropd [sic]. All the Highlands ring with a prophecy that when there should be a deaf Caberfae the clan and chief should all go to wreck, *but these predictions are very apt to be framed after the event*' (emphasis added).[105] This qualification from Scott suggests an ambivalence regarding the prophecy but D. S. Hewett writes, 'I think we must be wary of the use we make of his letters in determining his views and opinions, for what he says is *always* contingent upon his correspondent. No statement can ever be taken at face value' (original emphasis).[106] Scott's letters are what the recipient wants to hear. His manly discussions with Morritt would be less inhibited and not necessarily an exhibition of belief, just an exchange of stories. Scott's letter to the Marchioness is more circumspect regarding any revelation of Scott's own belief but both letters suggest that a prophecy existed.

The prophecy featured in the conversations of the social circle in which Davy, Scott and Morritt moved. This is confirmed by a young acquaintance of Scott's, Elizabeth Grant of Rothiemurchus, who wrote her memoirs as a gift to her grandchildren several years after the events she describes. She started writing in 1845 and finished in 1854. She wrote

104 Ibid., p. 19. 21 January 1815.

105 Ibid., p. 22. And W. Fraser, *The Sutherland Book* Vol. II (Edinburgh, 1892), pp. 323–324.

106 D. S. Hewitt, 'The Survey of the Letters of Sir Walter Scott,' *The Scottish Literary Journal* (Aberdeen, 1980), pp. 7–18, pp. 17–18.

in chronological order, letting her sister, former governess and other close confidantes see each chapter as it was completed so that they could pass comment on the accuracy of her recollections.[107] Grant recalled the events of the year 1815:

> The Inverness Meeting ... was a very bad one, I recollect, no new beauties, a failure of old friends, and a dearth of the family connexions. Mr [Thomas] Mackenzie of Applecross [who later succeeded William Frederick as MP for Ross-shire] was at this meeting, more agreeable than ever, but looking extremely ill ... [108] He was a plain man, and he had a buck tooth to which some one had called attention, and it was soon the only topick spoken of, for an old prophecy ran that whenever a mad Lovat, a childless Chisholm, and an Applecross with a buck tooth met, there would be an end of Seaforth. The buck tooth all could see, the mad Lovat was equally conspicuous, and though Mrs Chisholm had two handsome sons born after several years of childless wedlock, nobody ever though of fathering them on her husband. In the beginning of this year Seaforth ... boasted of two promising sons; both were gone, died within a few months of each other. This made every one melancholy, and the deaths of course kept many away from the meeting.[109]

The Inverness Meeting to which Elizabeth Grant refers was the high point of the social calendar, a series of balls and gatherings held over a week in October of each year. Grant is recounting events which occurred some ten months after what was seen by many as a welcome end for the elderly Lord Seaforth and the meeting of the contemporaries with distinguishing features could not be seen to presage what had already happened. The death of William Frederick occurred two months prior to the 1814 Meeting. This, following so soon after the tragic death of his younger brother, and with the father lingering in poor health, could have had a depressing impact on the demeanour of the revellers. Yet, Grant 'came out' in 1814, and recalls her entry into society with obvious pleasure, in contrast to the subdued affair of 1815.[110] Grant had met Thomas

107 A. Tod (ed.), *Elizabeth Grant of Rothiemurchus: Memoirs of a Highland Lady* 2 Vols. (Edinburgh, 1988) Vol. I, p. viii.

108 Ibid., Vol. II, p. 30.

109 Ibid.

110 Ibid., Vol. I, pp. 345–349.

Mackenzie the year before and though she thought him 'very plain' and 'very sickly,' she passed no other comment on his physical appearance.[111] Osgood Mackenzie relates that his grandfather, Sir Hector Mackenzie of Gairloch, was universally known among Highlanders as '*An tighearna Storach*' (the buck-toothed laird).[112] Sir Hector was a contemporary and associate of the last Lord Seaforth and it may be that any prophecy linking Seaforth to a man with this peculiarity originated with him. The Grant and Chisholm parents had fallen out some years earlier. The unfortunate Mrs Chisholm had given Elizabeth substantial gifts prior to the 1815 ball in what was seen as an unsuccessful attempt at reconciliation.[113] Grant's seeming candour at naming Mrs Chisholm may have been driven in part by this feud. The circumstances of the prophecy could only be made to fit by impugning the lady's reputation.[114]

Prophecies were in circulation referring to lairds with distinguishing features including a deaf Mackenzie but they appear to have been revised, re-invented and relocated to suit different circumstances. R. C. Macleod recounts a prophecy relating to a branch of his family and which he attributed to Coinneach Odhar. 'When we shall have a red-haired Lovat, a squint eyed, fair haired Chisholm, a big, deaf Mackenzie, and a MacGille-challum [MacLeod of Raasay] is crooked legged, and is the great-grandson of John beg of Ruigha [a place in Skye], that Mac-Gille-challum will be the worst that ever came or ever will come.'[115] Raasay was sold in 1846 through the foolishness and extravagance of this last named. Alexander Nicolson provides from Skye a variation on this same

111 Ibid., Vol. I, p. 348.

112 O. Mackenzie, *A Hundred Years in the Highlands* (London, 1921), pp. 139, 149 and 142.

113 Tod (ed.), *Elizabeth Grant of Rothiemurchus*, Vol. II, p 30.

114 It is only since the 1988 edition of Elizabeth Grant's memoirs, edited by Andrew Tod, that Mrs Chisholm's name actually appears. All previous editions, beginning with that of Grant's first editor, her niece, Lady Strachey (1898), left the name blank.

115 R. C. MacLeod, *The MacLeods: Their History and Traditions* (Edinburgh, undated), p. 149.

prophecy in Gaelic verse which he attributed to '"Coinneach Odhar" the "Brahan Seer."'[116]

None of the elite contemporaries of the last Seaforth named Coinneach Odhar as the seer who predicted the family's downfall though their accounts demonstrate belief in a prophecy. Their narratives, initially private, entered the public domain; Davy's in 1836, Scott's in 1838 and Grant's in 1898. Carruthers was the first to link seer and prophecy in print in 1863, indicating that by then the association had been made. By the time *The Highlander* began circulating that association was enshrined in the 'Traditions and Legends of the Black Isle.' A column of this name, written by Mr A. B. Maclennan, police constable in Croy and a folklorist in the area, had been running intermittently in the paper since its inception.[117] He responded to N. M.'s Gaelic 'effusion' by giving 'an unvarnished narrative of Coinneach Odhar's cruel death, as handed down to us by our forefathers.'[118] Maclennan's narrative is anything but unvarnished. He relates that 'some two hundred years ago ... Coinneach Odhar, the greatest revealer of future events ever known in the north of Scotland' had such a reputation that he was 'invited ... by the nobility of the land' to reveal the future for themselves, their families and their guests. 'Having been born on the Seaforth estate, he was more associated with that family than with any other.'[119] Once, at the grandest of balls, Lady Seaforth asked the seer's opinion of the pretty ladies dancing before him. Coinneach, 'who by the way, had no liking for that kind of amusement,' gave her an answer that was so rude that Maclennan declined writing it. The proud lady vowed that he would never insult her like that again. [120]

116 A. Nicolson, *A History of Skye: A Record of the Families, the Social Conditions, etc.* (Glasgow, 1930), p. 449.

117 A. B. Maclennan, 'Traditions and Legends of the Black Isle,' *The Highlander*, 1873, passim.

118 Maclennan, 'Traditions No. XII,' *The Highlander* Vol. I. No. 28 22 November 1873, p. 7.

119 Ibid.

120 Ibid.

A few days later, when the laird was absent, Lady Seaforth ordered Coinneach Odhar to be 'bound hand and foot,' and taken immediately to the Ness of Chanonry. There, 'despite his pitiable looks and lamentable cries ... he was inhumanly thrown, head foremost, into a barrel of burning tar,' despite the valiant efforts of the returning laird who had rushed to the spot, his horse expiring on the way.[121] Maclennan identifies with some precision, a spot where 'a large stone slab, now covered by sand ... marks the place where the terrible tragedy was consummated.'[122] Quite how he can be so sure of the location of something no longer visible is unclear but there may very well have been a stone in the vicinity to commemorate burnings, the only historical evidence for which is that from the time of the Fowlis affair. If this memorial exists it appears to be the only tangible link with those events. The passage of time has changed the narrative.

Conclusion

The content of oral narrative is influenced by memory and by the desires and expectations of storyteller and audience. The experiences of nineteenth-century collectors highlight the difficulties inherent in obtaining oral traditions when the practice of ceilidh gathering was in decline. Paradoxically, it is through the medium of the written word that tales of Coinneach Odhar have come down to the present. These show that accounts of his birth, how he acquired his supernatural powers and the prophecies attributed to him were located in time and place to suit local circumstances. Once these tales were committed to print they became accessible to a wider audience which looked to the text as the authoritative source of information. The storyteller's ability to adapt the narrative

121 Ibid.

122 Ibid.

diminished. Coinneach Odhar's prominence is a literary, rather than a purely 'oral' achievement. A. B. Maclennan's elaborate account, with its wealth of detail, of Coinneach Odhar's connection to the Seaforths, is in sharp contrast to the relatively simple tales of oral tradition collected from earlier sources. These, in turn, appear to have linked the events surrounding the demise of the family to prophecies involving lairds with distinguishing features which had existed since the seventeenth century. These old prophecies have been relocated in time and place to explain contemporary events of local significance. Maclennan's dating in print of 'some two hundred years ago' places the tale in a historical context. This is no different to the practice of oral tradition excepting that identifiable historical names can be added to the narrative. People supplied the columns of newspapers, the historians and folklorists with their recollections. Editors and writers committed the stories to print. The mediation of agents and the printed word affect how a story is recorded and the committing to print of oral tradition is a further link in the recurring theme of the complex interrelation between elite and popular culture at the heart of this story. Despite Maclennan's claim that his account was 'handed down from our forefathers,' and there is no grounds for thinking he obtained it from other than oral sources, those sources themselves had become influenced by the intervention of a 'Gothic phantasist' who had drawn from the raw materials of history and oral tradition to create in print a Romantic legend of his own. The next chapter turns to this Romantic legend, and the local response to it.

CHAPTER 6

The Making of a Legend

Introduction

Having examined the place of Coinneach Odhar in oral tradition it is now time to examine how that oral tradition was transmuted into Victorian literature and the affect that this had on the legend. A romanticised version first appeared in the literature in 1863 and forms the basis of the legend that has come down to the present day. Written by an aristocratic Anglo-Irishman, Sir Bernard Burke, it was modified some years later to suit local perceptions of the past by Alexander Mackenzie and fellow collectors of traditional lore who were active in 'rescuing from oblivion' all aspects of Celtic culture.[1] This chapter examines the nature of this transmutation from a cultural historical perspective.

Writers from the 1970s and 1980s provide an interpretation of history which portrays Scotland and the Highlands as the subjugated periphery of a metropolitan ideology. Culture was seen as a power struggle and the product of class divisions; everything, in short, was reduced to the political. Eric Hobsbawm examined the invention of practices which take on a symbolic nature and are adopted by emerging nation states to provide them with tradition and cohesion. The celebration of national days, coronations and annual rallies are broad examples of invented tradition. Their purpose, unlike custom which does permit some element of

1 B. Burke, *Vicissitudes of Families* 3 Vols. (London, 1860–63) Vol. III 'The Fate of Seaforth' pp. 266–281. A. Mackenzie, *The Prophecies of the Brahan Seer* (London, 1977 (1877)). A. Mackenzie, 'The Prophecies of the Brahan Seer,' TGSI Vol. I, 1871, pp. 196–211.

change, is to create 'invariance' in an ever changing society by imposing formal rules as to how the practice should be conducted.[2] Hobsbawm identified three broad, overlapping categories of invented tradition: those which determine or represent shared unity within particular groups; those determining or justifying organisations and their authority and 'those whose main purpose was socialisation: the inculcation of beliefs, value systems and conventions of behaviour.'[3]

An example of invented tradition which encapsulates these categories is the kilt. The wearing of the kilt and tartan is, according to Hugh Trevor-Roper, a relatively new (early eighteenth-century) concept and he identifies two principal reasons for its success: the influence of the Romantic Movement and the formation of Highland regiments in the British army. Both of these external influences originate in the environs of elite (rather than popular) culture: the first driven by Romantic perceptions, the second driven by political pragmatism.[4] For some historians the Highlands are portrayed in the sentimental iconography of tartanry, James Macpherson's poems of Ossian and the Jacobite failure, most of which are remnants or additions to the Romanticism which pervaded perceptions of the Highlands during the latter part of the nineteenth century. Malcolm Chapman suggests that much of what is perceived as Gaelic culture was imported from elsewhere and he raises questions not just about its authenticity but about the 'false consciousness' this engenders in those living in the region who take up such cultural practices.[5] For Peter Womack the Highlands of Scotland is an imaginary place on the periphery of the real world, so created in the age of discovery to provide

2 E. Hobsbawm and T. Ranger (eds), *The Invention of Tradition* (Cambridge, 1983), p. 2.

3 Ibid., p. 9.

4 H. Trevor-Roper, 'The Invention of Tradition: the Highland Tradition of Scotland' in Hobsbawm and Ranger (eds), *The Invention of Tradition*, pp. 15–41. Not all historians accept Trevor-Roper's view on the relative modernity of the kilt; Hugh Cheape, in his *Tartan: The Highland Habit* (Edinburgh, 1991) deals with the suggestion by simply ignoring it.

5 M. Chapman, *The Gaelic Vision in Scottish Culture* (London, 1978), p. 53.

the residents of the real world with a place of escape. He goes so far as to state that improvement and Romanticism were 'twins,' the former the economic necessity to change the region for the better, the latter assisting to effect that change through the construction of a myth about an imagined society.[6] Womack sees literature, poetry in particular, as the principal medium for propagating the myth, a process he calls *literarisation* through which the Highlands were 'admitted to the privileges, and condemned to the marginality, of fiction.'[7]

More recently, Sharon Macdonald has taken a more optimistic view. Working from a social anthropological perspective, she writes that the Romantic Movement and 'Macpherson's "search" [for old manuscripts] ... reinforced the idea that some aspects of Gaelic culture – the old and traditional – were valued by the outside world.'[8] Her studies indicate that people living in the Highlands 'have drawn on their own cultural preoccupations to challenge, make use of, or appropriate outside forms.'[9] Michael Newton argues that Gaelic culture has survived the impositions of language, education, economic and political changes during the past six centuries. The continued existence of the modern *Gàidhealtachd* is due to its strength at the grass roots. Newton suggests that those theorists who focused on class oppression have failed to adequately explain Highland-Lowland cultural differences. These he explores in what he refers to as a cultural invasion model, comparing them with colonial experiences.[10] The inhabitants of the region being encroached upon, he writes, can be classified broadly as either *traditionalists* who wish to maintain or restore their existing culture, *syncretists* who incorporate some aspects of the

6 P. Womack, *Improvement and Romance: Constructing the Myths of the Highlands* (Basingstoke, 1989), p. 3.

7 Ibid., pp. 179–180.

8 S. Macdonald, *Reimagining Culture: Histories, Identities and the Gaelic Renaissance.* (Oxford, 1997), p. 54.

9 Ibid., p. 248.

10 M. Newton, *A Handbook of the Scottish Gaelic World* (Dublin, 2000), p. 38.

encroaching culture into their own, and *assimilationists* who wish to adopt the new culture in its entirety at the expense of their own.[11]

These more nuanced approaches suggest that the assumption that cultural change is enforced by one homogenous mass on another homogenous mass is misleading. Several writers, among them I. F. Grant, have stressed the homogeneity of culture in different parts of the Gaelic region especially in the similarity of songs and folk tales from oral tradition.[12] The different versions of the Coinneach Odhar legend from within the separate areas of the Western Isles and Easter Ross show similarities. Without some such defining homogenous features it would be difficult to identify any culture as being distinct from another. Newton argues that '[n]o healthy society silently succumbs to pressure from external forces, nor does it entirely reject all external stimuli. Rather, a fully functional and self-confident society assesses ideas from outside sources according to its own internal value and belief systems, adapts those ideas which are perceived to be beneficial to it, and rejects those which disturb or conflict with its own norms and aesthetics.'[13] However, it is also true that a society under threat and in search of an identity will select and adapt ideas from outsiders which resonate with its perception of itself and this, it is argued, is what happened in the case of the Brahan Seer legend. Newton's model would require a fourth category, *synthesists*, to accommodate those who wish to maintain a threatened culture but incorporate aspects from an encroaching culture to enable them to do so.

People from different social groups and classes, in sufficient numbers to ensure continued dissemination, took up the legend of the Brahan Seer, modified and embellished it to suit their understanding of local culture. Had the legend not held meaning and value for them they would have rejected it, just as they would have rejected the kilt and the poems of Ossian. These productions all had their roots in Romantic conceptions of the Highlands; the people of the Highlands accepted all three with different degrees of endorsement. The raw materials for the invention of

11 Ibid., p. 23.
12 Ibid., p. 38.
13 Ibid., p. 275.

these productions were acquired locally; their appropriation by groups within Highland culture was partly due to this. They came to signify different things to different groups within Highland culture. The kilt was primarily adopted by elite classes of society, not all at the one time and not with universal approval; the poems of Ossian were adopted by those, including writers and poets, who sought a classical past for their literary culture. The legend of the Brahan Seer helped to explain the demise of a once great family and gave credence to the phenomenon of second sight because of the seer's apparent success. In all three cases it does not matter whether or not they are based on truth or error, they have influenced human behaviour and changed the nature of Highland society to a greater or lesser degree because they were perceived to be of value to people in the region.

By appropriating literary romance into history and oral tradition and committing it to print, the revised legend of the Brahan Seer has become not only the definitive version but the events depicted have become real for those who choose to perceive them in that light. History and oral tradition were transmuted into literature and the legend became imbued with a Romantic perception of the past. This was only possible because the prevailing vision of the Highlands during the nineteenth century enabled accounts of the region to be portrayed in a Romantic light. This vision was shared by those who collected the folklore surrounding the legend and enabled them to present it in a similar way. By transforming literary romance into folklore the collectors made the Seer real and attracted to his person numerous prophecies relating to other events in the region. Their perceived accuracy helped perpetuate the legend and confirmed the existence of second sight. This was in contrast to how second sight was generally portrayed in Romantic literature by writers from outside the area; as a superstition from a bygone age.

The Romantic invention of the Brahan Seer

In the early 1860s Sir Bernard Burke provided dramatic and largely imaginary literary accounts of how once great families had disappeared.[14] The accounts were written in an effusive style and directed towards an audience with a hunger for 'bogus medieval romanticism.'[15] In a short biography issued to celebrate a hundred and fifty years of publications by *Burke's Peerage* the company's own editor states of Sir Bernard that, '[h]e loved a flowery phrase and, if not a charlatan, took on too much and was undoubtedly uncritical to a degree.'[16] This restrained criticism is primarily directed toward his work in genealogy which became so 'tainted with the stigma of snobbery' that accurate academic research was compromised. *Burke's* was in the forefront of trying to satisfy a heavy demand for genealogical work and 'some lamentable exercises in "Gothick phantasy" were perpetrated.'[17] Only when scholars led by Horace Round exposed the inaccuracies did *Burke's,* under Sir Bernard's son, Henry, establish themselves as an objective source of information.

Among the accounts of family misfortune was 'The Fate of Seaforth.' The story of the demise of the Seaforths and a prophecy linked thereto, seem to have been common currency among the upper reaches of Highland society. Burke received a version of the story from the Earl of Ellesmere, who died in 1857, although there is no evidence that this contained any reference as to how the prophecy originated.[18] Ellesmere was the second and eldest surviving son of Elizabeth, Marchioness of Stafford and Countess of Sutherland, who was a close friend of Mrs Stewart Mackenzie and one of Sir Walter Scott's correspondents at the time of Lord Seaforth's

14 Burke, *Vicissitudes of Familes*, 3 Vols (London, 1860–3).
15 R. Pinches (ed.), *Burke's Family Index* (London, 1976), p. xi.
16 Ibid.
17 Ibid.
18 Burke, *Vicissitudes* Vol. III, p. 275.

death.[19] Burke was the first to identify in print Lady Isabella Mackenzie as the tormentor of '"The Warlock of the Glen," ... a clairvoyant and a medium; for he united in his person the characteristics of both these branches of the mysterious gifts ... possessing ... what in the days of our fathers would have been called the second sight.'[20] In common with many writers of his time, Burke does not usually specify his sources although he cites village legend and the peasants' tale as his 'constant helps' in fleshing out his narratives.[21] Burke quotes from James Fraser's *Wardlaw Ms.*, large extracts of which had been published in the *Inverness Courier*.[22] He may have been influenced by Fraser's description of the unpopular Isabella, although Fraser does not mention the Countess by name.[23] The Restoration was perceived as a defining moment in history, as were the numerous witchcraft trials of the period. The Restoration was also a Romantic period with its focus on the monarchy and court life: a time and place of special relevance to Burke's audience with its interest in the peerage, heraldry, and genealogy.

According to Burke, Lady Isabella called for the 'Warlock' during her husband's absence in Paris, and asked him to tell of the earl's whereabouts. On being told, after much prompting, that he was in the arms of a lady and had no thought for her, she determined to make an example of the seer's insolence. 'The gallows were forthwith erected and the miserable Warlock of the Glen was led out for immediate execution' though not before he had time to predict the fate of the Seaforths. After the last deaf and dumb chief 'shall sink into the grave ... the remnant of his possession

19 J. B. Paul, *The Scots Peerage: A History of the Noble Families of Scotland* 9 Vols. (Edinburgh, 1911), Vol. VIII, pp. 361–362.

20 Burke, *Vicissitudes* Vol. III, p. 269.

21 Ibid., Vol. II, p. 13.

22 J. Barron, *The Northern Highland in the Nineteenth Century* Vol. II (Inverness, 1907), p. 202. The *Wardlaw Ms* was first identified to readers of the *Inverness Courier* on 31 December 1834. The paper's editor later published the extracts in book form. R Carruthers, *The Highland Note-Book or Sketches and Anecdotes* (Edinburgh, 1843), passim.

23 Burke, *Vicissitudes*, Vol. I, p. 7. Ibid., Vol. III, p. 268. J. Fraser, *Chronicle of the Frasers (The Wardlaw Manuscript)*, p. 421.

shall be inherited by a white-hooded lassie from the east. She is to kill her sister ... '[24] The seer then gave the names of four great lairds, Mackenzie of Gairloch, Chisholm, Grant and MacLeod of Raasay, who would be buck-toothed, hare-lipped, half witted or a stammerer. Seeing these distinguishing features among his peers Seaforth would know his line was to end. The seer finally threw his stone into a nearby loch, proclaiming that the finder would have prophetic powers. Immediately thereafter 'he was hung up on high.'[25] Burke could not resist squeezing the last drop of romance and intrigue out of his tale. The prophecy was 'uttered it in all its horrible length; but I suppress the last portion which is yet unfulfilled and which therefore I am unwilling to relate ... The last clause ... is well known to many of those versed in Highland family tradition; but it must not be published, and I trust that it may remain unfulfilled.'[26] The romance is perpetuated because whatever happens to the Mackenzies can be construed as fulfilment of the prophecy.

The death of the last Lord Seaforth was not the last misfortune to befall the family. Sadly for all concerned, Lord Seaforth's daughter, Mrs Stewart-Mackenzie, who had inherited the estates, and her sister, Lady Caroline, were involved in a fatal accident. They had accompanied the laird and his grieve on the morning of 29 March 1823 while they marked out some trees which needed to be cut.[27] The two ladies sat in a 'little garden chair' pulled by a pony which Mr Stewart-Mackenzie led by the head. After about an hour they were returning to the Castle when Mr Stewart-Mackenzie asked if they could make their own way back because the men had business on another part of the estate. Mrs Stewart-Mackenzie took the reins but on coming down an incline the pony broke into a gallop which she could not control. Lady Caroline considered jumping but was impeded by the chair's leather apron. When the pony swerved

24 Burke, *Vicissitudes* Vol. III, pp. 273–274.

25 Ibid., p. 274.

26 Ibid., pp. 274–275.

27 *The Seaforth Muniments*, NAS GD 46/15, f.135, 12. A narrative of the accident and the illness of 'our dear angel' in the hand of Mr. Stewart-Mackenzie but told partly from the viewpoint of his wife.

suddenly both ladies were thrown into a rock-strewn ditch. Mrs Stewart-Mackenzie's first recollection on regaining consciousness was seeing her sister standing, dazed and blood splattered, in the road.

Although Mrs Stewart-Mackenzie made a full recovery her sister died on 24 April 1823 after a series of relapses. She had suffered head injuries and was attended by doctors from Dingwall, Inverness and a London practitioner who was on a visit to Strathpeffer. Very likely she had sustained internal lesions which the doctors could do nothing about and following the medical practice of the period she was bled several times. An already weakened patient was put on a liquid diet, 'just enough to keep above starvation,' in a futile effort to save her life.[28] There was much bitterness between the surviving sisters over who was to blame for Caroline's death. 'As to the death of relations, where the nerves are concerned, they do play strange tricks with us,' wrote Mrs Stewart-Mackenzie. 'You hear in the 1st month how admirably everybody has behaved, and in the 2nd you are astonished to find the whole family at variance, possessed with heart-burnings and discontent.'[29] Their mother tried to act as a mediator with less than enthusiastic support for her eldest daughter.[30] Mrs Stewart-Mackenzie denied telling her sister, Augusta, that her coming to Brahan had hastened Caroline's death. She had always blamed Caroline's exertions on her behalf at the time of the accident as the source of her illness. 'I have,' she wrote, 'expressed this to every person who has talked to me.'[31]

This is borne out by Sir Walter Scott who wrote from Abbotsford, 11 May 1823, 'My Dear Morritt, – All you have heard is too true. Mrs Stuart Mackenzie was driving her sister's curricle which from some unhappy

28 *The Seaforth Muniments*: NAS GD 46/15; f.135, passim.

29 *The Seaforth Paper:* NAS f415.080.

30 *The Seaforth Muniments*: NAS GD 46/15, f.26, 5–11. The mother put off seeing her daughter on one occasion at her Charlotte Square home, saying she was not well. Letter dated 22 September 1823.

31 *The Seaforth Muniments*: NAS GD 46/15, f.26, 5–11. The correspondence took place in September and October 1823. Mrs Stewart-Mackenzie's letter to her mother of 4 October 1823.

accident was overset. [She] was much hurt and senseless – her sister ran to procure assistance and exerted herself perhaps too much – at least after two days her complaints took an alarming turn and the consequences have been fatal. Mrs Stuart Mackenzie's agony of mind is inconceivable … surely the house of Seaforth have [sic] had their full share of domestic calamity.'[32] Scott shows evident sympathy for the misfortunes of his 'Patagonian Baby' and her family but makes no reference to this accident being the fulfilment of any prophecy.[33] Nor do the ladies, in all their obvious distress, make such a suggestion. However, the family erected a large, six-sided monument overlooking the River Conon to mark the spot where Mrs Stewart Mackenzie and her sister had their awful accident. It bears a Latin inscription: 'Here, according to her prophesied fate, Caroline Mackenzie, daughter of Francis, Baron of Seaforth, was snatched from us. Her sister, who shared in the same peril, survived as the last hope of rebuilding her family, 1823.'

The family had certainly come to believe there was a prophecy concerning this accident although there is no evidence to suggest it existed prior to the event. Duncan Davidson of Tulloch, Lord Lieutenant of the County of Ross, wrote to Alexander Mackenzie after reading the second edition of *The Prophecies of the Brahan Seer* advising him that he had been a regular visitor to Brahan Castle while the last Lord Seaforth was still alive and had often heard the family discussing the prophecies. In his letter, dated 21 May 1878, he wrote 'many of these prophecies I heard of *upwards of 70 years ago*, and when many of them were *not* fulfilled, such as the late Lord Seaforth surviving his sons, and Mrs Stewart Mackenzie's accident … by which Caroline Mackenzie was killed' (original emphases).[34] Seventy years is a long time to recall. Davidson, a contemporary and particular favourite of Elizabeth Grant of Rothiemurchus, would have been a boy

32 H. T. C. Grierson, *Letters of Sir Walter Scott* (London 1933–35) Vol. VII, pp. 385–386.

33 Scott describes her thus in a letter to Charles Kilpatrick Sharpe, 4 November 1811. Grierson, *Letters of Sir Walter Scott* Vol. III, p. 29.

34 A. Mackenzie, *History of the Mackenzies, with Genealogies of the Principal Families of the Name* (Inverness, 1894) p. 267.

at the time.[35] His memory may have been influenced by hearing of, and reading about, the events after they had occurred. His letter suggests that the prophecies relating to the extinction of the male line and Lady Caroline's accident are not one and the same.

A granddaughter of Mrs Stewart Mackenzie, recalling from memory her childhood in the Highlands, recollects that there was a prophecy within the family originating with the wife of the fourth earl in the early part of the eighteenth century.[36] When the earl was absent on business in Edinburgh, the countess demanded that the family seer, Kenneth Ogh, tell her how her husband was faring. He told her the earl was enjoying himself in the company of two young ladies. Enraged at the insult, she demanded retribution and the unfortunate seer was taken to Chanonry and 'burned for a wizard.'[37] Her story ends with the prophesied arrival of a white-coifed lassie from the east, understood to mean her grandmother returning from India in her widow's cap. She makes no reference to her beloved grandmother causing the death of her sister. Burke's account conflates the two prophecies. By placing them in the mouth of the warlock who died at the hands of Countess Isabella he provides a common and romantic source which predates the events.

On 18 March 1875, Alexander Mackenzie, secretary and founding member of the Gaelic Society of Inverness, presented a paper entitled, 'The Prophecies of Coinneach Odhar Fiosaiche, the Brahan Seer.'[38] Mackenzie began his paper by stating that in the present scientific climate to confess to a belief in second sight was taken as evidence of 'looming if not actual insanity' and he did not wish his audience to think for a moment that he believed in what he was about to present.[39] 'We have all grown so scientific,' he said, 'that the mere idea of anything being possible which

35 A. Tod (ed.), *Elizabeth Grant of Rothiemurchus: Memoirs of a Highland Lady* Vol. II (Edinburgh, 1988 (1898)), pp. 77, 162 and 188.

36 Lady St. Helier, *Memories of Fifty Years* (London, 1909), pp. 5–10.

37 Ibid., p. 7.

38 A. Mackenzie, 'The Prophecies of Coinneach Odhar Fiosaiche, the Brahan Seer,' TGSI, 1875, Vol. III, pp. 196–211.

39 TGSI Vol. III, p. 196.

is incomprehensible to our cultured scientific intellects cannot be entertained' even though there were things known to science which had yet to be explained.[40] The prophecies were attributed to Coinneach Odhar 'the great prophet of the Highlands who lived near Loch Ussie, on the Brahan estate, some 200 years ago.'[41] He presented his paper because the prophecies existed among the people and he thought that, by placing them on record, he would allow future generations to test their faith in second sight – by comparing events with unfulfilled prophecies. Mackenzie provided several prophecies which he had culled from a variety of sources including the pages of *The Highlander*. The core of his paper was a near verbatim recounting of Burke's story regarding the seer's connection to the Seaforth family with small, but important, alterations such as substituting the name 'Coinneach Odhar,' 'Coinneach' or 'Kenneth' where Burke had used the word 'Warlock.' No effort was made at this stage to change the method of the seer's death from the hanging more familiar to an Anglicised audience. Another large segment of his paper was an account of second sight taken verbatim from Armstrong's *Gaelic Dictionary* where the sympathetic opinion of Dr Johnson is compared favourably with the scepticism of James Beattie.[42] Mackenzie's paper was well received by the members of the society and they provided additional prophecies during the discussion which followed.

After the success of his talk Mackenzie serialised an extended version of the paper in *The Celtic Magazine*, of which he was editor.[43] One of the most durable of regional publications, the magazine ran monthly from 1875 to 1888. It had a broad ranging remit very similar to that espoused by the Gaelic Society of Inverness, being 'devoted to the literature, history, antiquities, folk-lore, traditions, and the social and material interests of the Celt at home and abroad.'[44] Mackenzie's introductory disclaimer of

40 Ibid.

41 Ibid.

42 R. A. Armstrong, *A Gaelic Dictionary in Two Parts* (London, 1825), pp. 536–537.

43 A. Mackenzie, 'The Prophecies of Coinneach Odhar Fiosaiche, the Brahan Seer,' *The Celtic Magazine*, No XIII Vol. II (1876), pp. 18–25, p. 18.

44 From the magazine's cover.

personal belief in second sight was retained but his sympathies for the phenomenon are more obvious. He allows that 'We have had some slight experiences of our own which we would hesitate to dignify by the name of second sight.'[45] He did not elaborate. Mackenzie's discretion in the prevailing scientific climate was matched by that of Queen Victoria who, while holidaying at Loch Maree, thanked him through her secretary for copies of the magazine containing the Brahan Seer articles.[46]

Mackenzie gathered numerous prophecies attributed to the Brahan Seer and other versions of the legend including Hugh Miller's from *Scenes and Legends* and A. B. Maclennan's from the columns of *The Highlander*. From his friend, Donald Macintyre, schoolteacher at Arpafeelie, he obtained a version from the Black Isle which owed much to Miller's account with regard to the seer's acquisition of his prophetic powers while collecting peats. It was similar to Maclennan's account with respect to the events leading up to the seer's death. Only when his account was in book form did Mackenzie provide the Lewis version of the seer's birthplace in Uig which had appeared in *The Highlander*. He reiterated it, without acknowledgement, as a matter of fact.[47] Mackenzie reiterated Burke's account in full, including the manner of the seer's death by hanging. Macintyre's account was the first to record that the church was responsible for meting out the salutary punishment. 'The poor prophet was then taken to Chanonry Point, where the strong arm of ecclesiastical authority with unrelenting severity burnt him to death in a tar-barrel for witchcraft.'[48] Mackenzie concluded Macintyre's account by writing that 'When Coinneach Odhar was being led to the stake (not the gallows mark) fast bound with cords,' Lady Seaforth gloated that he was bound for hell. The seer responded that a raven and dove would circle over his pyre and the dove alighting on the embers would signify the innocent seer's elevation to heaven, rather than descent to hell; the destination

45 Mackenzie, *Celtic Magazine* No XIII Vol. II, p. 18.

46 *The Celtic Magazine*, No XXV Vol. III (1877), p. 38 and p. iv.

47 Mackenzie, *Prophecies*, p. 27–28. *The Highlander* Vol. I, No. 11, 26 July 1873, p. 3. See also chapter 5.

48 Mackenzie, *Celtic Magazine* No XVII Vol. II (1877), p. 172.

predicted for his persecutor.[49] It is not clear if this embellishment was Mackenzie's own but he did think that Coinneach Odhar was a 'pious man' of 'Christian orthodoxy' who was being badly treated by 'the highest dignitaries of a corrupted Church.'[50] This part of the legend, with its religious connotations, appears to have been borrowed from that linked to Michael Scot, the Scottish sage who 'may be regarded as the leading intellectual in western Europe during the first third of the thirteenth century.'[51] Scot, translator of Arabic, Greek, Hebrew and Latin texts, whose knowledge of magic has seen him depicted in legend as a magician – although it is unlikely he actually practiced – made predictions using astrology; the 'supreme science' of his day.[52] Following the success of the serialisation Mackenzie produced the prophecies of the Brahan Seer in book form. The above note in parenthesis '(not the gallows mark)' was omitted. It was no longer required. Burke's account, containing the earlier substitutions identifying Coinneach Odhar as the warlock, was again included, but when the seer was taken away for 'immediate execution' Mackenzie stopped short of specifying how this was done; leaving readers to assume that it was by burning as described by his other contributors.[53] The appropriation of Romantic literature into oral tradition had been completed.

Burke's romantic description of the encounter between Countess and seer has become the definitive version of what precipitated the doom of the Seaforths. His account had been in print for twelve years before the work of Mackenzie and his fellow collectors appeared. The appellation *The Brahan Seer* was coined by folklorist A. B. Maclennan and applied

49 Ibid., p. 173.

50 Mackenzie, *Celtic Magazine* No XVII Vol. II, p. 55; XVIII Vol. II p. 221. Mackenzie, *Prophecies*, p. 55.

51 L. Thorndike, *Michael Scot* (London and Edinburgh, 1965), p. 1. D. Mackenzie, 'The Brahan Seer', in L. Spence (ed.) *An Encyclopaedia of Occultism: A Compendium of Information on the Occult Sciences, Occult Personalities, Psychic Science, Magic, Demonology, Spiritism and Mysticism* (London, 1920), p. 78 and for Michael Scot, p. 356.

52 Thorndike, *Michael Scot*, pp. 13 and 116.

53 Mackenzie, *Prophecies*, pp. 115 and 109.

to Burke's 'wizard.' The name of Coinneach Odhar and the burning at Chanonry Point were provided from within the context of oral tradition – word of mouth anecdotes believed to be true about a community's past – and became the definitive account of how the seer met his death. Together with the events surrounding the downfall of the Seaforth family they form a synthesis between Romantic literature, history and oral tradition. The romantic language and attention to detail used by Mackenzie and his colleagues are a far cry from the simple language of earlier oral versions. Their acceptance of Burke's account was only possible because they had their own Romantic conception of the Highlands.

The Romantic vision of the Highlands

Over the centuries the Highlands were explored by different travellers whose main interest was in studying the region for scientific purposes. In the late eighteenth and early nineteenth centuries people such as Johnson and Boswell began to visit the region not for scientific exploration but for personal experience.[54] Many travellers showed a preference for emotions rather than rational thought, for imagination over common sense and for intuition over intellect. They favoured the real over the abstract, freedom and variety over restraint and orderliness, the natural and the organic over the mechanical and contrived.[55] They were, in effect, members of the Romantic Movement which arose across Europe as a reaction to industrial, political and religious changes driven by scientific discovery and exploration during the Enlightenment. The most visible illustration of these changes was the demographic shift from agrarian to urban living.

54 J. Glendening, *The High Road: Romantic Tourism, Scotland, and Literature, 1720–1820* (Basingstoke, 1997). T. C. Smout, 'Tours in the Scottish Highlands From the Eighteenth to the Twentieth Centuries,' *Northern Scotland* Vol. 5 No 2 (1983), pp. 99–122.

55 B. Russell, *A History of Western Philosophy* (London, 1988), pp. 651–659.

Romantics looked to 'Nature' to escape the changes in their environment and they looked at human development elsewhere to escape the changes in their own culture. They went back to 'folk culture' to reclaim something which has been lost, as they saw it, through scepticism and science.

However, the cleavage between science and Romanticism was not clear-cut. Many of the *literati* of the Scottish Enlightenment had Romantic tendencies, evincing a strong desire to see 'Nature' not as some untamed wilderness but as an environment which had been cultivated and moulded to man's design.[56] They had a particular way of looking at nature which was based on an aesthetic taste acquired through appropriate education. Scottish intellectuals such as Dugald Stewart and James Beattie assumed that an individual was formed through his environment and education. Their association theory offered an explanation of aesthetic pleasure as a particular function of the imagination, a disinterested pleasure produced by certain trains of associated ideas stimulated either by objects in the world or by their representation in works of art.[57] The consequence was a mode of aesthetic appreciation which regarded the natural world as if through the distancing, objectifying gaze of the scientist. This laid the foundation for the concept of the sublime by which even the most threatening of nature's manifestations, such as storms, mountains and wilderness, could be distanced and appreciated rather than simply feared and despised. Disinterestedness and the sublime together underpinned the idea of the picturesque through which the Romantic artists of the nineteenth century represented nature.[58]

The landscape in the Highlands could be viewed in a Romantic light, where pleasure could be invoked in those areas where man had shaped the environment and those areas whose scenic grandeur invoked feelings

56 A. Hemingway, *Landscape Imagery and Urban Culture in Early Nineteenth-Century Britain.* (Cambridge, 1992), p. 72.

57 Ibid.

58 D. Daiches, P. Jones and J. Jones (eds), *A Hotbed of Genius: The Scottish Enlightenment 1730–1790* (Edinburgh, 1986), pp. 40, 153, 154. A Broadie, *The Scottish Enlightenment* (Edinburgh, 2001), pp. 175–177 and 185.

of the sublime.[59] The past was brought to life for travellers and for their audiences through the use of Romantic literature and the use of Romantic concepts of the visited culture. The conception of the Highlands and its people received a fillip with the adoption of the kilt as the national dress of Scotland. The concept itself was an appropriation from within Highland culture of an identifiable precursor in the shape of the plaid. The kilt was born in 1720s Lochaber of the necessity to clothe foundry owner Thomas Rawlinson's forestry workers who wore a 'cumbrous, unwieldy habit' which they often preferred to throw off and work naked.[60] To such mundane utilitarian origins were grafted Romantic conceptions of the Highlander as the embodiment of martial virtue. John MacCulloch observed that the kilt was of modern introduction, 'and, what is worse, that it was the invention of an Englishman.'[61] He criticised the gentlemen of the Celtic societies, who wore it 'because it is handsome.' It was all very fine for them, wearing it at dinner once a year in a warm room but that they should think of imposing it on the Highlanders, outdoors in all weathers, did not bear thinking about. 'The project does not take, has not taken, and is not likely to take.'[62] Sir Walter Scott, to whom this letter was addressed, was to be the prime motivator in proving his friend wrong.

Scott was the orchestrator and artistic director of the visit to Edinburgh of King George IV in August 1822. Assisted by Colonel David Stewart of Garth, he appropriated Highland culture and made it accessible

59 S. Murray, *A Companion and Useful Guide to the Beauties of Scotland* (London, 1799), pp. 227 and 219. W. Gilpin, *Observations on the Highland of Scotland* 2 Vols. (Richmond, 1973 (1789)) Vol. II, pp. 117 and 141.

60 Trevor-Roper, 'The Invention of Tradition,' p. 22. J. T. Dunbar, *History of Highland Dress: With an Appendix on Early Scottish Dyes*, by Annette Kok. (London, 1979 (1962)), pp. 12–13. The reference to nakedness is contained in a letter dated 15 May 1796, some sixty years after the events, from Sir John Sinclair to John Pinkerton. J. Pinkerton, *The Literary Correspondence of John Pinkerton, Esq.* (London, 1830), p. 404.

61 J. Macculloch, *A Description of the Western Isles of Scotland, Including the Isle of Man* (London, 1819), Vol. I, p. 181.

62 Ibid., pp. 187–188.

to the rest of the nation by decorating the city and its people in tartan. Scott had written to every Highland chief of note requesting them to bring their clansmen, suitably attired, for 'Highlanders is what he likes best to see.'[63] The clans were pre-eminent in the processions and the garb of the Highlander, previously proscribed as a result of the '45 rebellion, feted as a dress fit for a king. The preponderance of tartanry was not universally welcome. Elizabeth Grant noted that, 'A great mistake was made by the Stage Managers – one that offended all the southron Scots; the King wore at the Levée the highland dress. I daresay he thought the country all highland ... did not know the difference Between the Saxon and the Celt.'[64] The offence was relatively short lived. Scott's efforts at reconciliation between Saxon and Celt was a resounding success and the kilt had come to symbolise the whole nation by the time Queen Victoria added her imprimatur by buying Balmoral in 1848 to use as a holiday retreat and decorating it in a tartan of Prince Albert's design.[65]

Prior to his involvement in 'The King's Jaunt' Sir Walter Scott's Romantic novels and poems such as *The Lady of The Lake* (1810) and *Lord of the Isles* (1815) had done much to entice tourists to view the scenes he described so vividly. Scott himself had been influenced by the accounts of earlier travellers and the involvement of one as famous as he did much to give the Romantic Movement added impetus. Another major influence was the literary work of a Highlander, James Macpherson. He published, to huge critical acclaim, a series of English prose works (*Fragments of Ancient Poetry* (1760), *Fingal* (1761) and *Temora* (1763), known collectively as *The Poems of Ossian*, purporting to be translations of Gaelic poetry from the third century AD. His writings provided an impetus to a dawning awareness of the Highlands as a place which satisfied the Romantic ideals, both in terms of the environment and the people in it.

63 *The Dunvegan Castle Muniments*: NAS, Ref 2950/683/S4.909, and cited in J. Prebble, *The King's Jaunt* (Edinburgh, 2000), p. 105.

64 A. Tod (ed.), *Elizabeth Grant: Memoirs*, Vol. II. pp. 165–166.

65 C. Withers, 'The Historical Creation of the Scottish Highlands,' in I. Donnachie and C. Whatley (eds), *The Manufacture of Scottish History* (Edinburgh, 1992), pp. 143–156. p. 153.

He brought the region to the attention of a European-wide readership which no previous writer had been able to match. The controversy over the authenticity of the poems divided scholars. Dr Johnson, the exemplar of rational thinkers, was scathing in his condemnation of notions that primitive man, unencumbered by materialism and rationalism, led a happier life than modern man, and his opinion of Macpherson and his claims for high art in primitive society was unequivocal.[66]

Macpherson himself added to the controversy. He failed to produce the original manuscripts when asked, and when the authenticity of the poems was challenged on historical grounds even before the publication of *Temora,* he countered by blaming Irish poems from the fifteenth century for corrupting Scottish oral tradition, which he held in low esteem.[67] The whole controversy acted as a forum in which to debate the various Celtic/ Saxon, primitive/modern dichotomies. Macpherson, who enjoyed the privileges of Saxon modernity, did not wish to see his Celtic/primitive roots disappear without trace. It was his good fortune that he presented his poems at the very moment a Romantic fascination was in place to welcome them.

The controversy did contribute to a search for authentic Gaelic material which may otherwise have been lost. Travellers with a Romantic conception, armed with Ossian's poems, toured the Highlands to see for themselves. The tourists' appropriation of Ossianic poetry, peopled by ghosts of long dead heroes and with supernatural dangers lurking in dark and dangerous corners, could be brought to life in the sublime landscape when all that was required to complete the picture was the observer's imagination, something which, according to Fiona Stafford, the fragmentary nature of the poems themselves required.[68] The appreciation of both landscape and poems was highly subjective. Bluestocking Mrs Elizabeth Montague, a staunch supporter of, and frequent London hostess to, Macpherson was able to exclaim with obvious delight that, 'We carry

66 Chapman, *The Gaelic Vision*, p. 50.

67 Ibid., p. 40.

68 J. Macpherson edited by H. Gaskill, *The Poems of Ossian and Related Works* (Edinburgh, 1996), citing the introduction by Fiona Stafford, pp. xv–xvi.

Ossian's Poems with us, as we shall see some of the Classic ground.'[69] On her return from her sortie to Argyle in 1764 her enthusiasm was undiminished. 'I have been in Ossian's land. A gentleman at Inverary, supped with us who had from his youth much of Fingal by heart.'[70]

Highlanders were not immune to such Romantic notions. As they witnessed the loss of Gaelic language and culture so they formed learned societies to reclaim a Highland 'Golden Age.' The Gaelic Society of Inverness was formed in 1871 with the aim of 'perfecting of the Members in the use of the Gaelic language; the cultivation of the language and music of the Scottish Highlands; the rescuing from oblivion of Celtic poetry, traditions, legends, books and manuscripts' and generally the furtherance of the interests of Gaelic people everywhere.[71] Among the thirty-five gentlemen who attended the inaugural meeting were John Murdoch, later to establish the bilingual, campaigning *Highlander*, and Alexander Mackenzie who were among the first to voice the need for such a society.[72] They were 'not bound up with the wishy-washy Romanticism of the type which seeks to make material backwardness a virtue.'[73] Industrial, agricultural and material changes were to be welcomed if they benefited the people but those elements of culture which were at risk of being lost were to be preserved. Fed up with the slipshod Gaelic heard in the streets of Inverness, Murdoch wanted the language taught properly in schools, 'where it is commonly laid aside,' and text books produced with practical instruction in the latest farming techniques.[74] Gaelic was to be reinstated as the everyday language of the people. The society lobbied Parliament for these educational imperatives and for the establishment of a chair of

69 R. Blunt (ed.), *Mrs Montague 'Queen of the Blues,' Her Letters and Friendships from 1762 to 1800* (London, 1992), p. 146.

70 Ibid.

71 TGSI Vol. I, 1871, p. vi.

72 Ibid., pp. 2–3.

73 J. Hunter (ed.), *For the People's Cause: From the Writings of John Murdoch Highland and Irish Land Reformer* (Edinburgh, 1986), p. 28.

74 Ibid., TGSI Vol. I, p. 2 and an essay by A. Farquharson 'Highlanders at Home and Abroad,' TGSI Vol. III (1873), pp. 9–25. p. 9.

Celtic Literature at a Scottish University.[75] The society's concern was the preservation of cultural identity in the face of changes which had seen the glens and straths denuded of people. Crofters were to be given security of tenure so that they could not be thrown off the land at the whim of landowners and their agents.[76] Those who connived at this were seen as the enemies of the people.

Murdoch agitated for land reform through peaceful means. He addressed meetings across the Highlands and Islands, walking everywhere and relying on the hospitality of the people to sustain himself. In the spring of 1882 he visited the school in Braes, Skye, to speak to local crofters who had been withholding rents because they had been denied the use of hill pastures. A few days later they fought a pitched battle with police sent to arrest the ringleaders. The affray precipitated rent strikes and land seizures across the Highlands, necessitating the deployment of the military. The Government was forced to respond. The passing of the Crofters' Act of 1886 brought to an end widespread clearances, giving crofters security of tenure and other safeguards.[77]

Despite their pragmatic aims, the Gaelic Society was imbued with a Romantic conception of the past. The old clan system, though not without detractors among society members, was seen in a favourable light, being conceived as based on kinship and with land ownership vested in the people.[78] The society elected honorary chieftains, a bard, a piper and a librarian. In the early years of the society the numbers representing each clan were identified from the subscription list.[79] Murdoch travelled everywhere clad in a kilt, a mode of dress he had adopted to 're-establish a Highland identity' while members railed at those who were not Highlanders and had no word of Gaelic but who wore Highland dress.[80]

75 TGSI Vol. III (1873–4), p. 188 and Vol. IV, 1874–5, p. 56.

76 Hunter, *For the People's Cause,* p. 28.

77 Ibid., pp. 9–10.

78 J. Murdoch, 'The Clan System' TGSI Vol. I, pp. 31–43. p. 43.

79 TGSI Vol. III, p. 49.

80 Hunter, *For the People's Cause,* p. 30. Farquharson, 'Highlanders at Home and Abroad,' TGSI Vol. III, p. 9.

Since ordinary Highlanders did not universally wear the kilt the reformer became known as Murdoch of the Kilt. One schoolboy in Braes recalled that Murdoch was the first man he had ever seen in one.[81]

The members of the Gaelic Society of Inverness were patriotic. They saw the teaching of Gaelic and land reforms as necessary to retain their Highland identity but saw themselves as Highlanders within Great Britain and the Empire. The members were fully aware that many young people left the Highlands, they wanted to help them find friends wherever they may go. They listened to talks delivered in effusive and glowing terms on how well emigrants had succeeded in North America because of their Highland attributes of hard work, perseverance and diligence.[82] At the end of 1875 the annual membership stood at some 320. About half of these lived outwith Inverness and many of them were expatriates. The members included titled gentlemen, academics, professionals and artisans.[83] Murdoch was originally an exciseman; Mackenzie still an auctioneer. At their annual suppers, the room bedecked with clan tartans, they toasted the Queen in Gaelic, followed by toasts to Members of Parliament and other civic dignitaries. They toasted the armed forces in general and Highland regiments in particular, never without reference to their martial prowess and their accomplishments in the service of the crown.[84] The Gaelic Society of Inverness praised the Poems of Ossian, 'still cherished by thousands,' as exemplars of the richness of their literary past.[85] They also wanted to preserve the richness of their oral traditions. Alexander Mackenzie was part of a three man special committee formed to gather folklore in February 1875.[86] A month later he read his paper on the prophecies of the Brahan Seer.

The Brahan Seer legend, as distinct from the historical Coinneach Odhar, was largely the creation of an outside literary source, but the story

81 Hunter, *For the People's Cause*, p. 9.

82 TGSI Vol. III, pp. 1–7 and 26–45.

83 TGSI Vol. IV, pp. 40–41.

84 TGSI Vol. III, p. 46, 54–56, 140 and Vol. IV, p. 39.

85 TGSI Vol. I, p. xiii–xiv, Vol. III, pp. 8 and 127 and Vol. IV, pp. 97–110.

86 TGSI Vol. III, p. 187.

was adapted and carried forward because it was acceptable to Romantic perceptions of a people's own culture, partly because it was framed within the context of historical events which had taken place in the region, and partly because it was based on, and resonated with, their oral tradition. Importantly, the seer as victim of an evil aristocrat epitomised the grievances of the times against which the Gaelic Society protested. Charles Withers writes, 'For the Highlands, it is not a question of 'false perceptions' in opposition to a 'real' history for the region for the simple reason that many of the generally understood images of the Highlands were held to be 'real' by the people at the time.'[87] By appropriating Burke's romance into the realm of folklore Mackenzie and his colleagues made the seer real. The seer, identifiable in time and place and with an apparent success in prophesying the doom of the Seaforth family, attracted a mass of prophecies rooted in folk culture. These, in turn, added to his reputation and helped perpetuate the legend. By establishing the Brahan Seer as a successful prophet the legend reclaimed the reality of second sight from Romantic literature where it had become largely marginalised as a relic from a superstitious age.

Second sight in Romantic literature

The earliest Romantic literature treated second sight in a sympathetic light while later literature, separated by a greater gulf in time and space from the source of popular belief, marginalised it as a superstition held by unsophisticated Highlanders. It was used as a device to convey messages, often political, in the shape of warnings, hopes and aspirations, or portrayed as a counterpoint to more worthwhile virtues. When John Home, clergyman and later playwright, returned to Scotland from London some time during the winter of 1749, having been 'out' during the '45, he received a

87 Withers, 'The Historical Creation of The Scottish Highlands,' p. 155.

welcoming *Ode* from William Collins.[88] Influenced by Martin Martin's account, Collins romanticised the darker side of Highland superstitions, including second sight, to make them a source of fear. He wrote nothing of the 'jovial' aspects, such as predicting a wedding, mentioned by Martin. While Martin had described how many superstitions even in his day were already in decline Collins suggested ''Tis Fancy's land to which thou sett'st thy feet/ Where still, 'tis said, the fairy people meet ...,' as if such superstitions could still be found.[89] Home later assisted and encouraged James Macpherson to collect and publish his Ossianic fragments. The receipt of the *Ode* and discussions with Collins must have influenced him in this regard.[90] Macpherson himself thought that second sight emanated from the Druids but made no effort to romanticise it. He dismissed it as a 'ridiculous notion ... which prevailed in the highlands and isles.'[91]

Thomas Blacklock, a member of the Edinburgh *literati*, and blind since infancy, used second sight in his poem, *The Graham*, to demonstrate the advantages to both countries of Scotland being joined with England under the Treaty of Union of 1707. Although Blacklock wrote that he did not believe in second sight he 'takes the advantage of an opinion prevailing in an early and uncultivated age, to introduce his moral with greater importance and solemnity.'[92] The poem is set in the borders in the age of chivalry when Scottish and English knights, who are friends, clash over family honour. An English Knight, Howard, is distraught when his friend Elliot is struck down. How, he asks, could they not have been forewarned? He seeks a solution from a source which is conveyed as being

88 Wm. Collins, 'Ode to a Friend on His Return etc' but subsequently better known as 'An Ode on the Popular Superstitions of the Highlands of Scotland, Considered as the Subject of Poetry.' R. Lonsdale (ed.), *The Poems of Thomas Gray William Collins Oliver Goldsmith* (London, 1969), pp. 492–519. See also Womack, *Improvement and Romance*, pp. 87–94, where the poem is examined in detail.

89 Lonsdale, *The Poems*, pp. 503, ll,. 19–20 and 506. Womack, *Improvement and Romance*, p. 90.

90 Ibid., p. 500.

91 Macpherson, *The Poems of Ossian*, p. 433.

92 T. Blacklock, *The Graham: An Heroic Ballad in Four Cantos* (London, 1774), p. vi.

peculiar to Scottish culture and which, had it been utilised, could have prevented the tragedy. 'Oft of a seer the Scots have told/ Before whose Heav'n directed eyes/ Remote events of things, enroll'd/ By Destiny, successive rise/ Why could not he this stroke behold/ Which now to Heav'n for pity cries?/ But victims to the future blind/ We must pursue the course assign'd.'[93] Later, as the opposing armies are facing each other the soldiers reflect on the repercussions of the interminable wars between their two nations. When: 'From Scotia's bands a rever'd sage/ Half way between the troops advanc'd/ In all the dignity of age/ With ardent eyes, on both he glanc'd …'[94] The seer extols the virtues of the warring families and their respective countries. He predicts that by combining each others' virtues they will become great.

A friend of Blacklock's, James Beattie, whose scepticism has been noted, thought that second sight 'would make but an awkward figure' in history or philosophy, but 'may sometimes have a charming effect on poetry.'[95] He quotes a little known poem, *Albania*, to illustrate how he thought accounts of second sight may arise from a person's imagination. Set in the days of the Thanes of Ross when hunters with their hounds scoured the forests by day or night in search of deer, the wind would have carried the sounds of the hunt to distant glens, alarming those unsure of what they had heard. The Englishness of the language reveals its southern origins. 'Sudden, the grazing heifer in the vale/ Starts at the tumult, and the herdsman's ears/ Tingle with inward dread … To what, or whom, he owes his idle fear/ To ghost, or witch, to fairy, or to fiend/ But wonders; and no end of wondering finds.'[96]

In his pastoral comedy, *The Gentle Shepherd*, the poet, Allan Ramsay, writing in the vernacular, mocked palmistry as a form of fortune telling and showed that knowledge of a secret could be used to impart information about a person and future events. Despite his natural explanation for a pretence on which the story hangs he made a sympathetic reference to

93 Ibid., Canto II, verse XV, p. 24.

94 Ibid., Canto VI, verse V, p. 48.

95 J. Beattie, *Essays* (Edinburgh, 1776), p. 482

96 Ibid.

'thae second sighted fowk' who 'See things far aff, and things to come, as clear/ As I can see my thumb.'[97] Taking Ramsay's light-hearted lines as his inspiration, James Mylne, a poet of lesser note, penned some witty lines to a lady in England to whom, a year earlier, he had promised a letter. He claimed that what had prompted his writing was his having had a second sighted vision of 'Dear Kitty' castigating him before her aunt for his delay.[98] Mylne makes no serious claim to second sight; he is teasing and entertaining Kitty in the knowledge that she will know she is being teased. Mylne penned two tragedies in which a darker side to second sight is evident. In the first, *The British Kings,* set in a divided Arthurian Britain, a Druid seer, the last of his race, knows that Queen Emma of the Britons is not dead as commonly thought and when she is rescued all the minor kingdoms are united through marriage. The seer has the last word, predicting greatness for a united kingdom.[99] In the second Tragedy, *Darthula,* a 'Bard of The Second Sight' sees tragic events unfold in 'Temora's hall.'[100] The Bard warns against looking into the future: 'Invoke no ghosts to tell you this!/ Blindness, mortals, here is bliss!' He knows how painful knowledge of future events can be. Encouraged by the persistence of the Chorus to tell them what he knows he slowly and reluctantly reveals, through mounting tension and to universal grief, the slaughter of 'Erin's youthful nobles.'[101] The seers of Mylne's tragedies are influenced by, and based on, heroes from the poems of Macpherson's Ossian.

Sir Walter Scott took a keen interest in all aspects of superstition and the supernatural. He was always on the look out for anecdotes of local interest which he could weave into his poems and novels, often treating

97 A. M. Kinghorn & A. Law (eds), *Poems by Allan Ramsay and Robert Fergusson* (Edinburgh and London, 1974). *The Gentle Shepherd: A Pastoral Comedy,* pp. 42–104. p. 70.

98 J. Mylne, 'For a Lady In England, Who had Exacted the Author's Promise that He Would Write to Her a Witty Letter', in *Poems, Consisting of Miscellaneous Pieces, and Two Tragedies* (Edinburgh, 1790), pp. 19–20.

99 Ibid., p. 238.

100 Ibid., p. 283.

101 Ibid., pp. 283–286.

the use of witchcraft, charms, prophecy and second sight, as emanating from the same person. Like other writers before him, Scott attributed the popular belief in superstitions, including second sight, to a bygone age. He introduced generational and geographical distinctions to separate belief and non-belief in the supernatural, creating defining boundaries in space and time. Believers and practitioners are old and confined to the Highlands. In *The Lady of the Lake* the arrival of a stranger is predicted using second sight by 'Old' Allan-bane, a 'grey-haired sire' (grandfather). The young maid of the lake treats his prophecy lightly, providing a natural explanation of the fulfilment by suggesting that the seer had heard her father's distant horn announcing the stranger's arrival.[102] In his notes on the text Scott provided verbatim Martin's account of second sight from *A Description of the Western Islands* and concluded cheekily that 'in despite of evidence, which neither Bacon, Boyle, nor Johnson, were able to resist, the *Taisch,* with all its visionary properties, seems now to be universally abandoned to the use of poetry.'[103]

In many of Scott's tales he blended fact and fiction into a seamless web to revise the history of the Scottish nation. Scott contrasted the realities, often harsh, of the real world with the romanticism of the supernatural. Included in the novel *Redgauntlet* is a short story, '*Wandering Willie's Tale'* in which fact and fiction are used indiscriminately while the reader is reminded that the 'true' facts of the case may be quite something else. A vision plays an important role in the story.[104] Willie tells how his grandfather, Steenie Steenson, goes late at night to pay his rent to his landlord, Sir Robert Redgauntlet. The transaction is witnessed by a servant, Dougal, and Redgauntlet's pet monkey, Major Weir, dressed in a red lace

102 W. Scott, *The Lady of the Lake* (London, 1898 (1810)), p. 18.

103 Ibid., note V. pp. 187–189. Martin's account of second sight begins p. 300 in *A Description of the Western Islands of Scotland.* Johnson summarises second sight by stating 'that particular instances have been given, with such evidence, as neither *Bacon* nor *Boyle* has been able to resist.' *A Journey to the Western* Isles, p. 91. Scott is paraphrasing Johnson and including him in the list of notable believers.

104 W. Scott, *Redgauntlet* Waverley Novels No. 35 (Edinburgh, 1902 (1824)), pp. 161–193.

coat and wearing his master's wig.[105] While Steenie is downstairs having a drink Redgauntlet dies raging at the pain from his gout. Steenie, without his receipt, flees in fear at the commotion. Redgauntlet's heir, Sir John, refuses to accept that Steenie has paid the rent and when Dougal, following a night at the brandy, falls down dead after he sees what he thinks is the devil dancing on Redgauntlet's coffin, Steenie's only human witness can no longer testify on his behalf. Unable to borrow more money from existing creditors Steenie wearily stops at an inn, where, on an empty stomach, he drowns his sorrows in a mutchkin of brandy before riding off through the dark woods.

Steenie meets the devil in the guise of a mysterious stranger and accompanies him to hell. There, as a reward for playing the pipes for assembled notables from Scottish history, Redgauntlet hands Steenie the receipt and tells him where to find the rent already paid. Steenie wakes in a churchyard clutching the receipt with that day's date on it. He takes it to Sir John and they go together to a disused turret in the castle where they find the rent with other treasures hoarded there. Sir John burns the evidence of the posthumously dated receipt and gives Steenie another in his own hand. He urges Steenie to say nothing of his vision and suggests the monkey as an explanation for Dougal's seeing the devil and for stealing the money. That, however, according to Willie, was not the real story. Many years later 'my gudesire ... was obliged to tell the real narrative to his friends, for the credit of his good name. He might else have been charged for a warlock.'[106] By closing the tale on this note of ambiguity Scott leaves the reader to make her own interpretation of what was the

105 Major Thomas Weir had been burnt at the stake in 1670 for various crimes including adultery, incest and bestiality. Scott's application of his name to an animal responsible for the apparent supernatural troubles is inspired by some of the charges against Weir whom Scott thought the embodiment of evil. Weir was not charged with witchcraft. W. Scott *Letters on Demonology and Witchcraft* (London, 1830), p. 329 et seq. Weir and his sister Jean were tried on 9 April 1670. W. G. Scott-Moncrieff (ed.), *The Records of the Proceedings of the Judiciary Court of Edinburgh 1661–78*, 2 Vols. (Edinburgh, 1905), Vol. II, pp. 10–15.

106 Scott, *Redgauntlet*, p. 192.

true state of affairs. Further, by using Wandering Willie to report the tale of his grandfather Scott acknowledges that tales of superstitions, including second sight, are rarely first hand accounts. The revelation that his grandfather was 'bauld wi' brandy, and desperate wi' distress,' provide a natural substitute to account for his vision and his forgetfulness and to explain how the cash and receipt were recovered without supernatural agencies.[107]

Another short story of Scott's where superstitions and second sight play an integral role is that of *The Two Drovers,* based on hearing an account from an old friend who had been present at a murder trial in Carlisle.[108] The tale centres round the killing of an English friend by a Highlander, following a perceived slight to his honour after a dispute over grazing for their cattle. Central to the tale is that the event was foretold by a witch. When Robin Oig sets off with his herd on the drove road to England he does so with the good wishes of those he is leaving behind ringing in his ears. The last to speak is Robin's old aunt of whom he asks, 'What auld-world fancy has brought you so early from the ingle-side.'[109] She replies that she wants to perform the *deasil,* walking round him three times in the direction of the sun, as a blessing. In the course of her perambulation she exclaims that there is blood, English blood, on his hand and that he should not go. Robin signals to those around him that he has 'only complied with the old woman to soothe her humour' and that he was determined to be off. As a compromise he turns to a group of fellow drovers who had silently watched the performance. 'You Lowlanders care nothing for these freats [omens]' he says as he hands his dirk to one Morrison for safe keeping.[110]

The drovers set off south and near Carlisle Robin Oig arranges with a farmer to graze on his land unaware that an English friend, Wakefield,

107 Ibid., p. 182.

108 Scott's source was the late George Constable of Wallace-Craigie, near Dundee; identified in an introduction by Scott, *Highland Widow* Waverley Novels No. 41 (Edinburgh, 1903 (1834)), p. xxxvi.

109 W. Scott, *The Two Drovers* (New Jersey, 1971 (1827)), p. 5.

110 Ibid., p. 7.

has already contracted with the farmer's manager to graze on the same ground. Oig, arriving first, refuses to give up the grazing and in the inn that night a dispute arises during which he is taunted by English farmers after he refuses to fight Wakefield using nothing but his fists. He walks through the night to where the Lowland farmer has his herd and demands his dirk. Morrison suspects that Robin wants the dirk for some dark purpose and refuses to give it up until he is lied to by Oig who returns to the inn and stabs his friend before giving himself up to a bailiff. Robin had tried to ignore a warning because he thought it showed a belief in practices he was trying to put behind him. Paradoxically he killed his friend and surrendered himself to the gallows because of his continued belief in a code of conduct considered by Lowlanders and English to be outmoded.

This fascination with the past and the unwelcome changes wrought are evident in Scott's tale of the *Highland Widow*. Elspeth MacTavish, soured by the death of her husband in the Jacobite cause and by the subsequent encroachment of Saxon ways, fondly recalls when her husband's strength and status in the community had ensured she drew the respect her station demanded. When she considers the present she sees herself scratching a daily existence caring for her young son, Hamish, who would one day grow up and revenge his father. When he is old enough to look after his mother Hamish tries to deal with the realities of their situation by enlisting in the army. His mother is distraught and tells him that the army flogs deserters, a sentence she knows his proud Highland nature would not accept. On the eve of his departure she gives him a potion which makes him sleep through the next day and when he finds out he has been duped he hides to avoid the punishment his mother insists will be meted out. His best friend arrives with a party of soldiers to arrest him but rather than submit Hamish kills his friend before being overcome. Captain Campbell, who knows the Highland ways, tries to intercede on Hamish's behalf but the general, 'half a Lowlander, half an Englishman,' dismisses any notions of Highland chivalry with the words 'these are Highland visions, Captain Campbell, as unsatisfactory and vain as those of the second sight.'[111] Similar culture clashes where belief in second sight is prevalent among Highlanders of an older generation but given less credence among the young and dismissed by those from other parts of the country can be found in other of Scott's works.[112] In all these tales, notwithstanding the supernatural being central to the narrative, a plausible alternative explanation of unfolding events has been provided which does not depend on any supernatural agency.

In the stage play, *The Frozen Deep,* a collaboration between Wilkie Collins and Charles Dickens, the faculty of second sight plays a pivotal role at the beginning of the story but is marginalised at the climax. It is treated as a superstition not to be believed in, in contrast with a belief in the unfailing virtues of a brave Englishman who would rather give up his own life fighting the elements than succumb to acts unbecoming his noble spirit.[113] The play was a fictional account of explorers lost in the Arctic and was influenced by events surrounding Sir John Franklin's expedition which had become lost while trying to find a route through the Northwest Passage. No news had been heard of the expedition for two years and anxious families and friends waited at home in suspense. Several clairvoyants claimed to be in touch with the members of the expedition and one had claimed that the survivors had resorted to cannibalism

111 W. Scott, *Highland Widow*, p. 199.

112 See W. Scott, *The Black Dwarf* (London, 1993 (1816)), pp. 26 and 69–70 for a conversation between a grandmother and grandson when the latter says that witches and wizards do not have the power they once had. Despite this, it is the grandson who is prepared to consult a witch about the future; his grandmother says they should still be burned as the bible dictates. See also *The Bride of Lammermoor* (Edinburgh, 1995 (1819)) for a description of a triad of old witches based on those in Shakespeare's *Macbeth* and the dismissal of their second sight by the well spoken man who is doomed to die as predicted. pp. 192–193 and p. 261. Lady Ashton's use of prophecy by a witch to frighten her daughter into compliance, p. 238 et seq. See C. O. Parsons, *Witchcraft and Demonology in Scott's Fiction* (Edinburgh, 1964) and see Scott, *Demonology*.

113 R. L. Brannan, *Under the Mangement of Mr Charles Dickens: His Production of 'The Frozen Deep'* (Ithaca, 1966) The Dickens/Collins production was first presented on 6 January 1857 (coincidentally with another by the same authors called *Animal Magnetism*.)

in order to stay alive.[114] This suggestion so affronted the dignity of the Victorian Englishman that it was condemned in every drawing room in the country. The play is influenced by Scott's use of second sight in that geographical and generational distances are placed between those who believe in its efficacy and those who do not. Natural and plausible alternative explanations are evident to account for how information is obtained and how the prophecy is fulfilled. A plausible explanation is even provided to account for the failure of second sight. The old nurse who makes predictions is only Highland by descent and birth; she is 'Lowland by usage and education.' Her young charges are Southern ladies who do not believe in 'her barbarous nonsense about the Second Sight.'[115] When the nurse makes a prediction about the fate of her young mistress's fiancé she does so after appearing to eavesdrop on a conversation in which the secret engagement is revealed.

Conclusion

The assertion by Peter Womack that the Highlands as a whole had been 'literarised' would certainly seem apposite in the case of second sight. The phenomenon had been marginalised to other times and places, its believers treated as naive. However, this appeared only to be true for writers and their audiences for whom the Highlands were indeed an imaginary place. Those collectors who were trying to save aspects of a disappearing culture were not averse to incorporating Romantic literature into their own accounts of the past, after modifying them in the light of local knowledge. Alexander Mackenzie and his colleagues in the Gaelic Society

114 Brannan, *Under the Management*, p. 12. See the Bolton Clairvoyant in Wm. Gregory, *Letters to a Candid Enquirer on Animal Magnetism* (London, 1851), pp. 410–414. A. Winter, *Mesmerised: Powers of Mind in Victorian Britain* (London, 1998), pp. 122–124.

115 Brannan, *Under the Management*, p. 104.

of Inverness gave real and valued identity to the Brahan Seer. People across different strata of society believed he had existed, that he had had the power of second sight and had used it successfully. Committing the romanticised folklore to print fixed the seer's identity in time and place and created the definitive version of events. It was to literature, rather than oral tradition, that people turned to obtain an understanding of the events surrounding the acquisition and consequences of the seer's prophetic abilities. The literary seer provided a focal point for the proliferation of popular prophecies which existed at the time of Mackenzie's collection. These prophecies, by appearing to be fulfilled, enhanced the seer's reputation and helped perpetuate the legend.

Alexander Mackenzie and those who furnished him with prophecies of the Brahan Seer helped maintain an interest in second sight, a faculty which still had a place in their real, rather than imaginary, world. Despite Mackenzie's public, but hardly emphatic, disavowal of personal belief in second sight the appearance of the legend of the Brahan Seer in the literature provided a real and successful exponent of the faculty as conceived in the context of the time. Changing conceptions of scientific orthodoxy were to make later studies of second sight less subject to ridicule and further enhance his reputation. Popular culture has continued to appropriate the Seer by adding to the mass of prophecies attributed to him. Such prophecies are created by people to comment upon the changing circumstances of their time. Their successful fulfilment contributes to the reputation of the Seer whose fame extends beyond the Highlands, as do the events he is said to pronounce upon. The contemporary conception of second sight and the creation and use of popular prophecies continue to be determined according to a people's world view.

CHAPTER 7

The Power of Prophecy

Introduction

The preceding chapter showed how the legend of the Brahan Seer familiar to contemporary culture was created in the nineteenth century through a combination of historical events, oral tradition and Romantic literature. The legend is now on the primary school curriculum throughout Easter Ross, and is taught as part of a class four project.[1] Such is the power of the legend that people believe 'this wonderful man' existed.[2] Two families with Mackenzie antecedents – one family of medical practitioners, the other of former Seaforth estate workers – are known to have recently instituted genealogical studies supposing themselves to be descendants of the Brahan Seer.[3]

Belief in legend and prophecy is never better demonstrated than in the Brahan Seer Festival which took place in Easter Ross and the Black Isle during the period 5 – 15 September 2001. The festival organisers had several aims. Among them was to celebrate the legend of the Brahan Seer in a variety of artistic ways, embracing the traditional and the contemporary, so that the broadest possible spectrum of the community could become involved as either direct participants or as interested spectators.[4] Traditional art was not confined to that of the immediate locality: a troupe

1 Personal communication.

2 The Seer was described thus by the Master of Ceremonies at the Brahan Seer Festival Ceilidh, Dingwall Town Hall, 7 September 2001.

3 Personal communication.

4 www.brahanseer.co.uk/news/pages/8.htm. Brahan Seer News Update 2 August 2001.

of four belly dancers of indeterminate age performed to enthusiastic applause during the festival's ceilidh.[5] Events included an animated film, *Coinneach Odhar Fiosaiche–The Brahan Seer*, made for and by children with adult supervision, and a ceilidh for which two songs in Gaelic were specially commissioned. There was a museum presentation, a children's prophecy parade, an art exhibition, plays, a storytelling walk and a torchlit procession and firework display which re-enacted the Brahan Seer's burning as a witch. An opera, *The Seer*, composed in English by the late John Bevan Baker, and an academic seminar on second sight were also included.[6] Venues included the school hall in Conon Bridge, the gardens and Pump Room at Strathpeffer Spa, the Town Hall and Tulloch Castle Hotel, Dingwall, and the village hall and beach at Fortrose. Around three hundred and sixty people of all ages took part in the events which attracted an aggregate audience of 2360.[7] In addition to these artistic endeavours a celebratory colour booklet was produced which provided information on the Seer's life, on second sight, and on some of the numerous prophecies attributed to him.[8] Four standing stones were later erected in the area, each inscribed with a prophecy in English and in Gaelic. The legacy of the commissioned works and the standing stones was another aim of the organisers of this one-off event. One of the inspirations behind the project has been the perceived resurgence of confidence in Highland culture, both contemporary and traditional. A third aim of the festival organisers was to fulfil a prophecy of the Brahan Seer regarding the economic regeneration of the Highlands. This chapter focuses on two aspects of the festival in order to demonstrate a continued intellectual interest in second sight and a popular interest in prophecy, its function, content and power.

An academic seminar on second sight was held as part of the festival celebrations at Tulloch Castle Hotel, Dingwall on 15 September 2001. The seminar is a reminder that although second sight had been

5 Brahan Seer Festival (BSF) 7 September 2001.

6 BSF events programmes.

7 Statistics from privately circulated BSF Report.

8 *The Brahan Seer Celebratory Booklet* (Dingwall, 2001)

apparently marginalised in Romantic fiction and subsumed under the general headings of animal magnetism or clairvoyance, there have been periodic renewals of interest at an intellectual level, as belief in second sight has persisted among sections of the learned community. For example, the Society for Psychical Research, founded in 1882, aimed to tackle a range of questions centring on paranormal phenomena which orthodox science, relying on empirical knowledge obtained from the five recognised senses, was failing to address. The society's remit was, and still is, 'to examine without prejudice ... and in a scientific spirit those faculties of man, real or supposed, which appear to be inexplicable on any generally recognised hypothesis.'[9] This approach, influenced by Romanticism, gave rise to an emphasis on subjective rather than objective responses which rely on observable 'matters of fact.' Among the papers presented at the festival seminar was one by Shari Cohn entitled *The Theory and History of Inherited Second Sight*.[10] Cohn is in the tradition of those nineteenth century researchers and her studies have suggested that second sight may be hereditary.[11] Such a hypothesis can only be made if there is a presupposition that second sight exists and Cohn's rationale for undertaking her study was her observation that psychic experiences symptomatic of 'true' communication ran in her own family.[12] An examination of the experiences of the seminar participants shows that they think of second sight as a generic term encompassing a range of psychic abilities.

A second feature of the festival is evidence of persistent belief in the veracity of the Brahan Seer's prophecies and this chapter examines contemporary belief in these within a historical and geographical context.

9 *Journal of the Society for Psychical Research* (JSPR) Vol. 63 No. 855 (1999), p. 128. The society's aims are stated in each issue of the journal.

10 Programme for The Seer Festival Seminar on Second Sight, 15 September 2001.

11 S. A. Cohn, 'A Survey on Scottish Second Sight,' JSPR Vol. 59 No. 853 (1994), pp. 385–400. S. A. Cohn, 'A Questionnaire Study on Second Sight Experiences,' JSPR Vol. 63 No. 855 (1999), pp. 129–157. S. A. Cohn 'Second Sight and Family History: Pedigree and Segregation Analyses,' *Journal of Scientific Exploration* Vol. 13 No. 3 (1999), pp. 351–372.

12 Cohn, 'A Survey on Scottish Second Sight,' p. 385.

John MacInnes writes that the perception of a seer's role in Gaelic tradition has changed over time. Whereas it is now thought that an event predicted by a seer will prove to be unavoidable, this was not always the case. Formerly, a seer 'had a duty to warn of approaching danger; evasive action was possible; fate was not fixed ...'[13] MacInnes suggests that this fatalism has been imbued into Gaelic culture after centuries of 'ethnocide.' However, as Keith Thomas argues, and this chapter will show, popular prophecies are created to record unfolding events and succeeding generations create their own prophecies or appropriate existing ones, redefining, reinventing and modifying them to make them relevant within a world-view proscribed by their contemporary knowledge and values.[14] The world-view in contemporary Easter Ross is one of optimism: the fatalism described by MacInnes is absent. The cultural shaping of prophecies is contingent on lived experience and where lived experiences are similar the prophecies describing them are similar, however different the cultures. Prophecies often have strong judgmental connotations closely linked to religious beliefs. When the prophecies of the Brahan Seer are compared with popular prophecies from Ireland – which has a similar cultural background to the Highlands and went through similar changes on its route to modernity – their content is seen to be identical. Popular prophecies from German literature show similarities to those of the Brahan Seer. A comparison of the prophecies of the Brahan Seer with prophecies from Native American Indians shows them describing shared experiences in the same way.

13 J. MacInnes, 'The Seer in Gaelic Tradition' in H. E. Davidson (ed.), *The Seer* (Edinburgh, 1989), pp. 1–23. p. 23.

14 K. Thomas, *Religion and the Decline of Magic* (London, 1973), p. 469.

Second sight enquiries in their historical context

Although during the eighteenth century second sight appeared to lose much of its attraction for educated elites, other than as a private pursuit, interest was renewed towards the end of the nineteenth century when it was examined within the orbit of psychical and spiritual studies. Moses William Stainton, of the London Spiritual Alliance, was convinced of the authenticity of second sight accounts, believing them to be evidence of the inherent power of the human spirit. He personally looked into a handful of instances, but in the main cites examples from Theophilus Insulanus's work of the previous century, 'a most obviously sincere book whose naïve quaintness is very enticing.'[15] The high proportion of cases featuring some aspect of death led him to surmise that the appearance of apparitions was proof of the spirit being liberated during the final crisis in a person's life.[16] Unfortunately, respondents were so 'morbidly adverse' to speaking about their death-linked experiences that Stainton found it difficult to obtain authentic cases.[17]

Reticence on the part of seers was a common feature of late nineteenth century enquiries into second sight. All enquirers provided their own reasons to explain why this should be so. A folklorist, Miss Dempster, gathered instances from Sutherland-shire in the summer of 1859 but they are few in number and refer in the main to events 'long ago.'[18] Her account was not published until 1888. 'It was difficult ... to make such a collection, it would be impossible now' she wrote, the passage of time seeing 'unwritten literature' being supplanted by 'readings,' the whole process accelerated

15 M. W. Stainton writing as 'M. A. (Oxon.),' *Second Sight: Problems Connected with Prophetic Vision, and Records Illustrative of the Gift, Especially Derived From an Old Work Not Now Available for General Use* (London, 1889).

16 Ibid., p. 33.

17 Ibid., p. 35.

18 Miss Dempster, 'Folk-Lore of Sutherlandshire' in *The Folk-Lore Journal*, Vol. 6 (1888), pp. 149–189 and 215–252.

by 'bigoted religious ideas and by modern progress in all its shapes.'[19] It was only those ordinary people with a 'genuine Highland mind' who preserved the 'language, associations, and the primitive life of the people,' the others being 'out of touch with their betters, and given over to social and polemical hatreds.'[20] The preservation of an idealised mode of life cannot be sustained contrary to lived experience. By its very nature culture is part of changing circumstances: there had been protests against evictions in Sutherland-shire within the living memory of Dempster's respondents.[21] The predominant feature in Dempster's second sight accounts is either a vision of a funeral procession or some other warning of impending death, such as seeing a body in a shroud or a wraith-like figure. Visions of people known to the seer could partly explain their reluctance to voice their foreknowledge but Dempster wrote that visions of funeral processions were so common that warnings often went unheeded; only in exceptional circumstances were they remarked upon.[22]

However reticent respondents might have been in divulging their experiences – and whatever the cause – accounts continued to emanate from the Highlands. Perhaps the most famous enquiry into second sight was carried out in the closing decade of the nineteenth century by the Society for Psychical Research (SPR). Funded by the Marquis of Bute, a wealthy member of the Society since 1889, the enquiry, begun in late 1892, was to end in failure and controversy. Under the supervision of the Gaelic speaking Rev. Peter Dewar of Rothesay, who was the enquiry's secretary, nearly two thousand questionnaires were sent throughout the Highlands asking if second sight was believed in and if the recipient knew personally of any cases or knew somebody who might be willing to help with the enquiry. It is noteworthy regarding the enquirers' own perception of second sight as being an anachronism that the first of the four questions initially read 'Is "Second Sight" *still* believed in by the people of

19 Dempster, 'Folk-Lore,' p. 149.

20 Ibid.

21 C. W. J. Withers, *Gaelic Scotland: The Transformation of a Cultural Region* (London and New York, 1988), pp. 359–360.

22 Dempster, 'Folk-Lore,' p. 238.

your neighbourhood?' (emphasis added).[23] The word 'still' was removed from the final draft at the insistence of Lord Bute.[24]

The questionnaires were sent to professional people in each area: the clergy, doctors, police, law officers, schoolteachers and to some of the landed proprietors. Some of these men (for they would have been men) were charged with stamping out what they perceived to be superstitious beliefs and were not favourably inclined to investigate cases of second sight. Although this attitude was not universal such professional men mediated between the enquirers and the people the enquiry was addressing. The circular elicited fifty-four responses of which twenty-six affirmed that belief in second sight existed in their neighbourhood. None of these provided 'any well-attested first-hand case.'[25] Despite this, a school inspector informed Rev. Dewar that 'belief in second sight is universally current in Sutherlandshire' and although he promised to gather information there is no evidence that it was ever forthcoming.[26] Disappointed with the response, a second round of questionnaires was issued, addressed in part to newspaper editors and accompanied by a personal letter from the Marquis. This resulted in 157 responses including 'forty-two replies which are more or less affirmative.'[27]

Realising that corresponding by letter was an unsatisfactory way of conducting research, the SPR decided to send someone to carry out the work in person. Rev. Dewar, who had already expended a great deal of effort on the enquiry, seemed best suited to the task but the SPR sent a close friend of the Society's leaders, Miss Ada Goodrich-Freer who thought that the force of her personality would achieve more success. In a paper read before the Gaelic Society of Inverness on 30 April 1896, she made no effort to disguise the fact that so far the enquiry had been a failure. She blamed this on the Highlanders' reluctance to discuss

23 J. L. Campbell and T. H. Hall, *Strange Things* (London, 1968), p. 29.

24 Ibid., p 30.

25 Ibid., Rev. Dewar's letter of 17 March 1893, to the Marquis of Bute, giving him a progress report, p. 30.

26 Ibid., p. 31.

27 Ibid., Dewar's letter of 25 April 1894, to Marquis of Bute, p. 34.

traditional matters with strangers on the one hand, and on the other suggested that, due to their oral tradition, they were unaccustomed to writing such accounts and would be more comfortable talking about them. Schoolteachers also inhibited the continuance of tradition, she alleged, as did Protestant ministers, who did not have the same ideological connection to antiquity as their Catholic or Episcopalian counterparts. Miss Goodrich-Freer – who probably had members of these maligned professions in her audience – appealed to them for accounts of second sight.[28] Her lecture received scathing reviews in the local press not least because she included an account of a séance she had attended and used a diagram, no longer extant, to show 'the space-time co-ordinates of second sight.'[29]

Known as Miss X at the start of the enquiry, it was only later that Goodrich-Freer revealed her name. Although born in Uppington, in the English Midlands, she tried to exploit an unfounded claim to Highland ancestry. She claimed falsely to be a clairvoyant and demonstrated an ability to take credit for material collected and translated by others, most notably Father Allan McDonald of the Isle of Eriskay.[30] He had provided her with notebooks in which he had recorded instances of second sight and other folklore. Goodrich-Freer used this material as if it were her own. Notwithstanding her explanations for the failure of the enquiry it seems the real reason was more colourful. Goodrich-Freer's principal interest was in ghosts and according to J. L. Campbell she is still referred to in South Uist and Eriskay as *Cailleach bheag nam Bòcan* – 'little old woman of the ghosts.'[31] She took part in an SPR investigation into Ballechin House in Perthshire, reputed to be the most haunted house in Scotland. Even before Goodrich-Freer had published her findings she was castigated in

28 A. Goodrich-Freer, 'Second Sight in the Highlands' in TGSI Vol. 21, 1896, pp. 105–115. p. 105.

29 Ibid., p. 110. Campbell and Hall, *Strange Things*, p. 83.

30 Campbell and Hall, *Strange Things*, p. 103. The exposure of Goodrich-Freer's indebtedness to Fr McDonald is one of the main purposes of their book. McDonald's note book on second sight was called 'Strange Things.'

31 Campbell and Hall, *Strange Things*, p. 63.

the national press over her claims and methodology. The SPR, to retain its credibility, rejected her findings.[32] She left the Society: the second sight enquiry was discontinued and its records destroyed.

Although a failure, the SPR enquiry did confirm the existence of a continued belief in second sight in parts of the Highlands even if authenticated cases were hard to obtain. Father Allan McDonald's Hebridean material conformed to the stereotypical examples identified elsewhere in the Highlands, being related to trivial events such as the appearance of a train engine where there was no railway, foretelling the arrival of visitors and foretelling deaths.[33] While Father McDonald collected accounts of second sight he did not appear to believe in the phenomenon. Even though an uncorroborated account credits him with developing the faculty late in life he was unforthcoming when it came to divulging his own experiences.[34]

No such reticence was shown by another Highland minister, Rev. Dugald MacEchern, who wrote about his own second sight experiences in response to the horrors of the First World War. He resurrected once again the question of whether the spirit could survive independently of the body.[35] MacEchern had no doubt that it could. He was a devout Christian who had grown up in a family where second sight experiences were part of the fabric of everyday life. His mother and grandmother – 'a simple, God-fearing, practical minded farmer's wife' – were both endowed with the faculty.[36] MacEchern was keen to find an explanation for second sight and examined various possibilities such as the appearance of the human aura and telepathic powers. He provided several accounts which conformed to the stereotypical, including those where coincidence would seem to offer a natural and plausible explanation. Each possibility fell short of explaining the prophetic component of second sight and MacEchern concluded that the only satisfactory explanation was 'communication

32 Ibid., pp. 166–196.

33 Ibid., see p. 326 for the motif-index of the stories.

34 Ibid., pp. 302–309.

35 D. MacEchern, 'Highland Second Sight' TGSI Vol. 29, 1919, pp. 290–314.

36 Wm. Morrison and N. Macrae, *Highland Second Sight* (Dingwall, 1908), p. 103.

with the unseen spirit world.'[37] Himself a theist, he believed such spirits came from God but he was sufficiently influenced by the occultists, theosophists and pantheists who flourished at the time to proffer, without criticism, their alternative explanation of a united universe consisting of the visible and the invisible.

Belief in second sight persisted through the twentieth century. The late Wendy Wood collected about thirty accounts in the 1920s. These conformed to the stereotypical accounts of approaching visitors, death shrouds and funeral processions.[38] Wood tried to obtain confirmation for the prophecy before the event. She had prophetic visions of her own and details one incident in her autobiography where she had written to people describing a man's death before it took place.[39] The intended book on second sight was never completed. More recently, staff and students from the School of Scottish Studies have collected 'hundreds of examples' of second sight accounts from the 1950s, many relating to experiences of the traditional type, such as the vision of a funeral or impending death. Many of these accounts are in Gaelic and are collected from the Hebrides, the mainland and from Orkney.[40] The accounts are often set in the past and have taken on the patina of folklore. They include 'an old story o[f] the olden days' of how a seer acquired his gift from a mysterious woman who left her mark on him by pinching his nose and another of how a seer, 'my father's grand-uncle ... when he was young' lost his unwanted powers when an old woman recited a spell over a piece of copper he gave her.[41]

As recently as the 1990s, nearly three hundred years after the phenomenon had been derided by sceptics, Shari Cohn conducted a series of phenomenological experiments on second sight. A sixty-five-point questionnaire was sent to people chosen at random from different

37 MacEchern, 'Highland Second Sight,' p. 313.

38 W. Wood, NLS, Acc. 8197, Files 10–14.

39 W. Wood, *Yours Sincerely for Scotland: The Autobiography of a Patriot* (London, 1970), pp. 170–171. Also cited in Cohn, 'A Historical Review of Second Sight', *Scottish Studies* Vol. 33 (1999), pp. 146–185.

40 Anon., 'Second Sight' in *Tocher* No 6, 1972, pp. 192–200.

41 Ibid., pp. 198–200.

regions of Scotland and throughout the world. Two hundred and eight questionnaires were completed and returned. Cohn concluded that 'second sight is experienced by people of diverse ages, occupations and religious and cultural traditions.'[42] Her findings suggest that women are apt to report more second sight experiences than men and a pronounced religious experience featured prominently in many responses. She also found that people who had religious sensitivity were twice as likely to report second sight experiences as those who had not.[43] Cohn noted that stereotypical experiences such as funeral processions were reported in seven out of ten cases obtained from the Highlands but elsewhere there was a diminution in the reporting of such instances.[44] In a follow-up experiment Cohn examined one hundred and thirty families and concluded that second sight could, in part, be hereditary although the data was such that a social and cultural explanation, orally transmitted, could not be ruled out. This was particularly true of the Highlands where Cohn found 'an acceptance of the existence of second sight within the community at large' and 'where the interpretation of experiences as being "psychic" is orally passed down in families from one generation to another.'[45] There was a higher reporting of second sight experiences from the Grampian Region, 33%, compared with the Western Isles, 10%, and the Highlands, 16%.[46] By examining four letters from Grampian which actually described experiences, Cohn concluded that people from that region were reporting experiences from a wider psychic range than second sight.[47]

This is borne out by the writer's own experience while attending the seminar on second sight, held at Tulloch Castle Hotel, Dingwall, on 15 September 2001, during the Brahan Seer Festival. Following the presentation of papers, an open discussion of second sight experiences

42 Cohn, 'A Questionnaire Study on Second Sight Experiences' JSP Vol. 63, No. 855, p. 129–157.

43 Ibid., p. 146.

44 Cohn, 'A Survey on Scottish Second Sight' JSPR Vol. 59, No. 836, p. 398.

45 Cohn, 'Second Sight and Family History: Pedigree,' pp. 354 and 368.

46 Cohn, 'A Survey on Scottish Second Sight,' p. 392.

47 Cohn, 'A Questionnaire Study on Second Sight Experiences,' p. 129.

was held among the twenty-four female and seven male participants (coincidentally the same numbers as appeared on the first warrant for the arrest of witches during the Fowlis affair).[48] Participants were principally Scottish, but some came from other parts of the United Kingdom, America, South Africa and Germany. It was evident from the descriptions of those who chose to share them that different psychic experiences were being treated as second sight. Early examples of experience followed the traditional path but began imperceptibly to include conversations with visible and animate relatives who had died. Many of the circle had tales of unexplained changes of travel plans which were later shown to have coincided with a road accident which they thought they would have been involved in but for their change of mind. One participant spoke of hearing footsteps in the upstairs part of her house which she thought was her husband returning from outdoors. She discovered that he was still away. One participant spoke of a building in Edinburgh being haunted and of her hearing the sound of a person moving around when nobody else was there. She told of a man visiting a castle open to the public who took a turning in a corridor and found himself in a room with people dressed as if from a different era. On rejoining the party he remarked to the tour guide how authentic the actors looked in the next room. The guide pointed out that the room he had just visited was walled up and inaccessible.[49]

Influenced by her participation in shared accounts, Lesley-Anne Thomas, a psychology graduate was moved to write a fifty-page manuscript in which she describes the different experiences she categorises as second sight.[50] An 'intuitive knowing – a deep internal or "gut feeling"'

48 Privately circulated BSF Report, np. Academic Seminar on Second Sight, Tulloch Castle Hotel, Dingwall, BSF, 15 September 2001. NAS Ref: E1/7 fol. 67(v)-69(r) and ERS Vol. XX, pp. 522–523.

49 Academic Seminar on Second Sight, Tulloch Castle Hotel, Dingwall, BSF, 15 September 2001. Among the contributors were Dr Shari Cohn, Dr Margaret Bennett and Elizabeth Sutherland.

50 L.-A. Thomas, unpublished and untitled Ms. on personal second sight experiences, np.

– is an awareness that something is going to happen. She contrasts this with 'instant knowledge – a flash of knowing which is more cerebral.' Thomas describes this as 'claircognance' to differentiate it from 'clairvoyance' which occurs in a dream-like state. Her first experience of an intuitive knowing occurred at the age of eight when she 'knew' that her half-brother was going to arrive home unexpectedly from the army in Germany having been given leave at short notice. The feeling lasted throughout the day until his arrival in the small hours. Her first experience of instant knowledge occurred in 1978 when she came home from work one day and had a sudden urge to change the television channel despite protests from her parents. Her half-brother, by now a lorry driver, was working in Iran and the tensions leading up to the Iranian Revolution made those at home fearful for his safety. He appeared, dishevelled, on the screen being interviewed on the Iran-Turkish border on his way out of the country. She describes her grandfather making visits to her grandmother and being seen by her granny sitting in his favourite chair long after he had died. Thomas recounts foreseeing two major tragedies which resulted in loss of life as well as knowing the exact time of her grandmother's death. She describes her mother's own intuitive abilities and raises the question of second sight being hereditary, all the experiences being from the maternal side of her family. Her narrative shows that the three generations of women were religiously sensitive. Thomas's mother visited her several times in the years following her death often when she needed her mother's advice and protection.[51]

The extension of second sight to accommodate experiences which are not constrained by the traditional stereotypes is exemplified by the definition used by Elizabeth Sutherland in the booklet to accompany the festival. 'In modern terminology second sight consists of three facets of the psychic crystal – pre-and retrocognition – the ability to look forwards and backwards in time. Clairvoyance – the power to see through space. Telepathy – the skill to read other minds. More simply ... the ability

51 Ibid.

to see ghosts and from that sighting make a prediction.'[52] Second sight was formerly seen as a subset of clairvoyance; the roles now seem to be reversed. Although second sight may have become 'de-particularised' in the nineteenth century as a consequence of Romantic literature, as argued by A. J. L. Busst, its elevation to a position of pre-eminence in the psychic field is an indication of its popular appeal to an audience beyond the cultural region where it was first recognised.[53] Part of that pre-eminence is attributable to a belief in psychic abilities and prophecy across all sections of society. Scientific experiments continue to be carried out with a view to establishing the existence of, and classifying, different psychic phenomena and providing explanations for how they arise. Belief in prophecies has persisted across all sectors of Highland society and the Brahan Seer Festival shows how they continue to be used to 'predict' and to pass comment on unfolding events.

Contemporary use of the Brahan Seer's prophecies

The earliest prophecies attributed to the Brahan Seer recount noteworthy occurrences such as battles, the more recent recount the many changes which have taken place, and continue to take place, in the Highlands. Prophecies are shaped by their culture in terms of content and in the way in which they are interpreted, and reinterpreted, in light of later events to which they are attached. They are based on the interpreter's world-view and an existing prophecy can be applied to changing circumstances, as that world-view changes. An example of this occurred in the public domain during the Brahan Seer Festival. A Gaelic singer, Mary Ann Kennedy, had been commissioned to write a song especially for the festival's ceilidh. The

52 E. Sutherland, 'Second Sight and Some Seers' in '*The Brahan Seer Celebratory Booklet* (Dingwall, 2001), np.

53 A. J. L. Busst, 'Scottish Second Sight: The Rise and fall of a European Myth' in *European Romantic Review* Vol. 5, part 2 (1995), pp. 149–177. p. 177.

song was about the seer's predictions and was developed round the Gaelic phrase for 'come the day' with which he allegedly began his prophecies. When Kennedy introduced her song she mentioned a prophecy by the seer in which he predicted that 'Policemen will become so numerous in every town that they may be met with at the corner of every street.'[54] Interpreting the prophecy both literally and figuratively, she pointed out that this had not yet happened but was now coming to pass with the introduction of closed-circuit television in many town centres.[55] This example of an existing prophecy being reinvented to suit changing circumstances is necessarily couched in pre-technological language to authenticate its utterance prior to the arrival of the innovation.

Two prophecies in particular were seized upon by the organisers of the Brahan Seer Festival to reflect the current mood of optimism created by the regeneration of the Highlands and while an examination of any number of the prophecies attributed to the seer shows them to be the recording of historical events as, or after, they happened, only these two will be examined here. Among the prophecies collected by Alexander Mackenzie are numerous fragments commenting on the theme of emigration before and during the Highland clearances. They include the following, 'the people will emigrate to Islands now unknown, but which shall yet be discovered in the boundless oceans after which the deer and the other wild animals in the huge wilderness shall be exterminated and browned by horrid black rains (*siantan dubha*). The people will then return and take undisturbed possession of the lands of their ancestors.'[56] A shorter version runs as follows, 'sheep shall eat men, men will eat sheep, the black rain will eat all things; in the end old men shall return from new lands.'[57] This prophecy is considered to be as yet unfulfilled, and is still feared in the Highlands, according to Elizabeth Sutherland.[58] One informant advised the writer that when oil was discovered in the North

54 A. Mackenzie, *Prophecies of the Brahan Seer* (London, 1977), p. 64.

55 BSF ceilidh in Dingwall Town Hall, Friday, 7 September 2001.

56 Mackenzie, *Prophecies*, p 49.

57 Ibid.

58 Ibid., Commentary by Elizabeth Sutherland, p. 50.

Sea during the 1960s, people in her native Ross-shire recalled the prophecy and thought an oil-related disaster was inevitable. She also confirmed there are those who think the reference to black rain is evidence that the Brahan Seer predicted the discovery of oil in the first place.[59]

Modern interpretations of the black rain prophecies show how they have been used to keep pace with current anxieties, having changed from fears of nuclear fall-out during the Cold War era to fears of acid rain as concerns focused upon environmental issues.[60] However, a look into the past shows that these prophecies have always been used to voice concern regarding immediate events. Showers of black rain are not unknown. Between 1862 and 1863, showers of black rain fell on the parish of Slains and were witnessed by the parish minister, Rev. James Rust.[61] Slains lies in the Grampian Region on the east coast midway between Aberdeen and Peterhead, about fourteen miles distant from each. The first shower occurred in the early evening of Tuesday 14 January 1862. The rain gave off a sulphuric smell and fell for some twenty miles inland. Several washerwomen had their laundry ruined and a photographer lost a batch of prints by using the contaminated rainwater. The shower was accompanied by enormous masses of pumice stone washed up on the beach. Rev. Rust immediately reported the incident to *The Scotsman* newspaper.[62] A second shower of black rain fell over a similar area on the afternoon of 20 May and a third at seven in the morning of Wednesday, 28 October 1863. A correspondent to *The Glasgow Herald* reported a shower of black rain in Carluke on Thursday, 1 May 1862, that is between the first and second showers which fell on Slains. Carluke is near Glasgow, about one hundred and forty mile south of Slains and is well inland.[63]

Black rain fell on the Clyde valley on 20 March 1828, another shower two days later; again on the same region on 1 and 3 March 1884. These

59 Personal communication.

60 Commentary by Elizabeth Sutherland in Mackenzie, *Prophecies*, pp. 49–50.

61 J. Rust, *Scottish Showers: The Scottish Black Rain Showers and Pumicestone Shoals of the Years 1862 and 1863* (Edinburgh, 1864).

62 Ibid., p. 11.

63 Ibid., p. 21.

could be the result of factory waste but showers have fallen on parts of the country remote from industrial areas and before the industrial revolution brought factories into existence. A black substance fell on Norway and Northern Europe on 31 January 1686. On 20 October 1755, a black dust fell over all Shetland, though more thickly in some areas than in others. 'It was very much like lamp black,' according to eye witnesses, 'but smelled strongly of sulphur.'[64] People working outdoors had their bodies and clothes blackened by it. Rain followed. At Scalloway an earthquake accompanied this phenomenon. At the same time showers fell on Orkney where it was called 'Black Snow.' The wind at the time was blowing from the southwest, that is, from the mainland. Three days later a shower of dust fell on a ship from Leith bound for Charlestown, South Carolina, while it was seventy-five miles off the coast of Shetland. The report by arrivals in the New World provided evidence of a widespread, prolonged fall of a black substance.[65] On 8 February 1837 Loch Erne (Earn) was reported to be covered in a black scum which by the following day had gathered on the shore. At the same time, at Miggar, a village eight or nine miles away there was reported some clothes left on the washing line overnight found on the morning to be covered in a black powder.[66]

Showers of black rain could and did occur. Other accounts within the Highlands may have been reported orally. The prophecy need not be feared; showers of black rain have already fallen. More mundanely, *siantan dubha*, the Gaelic expression used by Alexander Mackenzie, does not translate as black rain. It more accurately translates as 'black storms' and is used idiomatically to describe the elements at their very worst.

64 D. Milne, 'Notices of Earthquake-Shocks Felt in Great Britain, and Especially in Scotland, with Inferences Suggested by These Notices as to the Causes of Such Shocks,' *Edinburgh New Philosophical Journal* Vol. 31 (1841), pp. 92–122. p. 101.

65 Ibid., p. 101. R. Whytt, 'An Account of the Earthquake felt at Glasgow and Dumbarton: Also of a Shower of Dust falling on a Ship Between Shetland and Iceland; in a Letter From Dr Robert Whytt, Professor of Medicine at The University of Edinburgh, to John Pringle, M.D. F.R.S. Edinburgh, February 10, 1756.' *Philosophical Transactions of the Royal Society* Vol. XLIX Part II (1755), pp. 509–511.

66 Milne, 'Notices of Earthquake-Shocks Felt in Great Britain,' p. 121.

Such weather by itself would have been a cause for concern but the term may be a figurative way of expressing the dismal conditions blanketing the region and its people. Both versions of the prophecy end on a note of optimism and this has been used as a means of self-fulfilment for the organisers of the Brahan Seer Festival. One of the inspirations behind the festival and project as a whole has been the resurgence of confidence in the Highland economy, exemplified in Easter Ross by the building of the British Aluminium smelter at Invergordon and the oilrig fabrication yard at Nigg. The festival was more than a celebration of artistic talent; it was seen as a fulfilment of the Brahan Seer's prophecies. The festival's artistic director Lizzie McDougall said, 'the prophecy mentions this horrid black rain and then the people will return and that to me is the oil. People are returning to the Highlands ... it is the prosperity oil brings.'[67]

The festival organisers set out to fulfil particular prophecies which they recorded on their website and in their literature. It is said that on the way to his execution at Chanonry Point, Coinneach Odhar looked over the waters of the Moray Firth and declared, 'I see a shadow over Culloden. That shadow covers all Scotland but that shadow shall rise and the light shall shine over Scotland brighter than it was before.'[68] This prophecy is of very recent origin, first surfacing in the literature in the 1980s.[69] It owes its genesis to those in the Romantic movement of the nineteenth century who began to perceive Culloden in a way that earlier generations had not. Indeed, older versions of the prophecy more accurately describe what actually happened. Drumossie Moor would be 'stained with the best blood of the Highlands. Glad am I that I will not see that day, for it will be a fearful period; heads will be lopped off by the score, and no mercy will be shown or quarter given on either side.'[70] The unfolding changes in the perception of Culloden can be examined in the literature. The dismissive Thomas Pennant, visiting the site in 1769,

67 www.travelscotland.co.uk/features/seer_festival

68 www.brahanseer.co.uk/news/pages/the_story

69 E. Sutherland, *Ravens and Black Rain: The Story of Highland Second Sight* (London, 1985), p. 335.

70 Mackenzie, *Prophecies*, p. 64.

thought a 'veil [should] be flung over a few excesses' so much had the country benefited from the outcome.[71] No commemoration of the battle existed in 1826 when a correspondent to the *Inverness Courier* wrote to express surprise that there is 'neither a stick nor a stone' to mark the site.[72] On the centenary of the battle the people of Inverness picnicked and chased rabbits on the moor or listened to tales from those whose relatives had fought there. Only afterwards did the mood change from the 'carnivalesque' to the 'elegiac.'[73] The cairn commemorating the slain clansmen was first begun in 1849 but abandoned through lack of funds. After several false starts it was completed in 1881. It marks 'the graves of the gallant Highlanders who fought for Scotland and Prince Charlie.'[74] This transformation of the Highlanders into a national representation is, according to Colin McArthur, a 'travestying of the non-nationalist, dynastic, social-systemic issues at stake in the battle.'[75] The creation of a prophecy predicting events on a national rather than on a regional scale extends the seer's sphere of influence beyond the merely provincial. By changing prophecies to accommodate changing perceptions of events, people's perception of the seer has also changed. The Brahan Seer, from being a local legend, has grown through the different media of print, radio, television and the Internet to become 'Scotland's most famous seer.'[76]

For the festival organisers, the opening of the Scottish parliament and a perceived renaissance in Scotland's art, literature and music, suggest that 'the dreadful shadow cast by Culloden down the years has begun at last

71 T. Pennant, *A Tour in Scotland 1769* (Edinburgh, 2000), p. 103, Also cited in C. McArthur, 'Culloden: A Pre-emtive Strike,' *Scottish Affairs* No. 9 (1994), pp. 97–126. p. 104.

72 J. Barron, *The Northern Highlands in the Nineteenth Century: Newspaper Index and Annals* Vol. II (Inverness, 1903), p. 18.

73 McArthur, 'Culloden,' p. 106.

74 Ibid., p. 108

75 Ibid., p. 110.

76 So described by the newsreader on the BBC's 'Reporting Scotland' on Thursday, 15 May 2003, when reporting the death of a modern day Highland seer, Swein MacDonald.

to lift.'[77] Four standing stones with Gaelic and English inscriptions have been placed unobtrusively throughout the region to commemorate the festival and celebrate the foretelling of a brighter future. The inscription on one stone on Knockbain Hill overlooking Dingwall reads, 'The day will come/ First sheep, then deer/ After the black rains/ People will return.' A stone set near some old Scots Pine between Fortrose and Avoch on the Black Isle looks towards Culloden. It reads, 'The shadow over Culloden will rise/ and the sun will shine brighter than before.' The stones are pink to match the predominant colour of the area's sandstone. Since no local quarry presently produces stone of this colour the organisers used stone imported from India.[78]

The Brahan Seer Festival was a celebration of a region's culture through a synthesis of local traditions and more widespread artistic practices, using the legend as a theme. The artistic works, some of them created specifically for the festival, embellish, expand and enhance the tale through artists' conceptions of how the seer and his contemporaries spoke, how they acted and how they dressed. An optimism about the here and now has been translated by the organisers and participants in the festival into a self-fulfilling prophecy. Such use of prophecy in response to unfolding events is consistent with a tradition which can be traced through the region's history.

The use and content of prophecy in Highland culture

The church has always played an important role in Highland culture and the prophetic utterances of 'Scots Worthies' such as the Covenanting ministers, Alexander Peden (c1626–1686) and Donald Cargill, appeared in chapbooks shortly after their death and continued to be peddled in this

77 *The Brahan Seer Celebratory Booklet*, np.

78 Lizzie McDougall, artistic director of the BSF, personal correspondence 27 June 2002.

form until the close of the nineteenth century.[79] What gave the words of these Covenanters added appeal was that they were prepared to lay down their lives for their faith. Cargill was executed at Edinburgh on 17 July 1681, and his final words predicted God's wrath upon his persecutors.[80] Religious prophecies included an inculcation of moral doctrine based on the laws of God. They also functioned 'to admonish and reprove' and to warn of divine judgement. They were often used to console or to pardon, seldom to approve or praise.[81] The prophecies of relatively obscure late seventeenth-century Scottish divines such as John Porter of Crossibeig, whose religious visions included the 'ruin of the Romish Antichrist' and Allan Logan of Culross who made earth-shattering predictions based on his calculations of Revelations, were issued by different printers to satisfy the demand of the public. Even the inconsequential prophecies of an Aberdeenshire eccentric, Dr Adam Donald, found their way into print.[82] The prophecies of Yorkshire's Mother Shipton and Cheshire's Robert Nixon were published by Scottish printers from the early part of the eighteenth century and their continued popularity is confirmed by the number of times the various accounts of such legendary prophets were reissued by different printers and edited to suit changing circumstances. They were often accompanied by such introductory comments as 'this remarkable prophecy has been carefully corrected' while the relevance of the text to contemporary events, and the preservation of stocks, was maintained by such artifices as showing the date of publication as 'printed in this present year.'[83] Chapbooks serve as an indicator of the continued interest in prophecy at a popular level. Cargill excommunicated the King

79 W. Harvey, *Scottish Chapbook Literature* (Paisley, 1903), p. 24. J. Howie, *The Scots Worthies* (Glasgow, 1846 (1775)), biography of Donald Cargill, pp. 382–393 and pp. 502–515 for biography of Alexander Peden. University of Aberdeen, Chapbooks in Historic Collections Vols. H8, 2: H4, 3: H8, 3: H15, 6.

80 Howie, *The Scots Worthies*, p. 392.

81 J. Davison, *Discourses on Prophecy: In Which are Considered its Structure, Use and Inspiration* (Oxford and London, 1870) pp. 28 and 36.

82 Chapbooks: Historic Collections, Vols. H7, 9: H15, 2: H8, 2: H15, 4: H2, 6.

83 Ibid., Vols. H2, 1: H8, 1: H21, 13: H15, 6.

and other members of the establishment including the Lord Advocate, Sir George Mackenzie of Rosehaugh, predicting that 'they would not die the ordinary death of men.'[84] Cargill died on the scaffold after making a lengthy speech in which he committed himself fearlessly to God's care. Point of death speeches and predictions of doom delivered by those such as Christopher Love, who shared the same fate, were circulated in chapbook form.[85] They act as precursors for the final utterances of the Brahan Seer.

Although Coinneach Odhar was known as a prophet in different parts of the Highlands, there are no chapbooks in either Gaelic or English containing his pronouncements. It was a Lowland seer, Thomas the Rhymer, that the Gaels considered to be their true prophet and although folklorist Donald Mackenzie writes that 'the sayings of "True Thomas"' were hawked through the Highlands in Gaelic chapbooks, the evidence, such as it is, does not suggest that Gaelic chapbooks were commonly sold and read throughout the region.[86] The only chapbooks now extant in Gaelic are of poems, printed for and distributed by Peter Turner, a chapman from Inverary.[87] The dearth of chapbook evidence for readership among ordinary people could be attributed in part to the relatively low levels of literacy in Gaelic speaking areas and the importance of oral tradition in Gaelic culture.[88] A few chapbooks in English were printed in Inverness but many were printed in Stirling and Falkirk as well as the larger cities in the Lowlands. One can only infer that Gaelic speakers if they read of such prophecies did so in English. Chapbooks containing the prophe-

84 Howie, *The Scots Worthies*, p. 388.

85 Ibid., Vols. H8, 2: H15, 4. Love was executed in London on 22 August 1651.

86 D. Mackenzie, 'The Brahan Seer,' in L. Spence (ed.), *An Encyclopaedia of Occultism* (London, 1920), p. 78.

87 Only seven Gaelic chapbooks have been traced at the NLS. All are titled and in the same format – eight pages – with a woodcut on the title page. They contain songs/ ballads and were printed for Peter Turner, Inverary. Six are at shelfmark L.C. 2879. The seventh is at shelfmark Hall.133.h.3. I am indebted to Eoin Shalloo, Curator, Rare Books Division, NLS, for help on this.

88 Withers, *Gaelic Scotland: The Transformation*, p. 146.

cies of Thomas the Rhymer were produced in abundance during the early nineteenth century, indicating a need to meet popular demand.[89]

Some accounts relate that Thomas prophesied the return of a Sleeping Warrior who will save Gaeldom while other accounts relate that Thomas himself is the Sleeping Warrior.[90] The strong tradition of poetry in the Gaelic language, coupled to the belief in the prophecy, was utilised in support of the Jacobite cause. The 1745 rebellion elicited such poems of hope as 'The Song of the Clans' by John MacDonald which begins 'Here's the time when the prophecy/ Has been proven true to us …'[91] Even after defeat at Culloden, Jacobite Colonel John Roy Stewart, who spent five months hiding out in caves, penned 'John Roy's Prayer' which contains the words 'My faith's in the prophecy of long ago/ That the force we need will come over the sea.'[92] Such expectant belief in a prophecy perceived to be as yet unfulfilled was to persist in poetic form until all hopes for a Jacobite return evaporated.[93] This prophecy appears to have been used as a political instrument and added impetus was given to the output of prophetic verses with each phase of heightened Jacobite activity.

Prophecies of a more mundane nature had been in existence since Thomas's floruit in the thirteenth century and for the next several hundred years it 'appears to have been found a good stroke of policy on many occasions' to make up a prophecy under his name.[94] In 1826 Robert Chambers identified prophecies referring to recent agricultural improvements which he was certain had been made after the event. These included what he

89 Chapbooks: Historic Collections. Vols. H2, 5: H7, 10: H8, 4: H18, 9: H21, 12: H21, 13.

90 J. MacInnes, 'The Gaelic Perceptions of the Lowlands' in William Gillies (ed.), *Gaelic and Scotland: Alba agus a'Ghàidhlig* (Edinburgh, 1989), pp. 89–100. Also cited in M. Newton, *A Handbook of the Scottish Gaelic World* (Dublin, 2000), p. 40.

91 R. Black, *An Lasair: An Anthology of 18th Century Scottish Verse* (Edinburgh, 2001), p. 39.

92 Ibid., pp. 181 and 448.

93 R. Black, 'A Century of Coded Messages' in *West Highland Free Press* (13 February 1998), p. 19.

94 R. Chambers, *Popular Rhymes of Scotland* (Edinburgh, 1890 (1826)), p. 212.

euphemistically referred to as 'changes of tenantry' in the Highlands which Thomas is reputed to have predicted by saying 'The teeth of the sheep shall lay the plough on the shelf.'[95] This prophecy, or a version of it, 'the sheep's jaw will put the plough on the hen-roost' has also been credited to the Brahan Seer. Alexander Nicolson, citing Chambers, argues that the Brahan Seer did not make this prophecy because it had 'been made long before by no less a person than Thomas the Rhymer.'[96] This is not at all what Chambers is asserting. He is arguing that the prophecy is of comparatively recent origin and has been *attributed* to Thomas the Rhymer in the same way as numerous prophecies have been attributed to the Brahan Seer. The obvious failure of the Jacobite cause has tainted Thomas's reputation. Prophecies once attributed to him are now attributed to Coinneach Odhar, the Brahan Seer.

Thomas the Rhymer and the Brahan Seer were not the only seers recognised in the Highlands. The Lady of Lawers – 'perhaps the most remarkable of them all' – was a seventeenth-century seer who lived in Perthshire and made predictions, most of which have been 'fulfilled to the letter.'[97] She is credited with several prophecies regarding the changes and modernisation taking place in her part of the country, all of which are similar in tone to prophecies attributed to the Brahan Seer.[98] A version of the example cited above runs, 'the sheep's skull will make the plough useless.'[99] Versions of these and similar prophecies have been credited to the Isla Seer from the Hebrides to account for changes in that region.[100]

95 Ibid., pp. 219–220. J. A. H. Murray agreed with the recency of prophecies attributed to Thomas. He cited Chambers' observations on the Highlands in his introduction to *The Romance and Prophecies of Thomas of Erceldoune* (London, 1875)

96 A. Nicolson, *Gaelic Proverbs* (Edinburgh, 1881), p. 159.

97 A. C. McKerracher, 'The Lady of Lawers' in *The Scots Magazine* Vol. 117, No. 3 (1982), pp. 253–260. p. 253.

98 J. G. Campbell, *Superstitions of the Highlands and Islands of Scotland* (Glasgow, 1900), p. 275 and McKerracher, 'The Lady of Lawers' p. 256. A. Mackenzie, *The Prophecies of the Brahan Seer* (London, 1977), pp. 36–37.

99 Campbell, *Superstitions of the Highlands*, pp. 274–275 and McKerracher, 'The Lady of Lawers,' p. 253.

100 Mackenzie, *The Prophecies of the Brahan Seer*, pp. 37 and 139.

By attributing prophecies to a particular seer the people are using the seer as a repository for collective wisdom, while simultaneously enhancing the seer's reputation.

Such was the interest in prophecy with religious and moral overtones that A. B. Maclennan gathered the alleged prophetic utterances of an eighteenth-century minister, John Morrison, from the parish of Petty near Inverness, and published them in a slim volume in 1894, over a hundred years after the cleric's death.[101] Morrison – according to Maclennan – denied any claim to prophetic ability. The power had been conferred on him by parishioners astounded at his uncanny knack of correctly anticipating the consequences of their conduct.[102] One religious group in the Highlands contained within their ranks an unusually high proportion of those thought to have the power of prophecy. These were 'The Men' of the Evangelical Movement, so called because they were lay preachers, or 'laymen of the common people' to distinguish them from the ministers of the established church who normally came from landed elites.[103] The Movement was essentially a protest group, challenging the patronage of ministers; the poor state of church property and social injustices, grievances with which many ministers were thought to be colluding.[104] The Evangelical Movement, which began during the period of social unrest in the late eighteenth century, included many 'Men' who were religiously inspired and who made utterances of a prophetic nature from within the context of their faith. These included condemnations, exhortations and warnings on future conduct. Belief in this form of prophecy persisted among strong religious communities in the Highlands until the last decades of the nineteenth century.[105] Prophecies attributed to the

101 A. B. Maclennan, *The Petty Seer* (Inverness, 1894).

102 Ibid., p. 12.

103 J. MacInnes, 'Religion in Gaelic Society' in TGSI No 52 (1982), pp. 222–242. pp. 231–232.

104 Ibid., p. 232. See also E. Sutherland, *Ravens and Black Rain* (London, 1985), p. 184.

105 MacInnes, 'Religion in Gaelic Society,' p. 236. Sutherland, *Ravens and Black Rain*, p. 195. Morrison and Macrae, *Highland Second Sight*, pp. 116, 117, 125–128.

Brahan Seer referring to a proliferation of 'ministers without grace' and 'women without shame' may have originated with these men.[106]

A movement of a different kind also used prophecy as a means of protest. The tradition of poetry, especially from within the Gaelic panegyric code, lent itself to prophetic utterances which could be used to pass judgement on those responsible for upholding traditional values such as kinship and hospitality. Comment could be made in verse, satirising the changes taking place in the country and those who were implementing them.[107] In 'A Song to the Lowland Shepherds' Allan MacDougall sang that 'it was the essence of the prophecy/ that the plough would become redundant' before compiling a litany of the ills which had befallen the Highlands. The shepherds, with their disgusting ways, such as using their teeth to castrate lambs, were the epitome of those ills. The people should salute, and follow the lead of, the handful of lairds who had maintained the bonds of kinship.[108] John MacRae began his 'Song about the Crofters' Bill' by observing that 'the plough has indeed been placed on the cross beam/ and the arable lad has been laid waste,' before exhorting his audience not to submit to the legislation.[109] He predicted that good times would return. The poets were aware of the 'old' prophecy. Donald Meek observes that references to it are 'relatively common in verses of this kind' and suggests they provide both comfort and insight during unsettled times.[110]

When storytellers and poets use prophecy to speak of the future they are passing judgement on events 'in the here and now' that give them cause for concern. People in the Highlands have a tradition of using prophecy in a judgmental fashion to describe unfolding events. This is

106 Mackenzie, *Prophecies of the Brahan Seer*, pp. 47–48.

107 D. E. Meek (ed.), *Tuath is Tighearna: An Anthology of Gaelic Poetry of Social and Political Protest from the Clearances to the Land Agitation (1800–1890)*. (Edinburgh, 1995), *passim*. Black, *An Lasair*, pp. xvii–xxxix. M. Newton, *A Handbook of the Scottish Gaelic World* (Dublin, 2000), pp. 92–98. See especially J. MacInnes, 'The Panegyric Code in Gaelic Poetry and its Historical Background', in TGSI Vol. 50 (1978), pp. 435–498.

108 Meek, *Tuath is Tighearna*, pp. 47–51, 186–189.

109 Ibid., pp. 153–154, 256–257.

110 Ibid., p. 52.

closely linked to their strong religious beliefs and religious figures were often credited with having prophetic abilities. The Brahan Seer was a 'pious man' who went to heaven, rather than to hell, after passing judgement on his tormentor and her family. People elsewhere shared similar experiences during unsettled times. When they did, the prophecies they used to describe the changes were identical to those attributed to the Brahan Seer. This indicates that their concerns and uncertainties were the same and that they were responding to them in the same prophetic way as the inhabitants of the Highlands.

Comparative prophetic traditions

The Irish have a popular prophet called Brian Rua Ó Cearbháin (Red Brian Carabine) who has many similarities to the Brahan Seer in terms of the manner in which he acquired his mystical powers and in the type of predictions he made. According to oral tradition he is also a contemporary of the legendary Highland figure having acquired his prophetic abilities in 1648. Like the Brahan Seer, Red Brian was a religious man who placed his trust in 'The Almighty Father.'[111] Among his first prophecies was 'there would be a big house on every small hill ... boots on fools, and the children would speak English ... there would come a time of young women without shame ... a bridge on every stream ... there would be iron wheels on coaches of fire in the north and in the south.'[112] Red Brian predicted the construction of roads made of meal, a reference to the manner of paying the labourers during times of hardship, and that village priests would convert to Protestantism.[113] The foregoing are fragments of what is collectively known as The Prophecy of Ireland which

111 M. Timony, *Red Brian Carabine's Prophecy and Other Interesting Historical Matter* (Dublin, 1906), p. 4.

112 Ibid., pp. 4–7.

113 Ibid., p . 8.

was never written down and 'could only be had from the mouths of the people.'[114] Red Brian died at the time he had predicted, bemoaning that people who did not take account of The Prophecy were going badly wrong. The author, Michael Timony, collected the material from three 'intelligent, studious and clear-sighted (named) storytellers' from Co. Mayo and it was published in Irish in 1906.[115]

The fragments of prophecy show the types of changes, including economic, linguistic and religious, taking place in Ireland and voice the concerns of the people that such changes are occurring. The entirety of the prophecies, with minor adjustments for geography and specific historical events, are interchangeable with those attributed to the Brahan Seer. It is possible that the relative lateness of publication resulted in 'feedback' from Scottish sources as Alexander Mackenzie's book had been in print for thirty years. Moreover, the geographical proximity of Ireland and Scotland and their shared cultural similarities could have resulted in a cross pollination of oral accounts, with prophecies attributed to one seer being attributed to the other. This does not detract from their relevance in describing similar changing events in either region.

The potential for transferring almost identical prophecies from one seer to another is less likely between cultures that have considerable geographic and linguistic differences. However, when the prophecies of one such culture are examined the types of events described follow a similar pattern. William Gregory, the Scottish medical professor and proponent of magnetism, visited Germany in 1849 and was sufficiently interested in prophecies to examine instances popular there at the time.[116] Germany as a unitary nation state was not formed until 1871.[117] At the time of

114 Ibid., p. 16.

115 Ibid., I am indebted to Professor Colm O'Boyle of the Celtic Department at the University of Aberdeen for translating the entirety of this volume from the Irish.

116 Wm. Gregory, 'German Popular Prophecies' in *Blackwood's Edinburgh Magazine* No. 415, Vol. 67 (1850), pp. 560–72.

117 J. Breuilly, 'The National Idea in Modern German History,' in J. Breuilly (ed.), *The State of Germany: The National Idea in the Making, Unmaking and Remaking of a Modern Nation-state* (London and New York, 1992), pp. 1–28. p. 1.

Gregory's visit it consisted of a loosely bound Confederation of forty-one independent states and principalities formed at the Congress of Vienna in 1815 following the Napoleonic Wars. The Confederation's purpose was to act as a constraint against French and Russian efforts at dominating Europe. Austria in the south – for centuries the bulwark of Catholicism against the Turks – vied with the militarism of protestant Prussia in the north for control over the Confederation which included some six million people of non-German nationality.[118] The Confederation's unity had been threatened by a revolution in 1848. Wars, religious differences and political intrigue had impacted upon the people whose main concern was to seek peace and prosperity. These were the most important subject matter of the prophecies examined by Gregory. He was acutely aware that many were made after the event but he 'found everywhere, and among all classes, a firm conviction of the *genuineness* of many of the popular prophecies' (original emphasis).[119] Gregory's main source of information for the German prophecies was, however, literary, he having obtained a recently published book by a Catholic curate, whose purpose, according to Gregory, was to interpret the prophecies in such a way as to predict the re-establishment of the Roman Catholic Church and the destruction of Protestantism.[120]

Gregory's account shows that prophecies attributed to seers in different parts of Germany coincide with each other and the unfolding events to which they relate are consistent with the turmoil in the country at the time. The prophecies are often a mix of highly detailed descriptions of events from a particular locality combined with generalisations such as peace ensuing when all things predicted have come to pass. In common with the Scottish and Irish prophecies, references to technological changes, such as the coming of the railways or the building of bridges,

118 D. Langewiesche, 'Germany and the National Question in 1848,' in Breuilly (ed.), *The State of Germany*, pp. 60–79. p. 60. Wm. Carr, 'The Unification of Germany,' in Breuilly (ed.), *The State of Germany*, pp. 80–102. p. 82.

119 Gregory, 'German Popular Prophecies,' p. 560.

120 Ibid., p. 561. The book was entitled '*Prophetic Voices, with Explanations. A Collection as Perfect as Possible, of all Prophecies, of Ancient and Modern Date, Concerning the Present and Future Times, With an Explanation of the Obscure parts.*'

are widespread. The terminology used to describe them are couched in the language of the pre-technological age, 'On this road, carriages will run *without horses*, and cause a dreadful noise' (original emphasis). [121] No one source could account for the origin of all the prophecies, thought Gregory. He speculates that some could be 'derived from the reflections of sagacious men.'[122] In others, the frequency of scriptural language suggests the application of biblical prophecies to contemporary events. The original seers, he suggests, were monks and ascetics whose prophecies, based on an understanding of history and the human condition, had come down to the people by word of mouth to be modified by them to suit local circumstances. Knowledge of the visions, necessarily induced in a trance-like state to which monks and ascetics were predisposed, may have encouraged 'second sight among the peasantry' when they became aroused by their own religious passions.[123] Gregory also notes that the existence of prophecies may prepare people for sudden outbreaks of turmoil and that consequently they could influence events towards self-fulfilment. This necessitates the re-interpretation and re-shaping of prophecy in light of current events, the argument put forward in this chapter. Gregory's article was published in Edinburgh in 1850. The extent of its influence over later prophecies emanating from the Highlands is impossible to quantify. What Gregory's account demonstrates is that similarities in popular prophecies are evident in different cultures, if parallels exist in the lived experiences of the peoples concerned.

Such similarities can even be seen on a different continent and in very different cultures. Paul Nabakov has obtained testimony from Native American Indians of different tribes who have prophecies relating to the coming of European settlers and the cataclysmic changes this wrought to their established ways of life. Not only are the contents of prophecies from different tribes similar to each other, they are similar, in both content and presentation, to their European counterparts.[124] Premonitions

121 Ibid., p. 563.

122 Ibid., p. 571.

123 Ibid., pp. 571–572.

124 P. Nabakov (ed.), *Native American Testimony* (New York, 1991).

regarding the coming of the white man, 'strangers with hair on their faces coming from the direction of the rising sun,' are widespread.[125] These people, who appeared to have lots of things, would use any means to get whatever else they wanted, they would take everything. The Indians had to be forever on their guard. 'Listen! Listen! ... They are building an iron road' to speed up their conquest.[126] The adoption of the white man's ways would have dire consequences for the Indians; drinking coffee would make their teeth soft, smoking (a white man's habit acquired from Indians) would ruin their eyesight, sleeping in soft beds and wearing heavy clothes would make them weak and lazy. 'You will break up homes, and murder and steal.'[127]

This prophetic response to unfolding events persists to the present day. Tom Mould has recently studied the prophetic tradition of the Mississippi band of Choctaw Native American Indians.[128] His account is primarily concerned with demonstrating the continuance of prophetic narrative by borrowing from that of riddling, itself a practice well known in Highland ceilidh circles where men and women would vie for the title of *Ridire nan Ceist*, King of Riddles.[129] Mould found that in performing prophecy, specifically fulfilled prophecy, Choctaw narrators had to establish that a prophecy existed prior to an event's occurrence. They used different strategies for this, younger narrators consistently referring to past performances of the prophecy, usually culminating in a highly descriptive account of the events surrounding their hearing it for the first time as a child. Older narrators also referred to past performance but could place themselves in the past, prior to the advent of the innovation, and thus lay personal claim to having heard a prophecy prior to its fulfilment. Narrators also attributed the prophecy to a tribal elder and spoke as if quoting him or her. In terms of establishing authenticity, they under-

125 Ibid., p. 6.

126 Ibid., p. 14.

127 Ibid., p. 14–15.

128 T. Mould, 'Prophetic Riddling: A Dialogue of Genres in Choctaw Performance' in *Journal of American Folklore* Vol. 115 Nos. 457–458 (2002), pp. 395–417.

129 Newton, *Handbook*, p. 102.

pinned the prescience of the elder by using pre-technological language, 'machines, you know, flying like a bird,' to convey the impression that the words had first been uttered prior to the arrival of the new technology whose name would not then have been known.[130]

Conclusion

Popular prophecies are used as a means of explaining what is going on in the midst of change. They often provide warnings to those who are forcing the changes, promising retribution or a return to old ways. Prophecies are often a cry for help from people who have no other tool or weapon at their disposal. Prophecies empower because they can be used to advise, warn and threaten. They distance the speaker by placing the authority for such pronouncements in the mouth of a more powerful being. Fulfilled prophecies play an important role in the prophetic sphere in that they provide validity for unfulfilled prophecies, while confirming the wisdom of the elders to whom any narrator of prophecy within a culture defers. Choctaw narrators establish the authenticity of prophecies by the use of pre-technological language and deferring to the prescient wisdom of respected tribal elders.[131] Scottish, Irish and German narratives also use pre-technological language and defer to the prescient wisdom of respected, 'pious' figures. Contemporary believers in prophecy use similar strategies. By attributing fulfilled prophecies, couched in pre-technological language, to the archetype of Highland seers, their authenticity in pre-dating events is secured. This success, in turn, provides an impetus for the phenomenon of second sight and for the enhancement of the reputation of the Brahan Seer.

130 Mould, 'Prophetic Riddling,' pp. 402 and 404.

131 Ibid., p. 403.

This examination from historical and geographical contexts shows that, on the one hand, second sight is still believed to be part of the human condition and continues to attract the attention of those sections of the intellectual community who have an interest in psychic phenomenon. On the other hand, it shows that contemporary users of prophecy follow a historical tradition, not confined to Highland culture, in interpreting existing prophecies, or inventing or re-inventing them, in order to comment on, and make sense of, the changing circumstances of lived experiences.

CHAPTER 8

Conclusion

This book has traced the legend of the Brahan Seer from the Fowlis affair of the sixteenth century to the present day. It has examined the legend without passing judgement on relative truths or moral values, and has tried to set beliefs within the contexts of their time. Anthropological approaches to oral tradition and legend have been employed so that what is sought is not some 'objective, truthful knowledge' about the past, but a 'reliable' knowledge that is 'intended to be realistic and honest.' This exploration of beliefs and practices has provided new insights into witchcraft, second sight and prophecy and the development of a legend within different periods and cultural contexts. The study shows that past, present and future are inexorably linked through lived experience. What is valued from the past is determined by the world-view of the present which is, in turn, influenced by the fears, hopes and aspirations for the future and the beliefs and practices used to determine the outcome of future events. An examination of the people who held particular beliefs at particular times contributes to the debate on the distinction between elite and popular culture and shows that, far from being 'bi-polar' opposites, they are enmeshed within each other in what Bob Scribner has called 'complex processes of inculcation, appropriation, competition, assimilation or rejection of any given set of cultural values and practices.'[1]

Historical records from the sixteenth century show that a Coinneach Odhar was a 'leader of witches' in the locality of Easter Ross when a major witch-hunt took place against those involved in a plot to rid Lady Munro of Fowlis of her stepsons and daughter-in-law. The Fowlis affair

1 B. Scribner, 'Is a History of Popular Culture Possible?' *History of European Ideas* Vol. 10, No. 2 (1989), pp. 175–191. p. 182.

of 1577–78 provides many of the ingredients which have survived as part of the Brahan Seer legend, including the name of the principal witch; a central role for a resolute woman from the most powerful family in the locality; and executions by burning. These historical events have been suggested as a context from which the legend originated. In the context of the time, the affair shows that witchcraft was endemic to the region, and believed in and practised by men and women of all ages and all social classes. Witches were known to each other and to the community at large. The concerted efforts of such a broadly based social group runs counter to the description of a stereotypical Scottish witch – an old, poor woman who lived alone.[2] Rather, evidence from the Fowlis affair supports the view that a more cautionary approach to identifying witches be adopted as suggested by Hugh McLachlan and J. K. Swales whose statistical analysis of Scottish cases shows a much greater variation among defendants than the stereotype suggests.[3] The witches of the Fowlis affair and their clients believed that the casting of spells, performance of rituals and intercourse with the fairy world could produce the desired results. The plot resulted in death and injury through poisoning and after local lairds, led by Lady Munro's husband, Robert Munro of Fowlis, brought charges of witchcraft against the conspirators, records show that a total of ten witches were burnt for their involvement. Nine of these were sent to the stake at the Chanonry of Fortrose, the supposed site of the Brahan Seer's execution.[4]

Lady Munro escaped punishment and was only brought to trial in 1590 as a consequence of King James VI's personal involvement after he visited Easter Ross in July 1589, during a tour of Scotland meant to demonstrate his regal powers and his determination to improve the legal system. The king and central authority appear to have treated witchcraft

2 J. Goodare, 'Women and the Witch-Hunt in Scotland,' *Social History* Vol. 23 No. 3, 1998, pp. 288–308. p. 290. H. V. McLachlan and J. K. Swales, 'Stereotypes and Scottish Witchcraft,' *Contemporary Review* Vol. 234, part 1357, pp. 88–94. p. 88.

3 McLachlan and Swales, 'Stereotypes and Scottish Witchcraft,' pp. 93–94.

4 R. J. Adam (ed.), *Calendar of Fearn, Text and Additions, 1471–1667* (Edinburgh, 1991), p. 135.

as a crime of little consequence unless loss of life ensued.[5] Contrary to speculation that the Easter Ross witch-hunt was precipitated by the Kirk, clerical involvement in the prosecution of the witches was marginal.[6] The devil's pact, a prerequisite for later successful prosecutions is absent from the charges but at least one of the witches believed herself to be the devil's servant, suggesting that the concept was known to her before it became an integral part of elite ideology. There is no evidence that her inquisitors suggested this to her, as has been argued in an examination of Aberdeenshire witches of the same period.[7] Evidence from the Fowlis records supports the assertion that the devil's pact was known to witches and most likely introduced into the craft by witches themselves rather than imposed upon them by educated elites.[8] It has been suggested that King James VI's first meaningful contact with witchcraft occurred on his return from Denmark and his examination of the North Berwick witches who, it was alleged, had plotted against him. The threat posed to the king is thought to have hardened his view of witchcraft.[9] The events of the Fowlis affair appear to have been the king's first significant exposure to witchcraft and this enabled him to understand the distinction between harmful and healing kinds. He pursued Lady Munro because deaths had occurred. When he came to reflect on witchcraft in his *Daemonologie* that distinction had disappeared. The devil's pact now featured prominently to explain why witches, mostly women, acted as they did, and the seeking out and suppression of the pact were actively encouraged. The events of

5 RPC Vol. IV, pp. 217–218.

6 J. Wormald, 'The Witches, the Devil and the King,' in Terry Brotherstone and David Ditchburn (eds), *Freedom and Authority: Scotland c1050–c1650* (East Lothian, 2000), pp. 165 –180.

7 J. Goodare, 'The Aberdeen Witchcraft Panic of 1597.' *Northern Scotland: the Journal for the Centre of Scottish Studies.* Vol. 21 (2001), pp. 17–37.

8 P. G. Maxwell-Stuart, 'Witchcraft and the Kirk in Aberdeenshire, 1596–97,' *Northern Scotland: the Journal for the Centre of Scottish Studies.* Vol. 18 (1998), pp. 1–14. p. 4.

9 P. G. Maxwell-Stuart, 'The Fear of the King is Death: James VI and the Witches of East Lothian,' in W. G. Naphy and P. Roberts (eds), *Fear in Early Modern Society* (Manchester and New York, 1997), pp. 209–225. pp. 211–213.

the Fowlis affair and Coinneach Odhar's association as leader of witches may have influenced the relationship between witchcraft and the state of early modern Scotland more than heretofore recognised.

By the time Countess Isabella of Seaforth is thought to have had her confrontation with the Brahan Seer the impetus for initiating witchcraft accusations had shifted from local lairds to the church.[10] The national witch-hunts of 1661–62 coincided with the first years of Isabella's marriage and appear to have originated at local rather than central level. Although witches were pursued in the neighbourhood of Easter Ross with particular severity Isabella would have had to follow a legal process which militated against her carrying out an arbitrary execution. Many reasons have been put forward to explain why the hunts erupted as they did. They arose partly in response to a return to the familiar Scottish legal system as neighbours settled old and recent scores after a decade of English administration. It has been suggested that the leniency shown by the English Commissioners during the Interregnum contributed to the rush of witch trials after their departure.[11] This is a misconception based on an erroneous journal entry of the time when sixty cases of all kinds were brought before the commissioners and dismissed.[12] All were subsequently described as witchcraft cases and their dismissal used by scholars as evidence of English leniency. The record of cases brought before the English Commissioners show that they diligently went about their business and burned witches who came before them if evidence existed to find them guilty. Prior English leniency can be discounted as an explanation for the hunts of 1661–62. Diary entries by Alexander Brodie of Brodie, Robert Baillie and John Nicholl suggest that fewer charges were brought before the English commissioners through a reluctance of Scots law officers to collaborate in the justice system during the Interregnum because of a

10 J. Goodare (ed.), *The Scottish Witch-Hunt in Context* (Manchester, 2002), pp. 1, 2 and 123.

11 Levack, 'The Great Scottish Witch-hunt,' p. 93. C. Larner, *A Source Book of Scottish Witchcraft* (Glasgow, 1977).

12 Bulstrode Whitelock, *Memorials of the English Affairs* (Oxford, 1853), Vol. III, p. 458.

continuing loyalty to the king and from a suspicion of English motives across all levels of society.

Historical material illustrates two models of elite involvement in witchcraft trials following the Restoration: a rational reluctance as evidenced by some such as Brodie, and corrupt exploitation as evidenced from, among others, the pursuit of the Strathglass witches. Professional prickers were used to find the devil's mark during the 1661–62 witch-hunts and an admission of a pact with the devil, often obtained through torture, was mandatory in successful prosecutions. References to the pact are absent from the legend of the Brahan Seer suggesting that Countess Isabella could not have successfully pursued him without it. Pricking became discredited during the hunt. Several practitioners were imprisoned and the use of torture forbidden. Rather than the church and central authority acting in tandem to stamp out witchcraft evidence from contemporary records supports the view that central authority acted as a restraining influence on the church and local lairds. Once the witch-hunts of 1661–62 had subsided central control over the legal process was such that local prosecutions declined dramatically making it even more difficult to pursue a witchcraft case without good cause.[13] Members of the body politic, for example Sir George Mackenzie of Rosehaugh, the Lord Advocate, questioned some of the indigenous beliefs of witches but continued to pursue them principally because of an elite ideology based on the devil's pact. It was rational pragmatism in questioning the credibility of evidence that led the way in reducing witchcraft cases although they remained an issue for the church. However, the power of the state exceeded that of the church and such cases became rare and acquittals common.[14]

13 C. Larner, *Witchcraft and Religion* (Oxford, 1984), p. 26. J. Goodare (ed.), *The Scottish Witch-Hunt in Context* (Manchester, 2002), pp. 1, 2 and 123. B. Levack, 'State-Building and Witch-hunting in Early Modern Europe' in J. Barry, M. Hester and G. Roberts (eds), *Witchcraft in Early Modern Europe* (Cambridge, 1996), pp. 96–115. pp. 102–103.

14 W. G. Scott-Moncrieff, *The Records of the Proceedings of the Justiciary Court, 1661–1678*, 2 Vols. (Edinburgh, 1905), passim.

The late seventeenth century saw the dawning of the Age of Enlightenment in England, when men of science and philosophy such as John Locke (1632–1704), Isaac Newton (1642–1727) and Robert Boyle (1627–1691) used reason to determine the acceptability of beliefs rather than the orthodox authority of churchmen, sacred texts or tradition. In their examination of the natural world scholars sought observable matters of fact and were able to show that causes had effects that did not rely on supernatural powers explained by superstitions but occurred through probability and motion regulated by laws of nature. God was not displaced from his position as designer of the Universe but his role in the ongoing affairs of men was questioned. Science and magic were not mutually exclusive. Some magical practices were considered worthy of scientific study. Boyle was among the first of the members of the Royal Society to make enquiries into the phenomenon of second sight when he interviewed George Mackenzie, Lord Tarbat, Countess Isabella's brother, in his Pall Mall home in October 1678 and early enquiries into second sight provide compelling evidence against Countess Isabella's arbitrary execution of the Brahan Seer. Contemporary enquirers make no mention of such a character. More broadly, second sight was perceived by elite and indigenous groups to be distinct from witchcraft and not subject to the same harsh judicial punishment. Lord Tarbat provided Robert Boyle with several first hand accounts, most of which had occurred over twenty years earlier. Fearful of causing his friends ridicule, he was reluctant to provide accounts he had heard from others. Although one scholar has argued that educated elites had ceased to believe in the power of astrology and that 'only the prophecies of the bible continued to be taken seriously by the learned.' another has argued that interest in magical practices and popular prophecy continued among elites who, fearful of social ostracism, conducted their enquiries in a private, rather than the public, domain.[15]

15 P. Curry, *Prophecy and Power: Astrology in Early Modern England* (Cambridge, 1989), p. 274. M. Hunter, *The Occult laboratory: Magic Science and Second Sight in Late 17th Century Scotland* (Woodbridge, Suffolk, 2001), pp. 1–28. M. Hunter, *Robert Boyle (1627–91): Scrupulosity and Science* (Woodbridge, Suffolk, 2002), passim.

This view is supported in the present volume which shows that second sight was investigated by elites to see if future events could be predicted and if it could provide proof of an afterlife. However, accounts emanating from the Highlands were mostly anecdotal and often contradictory in defining the properties of the phenomenon and its practitioners. Lord Tarbat's discretion in his communications with Robert Boyle was not misplaced. Second sight could not satisfy the strict scientific criterion of the time by failing to be an observable matter of fact and sceptics from the scientific community as well as religious freethinkers such as John Toland and Lord Molesworth were able to provide natural explanations for the various accounts provided by such as Martin Martin, John Aubrey and James Garden.[16] Duncan Campbell, a deaf and dumb practitioner in the capital, drew large numbers of fee-paying clients from across the social spectrum to his fortune telling. The seer and his clients were lampooned on the stage, in the coffee houses and in the periodicals of the time by wits such as Joseph Addison and Richard Steele.[17]

In this sense scepticism triumphed over superstition: belief in second sight could not be openly admitted by the educated elites. That said, the correspondence of Henry Baker in the mid eighteenth century showed that it was still of private interest to some among the scientific community, including members of the Royal Society.[18] The gathering of cases by the minister, Donald Macleod, writing as Theophilus Insulanus, suggests that second sight was still believed in by people in the Highlands, including

16 Toland's Marginalia in Martin's *Description of the Western Islands of Scotland*: British Library Ref: c. 45.c.1.

17 D. Campbell, *Secret Memoirs of the Late Mr. Duncan Campbel [sic] the Famous Deaf and Dumb Gentleman Written by Himself Who Ordered They Should be Publish'd After His Decease* (London, 1720). D. F. Bond (ed.), *The Tatler No. 14*. D. F. Bond (ed.), *The Spectator* 5 Vols. Steele's article is under the pseudonym of Dulcibella Thankley, No. 474. Addison, no. 323 under the name of Clarinda, no. 505 under the name of Titus Trophonius and no. 560.

18 Henry Baker Correspondence: the John Rylands Library, Manchester, *English Ms 19*, Vols. 3, 4 and 5.

some members of the clergy.[19] Insulanus's own interest was religious: his monograph, published in 1763, was a belated attack on freethinkers who had questioned the immortality of the soul and he thought second sight was a means of confirming that there was life after death. He cited sympathetic conversations held some forty years earlier with Richard Steele as the principal motive for his study. Steele's public denunciation of second sight appeared to contrast with his private interest. Travellers to the Highlands such as Dr Samuel Johnson and James Boswell continued to report instances of second sight. Johnson's interest was also religious and his open minded opinion on the existence of second sight was appropriated by later travellers such as John Carr to provide them with a rationale for making their own enquiries and for helping to propagate the knowledge of this distinctly Scottish phenomenon on the Continent. However, beginning in the late eighteenth century people across Europe flocked to private salons, theatres and university lecture rooms to view demonstrations of clairvoyance, a derivative of Franz Mesmer's animal magnetism. Clairvoyance was a particular favourite of an emergent middle class. Its widespread accessibility and similarity to second sight ensured that the Scottish phenomenon was no longer considered unique. Second sight had become, according to one scholar, 'de-particularized, de-localized and de-nationalized.'[20]

Second sight, however, was not 'becoming extinct in Scotland,' as has been suggested.[21] It continued to be accepted in the Highlands as part of the human condition, even though old beliefs and practices were under threat from emigration and programmes of improvement. Socio-economic changes had seen many inhabitants migrate to the towns and cities of the south or to distant lands in search of a better way of life. This did not mean that beliefs necessarily changed; but often those who held them were displaced. Belief in second sight, for example, continued among

19 T. Insulanus (Donald MacLeod), *A Treatise on the Second Sight, Dreams and Apparitions: With Several Instances Sufficiently Attested* (Edinburgh, 1763).

20 A. J. L. Busst, 'Scottish Second Sight: The Rise and Fall of a European Myth' *European Romantic Review,* Vol. 5, part 2 (1995), p. 163.

21 Ibid., p. 168.

Scots and Gaelic speaking communities in the New World.[22] For those who remained, ministers and schoolteachers were often in the vanguard of suppressing what they considered to be impediments to improvement. Oral tradition came under threat from spreading literacy. Gaelic was being superseded by English, the language of authority.

Oral storytelling is a shared experience between storyteller and audience in which a narrative is modified to suit local circumstances and the expectations of the participants. Oral tradition relies on memory and is continually being reinvented, due to 'selective forgetting and remembering.'[23] A study of oral tradition in Tiree shows that memory of communal events is limited to some two centuries. Events from the distant past take on the characteristics of folklore; they often become condensed and attached in time and place to some significant event, such as the battle of Waterloo, which acts as a mnemonic. The practice of 'non-remembering' was found among a community in Skye who wished to forget an episode that contained unpleasant memories.[24] People there obtained their information about events concerning the community's past from 'popular, accessible sources' such as newspapers, rather than relying on oral testimony.[25] The 'purity' of oral tradition has 'been replaced by ... a less discrete "popular culture" in which speech and writing interact.'[26] This study supports and extends these findings by showing how a different form of mnemonic device was used in oral tradition, one that could be

22 M. Bennett, 'Second Sight and Seers in the New World,' a paper presented at the seminar on second sight at Tulloch Castle, Dingwall, 15 September 2001, during the BSF. C. W. Dunn, *Highland Settler: A Portrait of the Scottish Gael in Cape Breton and Eastern Nova Scotia* (Cape Breton Island, 1991), pp. 47–48. D. B. Blair, *Coinneach Odhar am Foisaiche* (Sydney, Cape Breton, 1900). Abridged extracts from Alexander Mackenzie's *Prophecies of the Brahan Seer* serialised in *Mac-Talla*, an all-Gaelic weekly newspaper published in Cape Breton.

23 J. Goody, *The Power of the Written Tradition* (London, 2000), pp. 43–44.

24 S. Macdonald, *Reimagining Culture: Histories, Identities and the Gaelic Renaissance* (Oxford, 1997), pp. 112–114.

25 Ibid., p. 111.

26 P. Fielding, *Writing and Orality: Nationality, Culture, and Nineteenth-Century Scottish Fiction* (Oxford, 1996), p. 3.

moved around and modified to suit local circumstances. The 'four great lairds' with distinguishing features had been used in the seventeenth century as a sign that the Fraser family was coming to grief. They re-appear in different localities with different names and physical characteristics as a sign that unfolding events will come to pass as prophesied. They are attached to the Brahan Seer legend as a sign that the male line of Seaforth Mackenzies was coming to its premature end. Once the legend appeared in print and was disseminated to a wide audience, the four great lairds ceased their wanderings. Nineteenth-century historians and folklorists such as Hugh Miller and J. G. Campbell regretted the gradual diminution of oral tradition and they began to gather and record tales and legends. Miller maintained the tradition of oral narrators in that he was not averse to relocating events and characters in time and place if this improved the entertainment value of his tale. However, as with other collectors, once he had committed a story to print it became fixed in time and place and the capacity for relocation by an individual storyteller was removed. The performance of oral traditions such as the singing of waulking songs during communal work or storytelling at the social gatherings in ceilidh houses was in decline. The contents of oral tradition were being remembered by transcription. People turned for accounts of the past to the written word in books and newspapers.

A text is an immutable, fixed depository of shared knowledge which can be examined and challenged by any number of readers. When the oral tradition surrounding Coinneach Odhar was transmuted into Victorian literature the common core of his origins and acquisition of his supernatural powers became fixed in time and place and subject to the world-view of the writers of the time. Seventeenth century travellers to the Highlands had looked upon the region as a laboratory in which to conduct scientific enquiries. They were followed through the eighteenth and nineteenth centuries by visitors whose purpose was the fulfilment of a personal experience imbued with an aesthetic appreciation of nature and where imagination, free from the constraints of scientific reasoning, could be used to conjure up an idealised conception of the past.[27] When the Romantic conception of Highland witchcraft, second sight and prophecy surrounding the demise of the Seaforth family was fixed in text by the 'Gothic phantasist' Sir Bernard Burke, the core of the tale – that the prophecy had been precipitated by a seer who had insulted a particular identifiable Seaforth at a time and place when witches were known to have been prosecuted –resonated with local understanding of the past which was also susceptible to Romantic idealism. The circumstance of the seer's death was changed from hanging in the original text to the burning associated with Scottish witchcraft cases. The executions during the Fowlis affair appear to have been retained in folk memory through reference to a stone, now underwater, said to mark the site at Chanonry of Fortrose where Coinneach Odhar was thought to have been burnt. The oral tradition surrounding the seer's early life in Lewis, obtained from the pages of the *Highlander*, was grafted on to the romantic version of his death as was the oral tradition of the appearance of four lairds with distinguishing features which marked the end of Seaforth. Prophecies attributed to the seer were collected from a variety of sources, whether orally, from contributors to the pages of newspapers or the already published collection of Hugh Miller. Alexander Mackenzie's revised account, combining historical events, oral tradition and Romantic literature has become the definitive version of the legend which has survived to the present day. The legend of the Brahan Seer is an invention based on Mackenzie's conception of the past and as such is consistent with the kilt and Macpherson's Poems of Ossian, both of which are relatively recent inventions which rely on historical precedent, unverifiable connections to antiquity and Romanticism.

Romantic idealism and practical economic improvements were introduced to the Highlands from elsewhere. Some scholars see these as impositions by elite metropolitan ideologies, suggesting that because so much

27 J. Glendening, *The High Road: Romantic Tourism, Scotland and Literature, 1720–1820* (Basingstoke, 1997). T. C. Smout, 'Tours in the Scottish Highlands from the Eighteenth to the Twentieth Centuries.' *Northern Scotland,* Vol. 5. No. 2 (1983), pp. 99–121.

of Gaelic culture was imported its very authenticity is in doubt.[28] One argues that the Highlands represent an imaginary place of escape for the inhabitants of the real world and that the region has been 'condemned to the marginality of fiction.'[29] This writer takes a much more optimistic view, agreeing with those who suggest that people living in the Highlands continue to 'make use of, or appropriate outside forms.' and agreeing that Gaelic culture has survived due to its ability to adapt to ever-changing circumstances.[30] Local writers such as Alexander Mackenzie and his colleagues in the Gaelic Society of Inverness were capable of embracing Romantic conceptions of the Highlands without losing sight of oral traditions and local history and combining these to form a narrative acceptable to local sensibilities. While second sight may have been condemned to the marginality of fiction by Romantic writers in the south, Mackenzie, who considered second sight to be part of his real world, placed it squarely in the forefront of the legend of the Brahan Seer. Second sight continues to be part of the real world, as is evident from the enquiries conducted from the late nineteenth century to the present day.

Historical evidence shows that a Coinneach Odhar was engaged in witchcraft in and around Easter Ross in the century prior to Countess Isabella's encounter with the Brahan Seer. There is no evidence to suggest that an individual existed then who could be described as the Brahan Seer and consequently he could not have uttered his most famous prophecy regarding the fall of the House of Seaforth. However, it is necessary to look beyond historical verifiable truths; because the legend exists the Brahan Seer exists. He is a legendary character, the product of a synthesis of historical events, oral tradition and literary romance. He is now part of

28 H. Trevor-Roper, 'The Invention of Tradition: the Highland Tradition of Scotland' in E. Hobsbawm and T. Ranger (eds), *The Invention of Tradition* (Cambridge, 1983), pp. 15–41. M. Chapman, *The Gaelic Vision in Scottish Culture* (London, 1978), p. 53.

29 P. Womack, *Improvement and Romance: Constructing the Myths of the Highlands* (Basingstoke, 1989), pp. 179–180.

30 Macdonald, *Reimagining Culture*, p. 248. M. Newton, *A Handbook of the Scottish Gaelic World* (Dublin, 2000), p. 38.

Highland tradition; he fits historical circumstances and has been created from fragments of history stretching back to the witchcraft practised at the time of the Fowlis affair and the collective remembrance of the penalties imposed on the convicted. The Brahan Seer is not a person so much as a concept formed through the lived experiences of his local creators and the 'scientific' and literary mediations of visitors.

The Brahan Seer is a personification of a pious and forthright man betrayed and badly treated by his social superiors. His fate parallels the treatment of the crofters who were dispossessed during the clearances. The Highlanders see in him a person who embodies their traditions, who answers questions which they could not answer other than through the narration of his tale or through his prophecies. He has acted as a spokesman for the disenfranchised and he offers a better future than the fatalism – once absent – with which centuries of 'ethnocide' has imbued Gaelic culture.[31] Whereas a seer's pronouncement about future events used to be considered a warning which could be acted upon, fate is now fixed. Contemporary evidence contests this view. The prophecies of the Brahan Seer reveal a response to events which is more than merely observational, carrying moral overtones which are in the tradition of the panegyric code of poets or charismatic religious figures from the region. The prophecies describe unfolding events and the many changes which have taken place in the Highlands. Prophecies are interpreted in the here and now and are modified to suit and to reflect the interpreter's world-view. Contemporary economic improvements in the region around Easter Ross have prompted a celebratory feeling of wellbeing and optimism among many of the residents. That optimism has been translated by the organisers of the Brahan Seer Festival into a self-fulfilling prophecy. The vibrant artistic community living in Easter Ross chose to draw upon a particular aspect of their cultural past for artistic inspiration and moral values. That cultural icon has been created from historical events peculiar to the region, from folklore accounts peculiar to the region, and

31 J. MacInnes, 'The Seer in Gaelic tradition' in H. E. Davidson (ed.), *The Seer* (Edinburgh, 1989), pp. 1–23. p. 23.

from literary romance modified locally to make it culturally acceptable to the people of the region. The Brahan Seer legend is not a story that is verifiable but it is a true story in that it contains values which shape and influence human conduct.

Highland culture is mutable: it is at once responsive to new ideas and new technologies and grounded in shared history, folklore, experience and values. People do not need to subscribe to a belief in the Brahan Seer legend as such; they can discount any or all of the historical, folklore or Romantic constituent parts but believe more generally in any one or all of witchcraft, second sight and prophecy. Over the centuries people have availed themselves of belief in one or other when they have sought a particular outcome for events. People's desire for knowledge of what the future holds has sustained an interest in prophecy and in second sight to the present day, despite the phenomenon having been ridiculed in the Age of Reason. Changes in scientific, and indeed historical, approaches, most noticeably a shift from seeking objective to subjective truths, have ensured that personal experiences are treated as valid topics of intellectual enquiry. Contemporary first hand accounts suggest that people's perception of second sight has undergone changes and that it is now thought to include a wider range of psychic phenomenon than reported in the past. This suggests that Romanticism has triumphed over scepticism for at least some sections of the community and corroborates the argument that 'popular' culture is not antithetical to 'elite' culture but rather in constant (and complex) interaction with it.

Bibliography

Primary sources

Acts of the General Assembly of the Church of Scotland 1690–1713 (Edinburgh, 1843).

Adam, R. J. (ed.), *Calendar of Fearn: Text and Additions, 1471–1667* (Scottish History Society, Edinburgh, 1991).

Addison, J., *The Free-Holder* No. 27 (1716).

Allardyce, A. (ed.), *Scotland and Scotsmen in the Eighteenth Century: From the MSS of John Ramsay, Esq. Of Ochtertyre*. 2 Vols. (Blackwood, Edinburgh, 1888).

Baillie, R., *The Letters and Journals of Robert Baillie 1637–1662* (Ogle, Edinburgh, 1841).

Baker, H., Henry Baker Correspondence English MS 19. Vols. 2–4, John Rylands University Library of Manchester.

Bayne, R. (ed.), *The Life and Letters of Hugh Miller*. 2 Vols. (Strahan, Edinburgh, 1871).

Beattie, J., 'An Essay on Poetry and Music, As They Affect the Mind, Written 1772' in *Essays* (Wm. Creech, Edinburgh, 1776) pp. 347–580.

Blacklock, T., *The Graham: An Heroic Ballad in Four Cantos* (T. Davis, London, 1774).

Blanchard, R. (ed.), *The Correspondence of Richard Steele* (Oxford University Press, Oxford, 1941).

Bloch. G. (trs.), *Mesmerism: A Translation of the Original Scientific and Medical Writings of F. A. Mesmer* (Kaufman, Los Altos, California, 1980).

Blunt, R. (ed.), *Mrs Montague 'Queen of the Blues,' Her Letters and Friendships from 1762 to 1800* (Constable, London, 1923).

Book of Adjournal Series D, DI/66 process D/No. 3. NAS.

Bond, D. F. (ed.), *The Spectator* (Clarendon Press, Oxford, 1965).

——(ed.), *The Tatler* (Clarendon Press, Oxford, 1987).

Boswell, J., *Journal of a Tour to the Hebrides with Samuel Johnson,* R. W. Chapman (ed.) (Oxford University Press, London, 1951).

Brahan Seer Festival Bibliographical Directory of Participants (nd).

Brahan Seer Festival Report. Privately circulated report to organising committee and funding bodies (Dingwall, 2002).

Brewster, D., *Letters on Natural Magic Addressed to Sir Walter Scott, Bart.* (John Murray, London, 1832).

Brodie, A. and J., *The Diaries of the Lairds of Brodie 1652–1685* (Spalding Club, Aberdeen, 1863, reprint of part printed 1740).

Brown, P. Hume (ed.), *Tours in Scotland 1677 and 1681: Thomas Kirk and Ralph Thoresby* (Douglas, Edinburgh, 1892).

Burke, B., *Vicissitudes of Families*. Vol. III. (Longman, Green, Longman and Roberts, London, 1860/1863).

Burns Begg, R., 'Notice of Trials for Witchcraft at Crook of Devon, Kinross-shire, in 1662.' *Proceedings of the Society of Antiquaries of Scotland* Vol. 22 N. S. (1887–88), pp. 211–241.

Burt, E., *Burt's Letters from the North of Scotland* (Birlinn, Edinburgh, 1998 (1754)).

Calendar of Scottish Papers Vol. X. 1589–1593 (H. M. General Register House, Edinburgh, 1936).

Calendar of State Papers Domestic 1655 (H. M. Public Record Office, London, 1881).

Campbell, D., *Secret Memoirs of the Late Mr. Duncan Cambel (sic) the Famous Deaf and Dumb Gentleman. Written by Himself Who Ordered They Should be Publish'd After His Decease* (Attributed to Daniel Defoe) (J. Millan, London, 1732).

Campbell, J. F., *Popular Tales of the West Highlands.* 4 Vols. (Wildwood House, Hounslow, 1983 (1860)).

Carr, J., *Caledonian Sketches; Or a Tour Thro' Scotland in 1807* (Mathew and Leigh, London, 1809).

Chapbooks in Historic Collections, University of Aberdeen, Vols. H1–H21.

'Prophecies of Dr Adam Donald' Vol. H2, 6 (Buchan, Peterhead, nd).

'Prophecies of Allan Logan of Culross' Vol. H8, 2 (Ayr, 1797) and H15, 4 Robertson, Glasgow, 1804).

'Prophecies of Alexander Peden' Vol. H2, 2 (Johnson, Falkirk, 1818). Vol. H4, 3 (Edinburgh, 1799): H8.3 (Edinburgh, 1799): H18, 6 (Stirling, printed in the present year).

'Prophecies of Christopher Love' Vol. H8, 2 (Ayr, 1797) and H15, 4 (Robertson, Glasgow, 1804).

'Prophecies of John Porter of Crossiebeig' Vol. H7, 9 (Robertson, Glasgow, 1799): H15, 2 (Lumsden, Glasgow, 1820).

'Prophecies of Mother Shipton' Vol. 2, 1. (Randall, Stirling, nd).

'Prophecies of Robert Nixon' Vol. H8, 1 (Allison, Penrith, nd): H21, 13 (Johnson, Falkirk, 1814).

'Prophecies of Thomas the Rhymer' Vol. H2, 5 (Fraser, Stirling, early nineteenth century): H7, 10 (Edinburgh, 1821): H8, 4 (Edinburgh, nd): H18, 9 (Robertson, Glasgow, 1806): H21, 12 (Glasgow, copies from 1683 Edinburgh edition): H21, 13 (Johnson, Falkirk, 1814).

Chapman, R. W. (ed.), *Johnson's Journey to the Western Islands of Scotland 1775 and Boswell's Journal of a Tour to the Hebrides with Samuel Johnson, LL.D.* (Oxford University Press, London, 1951 (1924)).

Clarke, E. D., *The Life and Remains of the Rev. Edward Daniel Clarke* (George Cowie, London, 1824).

Cohn, S. A., 'A Questionnaire Study on Second Sight Experiences' in *Journal of the Society for Psychical Research* Vol. 63, No. 855 (1999a) pp. 129–157.

——'Second Sight and Family History: Pedigree and Segregation Analyses' in *Journal of Scientific Exploration.* Vol. 13, No. 3 (1999b) pp. 351–372.

Collins, Wm., 'Ode to a Friend on His Return etc' but subsequently better known as 'An Ode on the Popular Superstitions of the Highlands of Scotland, Considered as the Subject of Poetry.' R. Lonsdale (ed.), *The Poems of Thomas Gray, William Collins, Oliver Goldsmith* (Longman, London, 1969).

Colquhoun, J. C. (trs.), *Report on the Experiments on Animal Magnetism Made by a Committee of the Medical Section of the French Royal Academy of Sciences, 21st and 28th June, 1831* (Robert Cadell, Edinburgh, 1833).

Craigie, J. (ed.), *Daemonologie in Minor Prose Work of King James VI and I* (Scottish Text Society, Edinburgh, 1982).

Cregeen, E. R., 'Oral Tradition and History in a Hebridean Island' *Scottish Studies* No. 32 (1998) pp. 12–37.

Davy, J. (ed.), *Memoirs of the Life of Sir Humphry Davy* 2 Vol.s. (Longman, London, 1836)

Defoe. D., *The British Visions: Or Isaac Bickerstaffe, Senr; Being Twelve Prophecies For the Year 1711* (London, 1711).

Firth, C. H. (ed.), *Scotland and the Commonwealth*: *Letters and Papers Relating to the Military Government of Scotland from August 1651 to December 1653* (Scottish History Society, Edinburgh, 1895).

——*Scotland and the Protectorate: Letters and Papers Relating to the Military Government of Scotland from January 1654 to June 1659* (Scottish History Society, Edinburgh, 1899).

Fleeman, J. D. (ed.), *Samuel Johnson*: *A Journey to the Western Islands of Scotland (1775)* (Clarendon Press, Oxford, 1985).

Forbes, J., *Illustrations of Modern Mesmerism From Personal Investigation* (Churchill, London, 1845).

Fountainhall, Sir John Lauder of, *The Decisions of the Lords of Council and Session from June 6th 1678, to July 30th 1712* (Hamilton and Balfour, Edinburgh, 1759).

——*Fountainhall's Historical Notes*, 2 Vols. (Bannatyne Club, Edinburgh, 1848).

——(ed. D. Crawford) *Journals of Sir John Lauder of Fountainhall* (Scottish History Society, Edinburgh, 1900).

Franck, R., *Northern Memoirs Writ in the Year 1658* (Archibald Constable, Edinburgh, 1821)

Fraser, J., *Chronicles of the Frasers: The Wardlaw Manuscript entitled 'Polichronicon Seu Policratica Temporum' or, 'The True Genealogy of the Frasers,' 916–1674* (Scottish History Society, Edinburgh, 1905).

Fraser, J., *Deuteroscopia: A Brief Discourse Concerning the Second Sight* (Edinburgh, 1707).

Fraser, W., *The Sutherland Book, Vol. II, Correspondence* (Edinburgh, 1892).

Gilpin, Wm., *Observations on the Highlands of Scotland*. Two Vols. (Richmond Publications, Richmond, 1789 (1973)).

Gordon, C. A. (ed.), 'Professor James Garden's Letters to John Aubrey, 1692–5.' *Miscellany of the 3rd Spalding Club*, Vol. 3 (Aberdeen, 1960) pp. 6–56.

Grant, Mrs A. M., writing as 'By the author of "Letters from the Mountains,"' *Essays on the Superstitions of the Highlanders of Scotland*. 2 Vols. (Longman, Hurst, Rees, Orme and Brown, London, 1811).

Grant, J. P. (ed.), *Memoir and Correspondence of Mrs Grant of Laggan*. 3 Vols. (Longman, Brown, Green and Longman, London, 1844).

Gregory, Wm., 'German Popular Prophecies' in *Blackwood's Edinburgh Magazine* No. 415, Vol. 67 (1850) pp. 560–572.

——*Letters to a Candid Enquirer on Animal Magnetism* (Taylor, Walter and Maberly, London, 1851).

Grierson, H. T. C. (ed.), *Letters of Sir Walter Scott*. 12 Vols. (Constable, London, 1933/35).

Hume Brown, P. (ed.), *Tours in Scotland 1677 and 1681: Thomas Kirk and Ralph Thoresby* (Douglas, Edinburgh, 1892).

Hunter, J. (ed.), *For the People's Cause: From the Writings of John Murdoch, Highland and Irish Land Reformer* (HMSO, Edinburgh for the Crofters' Commission, 1986).

Hunter, M., *The Occult Laboratory: Magic, Science and Second Sight in Late 17th-Century Scotland* (The Boydell Press, Woodbridge, 2001).

Insulanus, T. (Donald MacLeod), *A Treatise on the Second Sight, Dreams and Apparitions; With Several Instances Sufficiently Attested* (Ruddiman, Auld, Edinburgh, 1763).

Inverness Burgh Records Vol. VIII, 1574–1576, transcribed 1900. f422, Original f347.

Inverness Courier.

Inverness Journal.

Johnson, S., *A Journey to the Western Isles of Scotland*, J. Fleeman (ed.) (Clarendon Press, Oxford, 1985).

Kinghorn, A. M. and Law, A. (eds), *Poems by Allan Ramsay and Robert Fergusson* (Scottish Academic Press, Edinburgh and London, 1974).

Kirk, R., 'The Secret Commonwealth or a Treatise Displaying the Chief Curiosities Among the People of Scotland as They are in Use to this Day' Transcribed by C. Campbell. Edinburgh University Library, Ms. Laing III, 551.

Kirk, T., *Tours in Scotland 1677 & 1681*, edited by P. Hume-Brown (Douglas, Edinburgh, 1892).

Lady St. Helier, *Memories of Fifty Years* (London, 1909).

Lee. E., *Report Upon the Phenomena of Clairvoyance or Lucid Somnambulism, to the President of the Parisian Medical Society* (Churchill, London, 1843).

Lockhart, J. G., *Life of Scott, Memoirs of Sir Walter Scott* Vol. II. (Macmillan, London, 1914).

Lonsdale, R. (ed.), *The Poems of Thomas Gray, William Collins, Oliver Goldsmith* (Longmans, London and Harlow. 1969).

Macculloch, J., *The Highlands and Western Isles of Scotland ... Founded on a Series of Annual Journeys Between the Years 1811 and 1821* (Longman, Hurst, London, 1824).

——*A Description of the Western Isles of Scotland, Including the Isle of Man*. 3 Vols. (Hurst, Robinson, London, 1819).

Mackay, Wm. (ed.), *Inverness and Dingwall Presbytery Records 1643–1688* (Scottish History Society, Edinburgh, 1896).

——'The Strathglass Witches of 1662,' *TGSI* Vol. IX (1888) pp. 113–121.

Mackenzie, A., 'The Prophecies of the Brahan Seer' in *TGSI* Vols. III and IV (1875) pp. 196–211. Mr Mackenzie's original paper to the society, presented 18 March 1875.

——'The Prophecies of the Brahan Seer, Coinneach Odhar Fiosaiche' serialised in *The Celtic Magazine* Vol. II, 1876 to June, 1877, No. xiii pp. 18–25, No. xiv pp. 54–61, No. xv, pp. 91–97, No. xvi pp. 128–135, No xvii pp. 168–173, No. xviii pp. 220–224, No xix pp. 258–263, no. xx pp. 297–304. Also Vol. III, No. xxv, p38. Nov. 1877.

——*The Prophecies of the Brahan Seer.* With a Foreword, Commentary and Conclusion by Elizabeth Sutherland (Constable, London, 1977 (1877)).

Mackenzie, Sir G., *Pleadings in Some Remarkable Cases Before the Supreme Courts of Scotland since the Year, 1661* (Swintoun, Glen & Brown, Edinburgh, 1673).

——*The Laws and Customs of Scotland in Matters Criminal* (James Glen, Edinburgh, 1678).

Maclennan. A. B., 'Traditions and Legends of the Black Isle No. XII.' *The Highlander* No. 28 (1873).

MacPhail, J. N. R. (ed.), *Highland Papers*, 3 Vols. (Scottish History Society, Edinburgh, 1914–1920).

Macpherson, J., *The Poems of Ossian* edited by H. Gaskill with an introduction by F. Stafford (Edinburgh University Press, Edinburgh, 1996 (1760, 1761, 1763)).

Martin, M., *A Description of the Western Islands of Scotland Circa 1695* (Eneas Mackay, Stirling, 1934 (1703)).

McInnes, C. T. (ed.), *Calendar of Writs of Munro of Fowlis* (Scottish Record Society, Edinburgh, 1940).

Mesmer, F. A. (trs. by G. Bloch.), *Mesmerism; a Translation of the Original Scientific and Medical Writings of F. A. Mesmer* (Kaufman, Los Altos, CA, 1980).

Miller, H., *Scenes and Legends of the North of Scotland* (B and W Publishing, Edinburgh, 1994 (1835)).

Mitchell, A. F. and Christie, J. (eds), *The Records of the Commissions of the General Assembly of the Church of Scotland, 1646–1647*, Vol. II. (Edinburgh, 1892).

Mitchell, A. (ed.), *Inverness Kirk Session Records 1661–1800* (Carruthers, Inverness, 1902).

Montgomery, H. R. (ed.), *Memoirs of the Life and Writings of Sir Richard Steele.* 2 Vols. (Nimmo, Edinburgh, 1865).

Mould, T., 'Prophetic Riddling: A Dialogue of Genres in Choctaw Performance' in *Journal of American Folklore*, Vol. 115 Nos. 457/458 (2002) pp. 395–421.

Mullan, J, and Reid, C. (eds), *Eighteenth-Century Popular Culture: A Selection* (Oxford University Press, Oxford, 2000).

Munro, R. W. (ed.), *The Munro Tree (1734): a Genealogy and Chronology of the Munros of Fowlis* (For the subscribers, Edinburgh, 1978).

Murray, S., *A Companion and Useful Guide to the Beauties of Scotland* (Printed for the author, London, 1799).

Mylne, J., *Poems, Consisting of Miscellaneous Pieces, and Two Tragedies* (W. Creech, Edinburgh, 1790).

Newes from Scotland (1591), reprinted in Pitcairn, R., *Ancient Criminal Trials in Scotland* Vol. I, Part II. (1833) pp. 213–223.

Nicholl, J., *A Diary of Public Transactions and Other Occurrence, Chiefly in Scotland from January 1650 to June 1667* (Bannatyne Club, Edinburgh, 1885).

Pennant, T., *A Tour In Scotland and Voyage to the Hebrides 1772* (Birlinn, Edinburgh, 1998 (1774/6)).

——*A Tour In Scotland 1769* (Birlinn, Edinburgh, 2000 (1771))

Pepys, S., *Correspondence of Samuel Pepys 1679–1700*. Two Vols. J. R. Tanner (ed.) (G. Bell, London, 1926).

Pinkerton, J., *The Literary Correspondence of John Pinkerton Esq* (Henry Colburn and Richard Bentley, London, 1830).

Pitcairn, R. (ed.), *Ancient Criminal Trials in Scotland* Vol. I, Part II and Vol. III. (The Maitland Club, Edinburgh, 1833).

Pottle, F. A. and Bennett, C. H. (eds), *Boswell's Journal of a Tour to the Hebrides with Samuel Johnson. LL.D.* (Heinemann, London 1936).

Records of Inverness Vol. I. Burgh Court Books 1556–86 (New Spalding Club, Aberdeen, 1911).

Redford, B. (ed.), *The Letters of Samuel Johnson*. Five Vols. (Clarendon Press, Oxford, 1992).

Register of the Great Seal of Scotland 1660–1668 Vol. II. (H. M. General Register House, Edinburgh, 1914).

Register of the Privy Council of Scotland Second series Vol. III, 1629, and Third Series Vols. I to VI. 1661–1680. (H. M. General Register House, Edinburgh, 1908–1914).

Register of the Privy Council of Scotland Vol. I. 1545–1569; Vols. IV and V, 1585–1599; Vols. X and XI, 1613–1616. (H. M. General Register House, Edinburgh, 1877, 1881, 1882, 1891 and 1894).

Rust, J., *Scottish Showers: The Scottish Black Rain Showers and Pumicestone Shoals of the Year 1862 and 1863* (W. Blackwood, Edinburgh, 1864).

School of Scottish Studies, Edinburgh: reel-to reel-tapes cited with reference to the Brahan Seer legend and prophecies. The first two digits refer to the year recorded.

SA55.78.A8; Anonymous man, Armadale, Skye
SA57.33.1: Jimmy Stewart, Dalmore, Inverness-shire
SA57. 75/76. 1; Mrs Christina Mackinnon, North Uist
SA63.21.A1; Peter Stewart, Barvas, Lewis
SA64.65.B4; Michael Mackintyre, Gerenish, South Uist
SA64.79.A1; Nan Mackinnon, Vatersay, Inverness-shire
SA68.231.A1; Joseph Macdonald, North Uist
SA71.158.B3; Donald Alisdair Johnson, South Uist
SA53.37.A4; Roderick Bowie
SA63.21.A2; Allan Walker, Killin, Perthshire
SA58.85.A6; Mrs P. MacDonald, South Uist.

Scott, J., *The Staggering State of the Scottish Statesmen from 1550–1650* MS. (Ruddiman, Edinburgh, 1754).

Scott, W., *Highland Widow: Chronicles of the Canongate*. Waverley Novels Vol. 41. (Constable, Edinburgh, 1903 (1834)).

——*Lady of the Lake* (Service and Paton, London, 1891 (1810)).

——*Redgauntlet*. Waverley Novels Vol. 35 (Constable, Edinburgh, 1902 (1824)).

——*Two Drovers: Chronicles of the Canongate* (Kindle Press, New Jersey, 1971 (1827)).

——*The Black Dwarf* Edinburgh edition of the Waverley Novels, Vol. 4. Edited by P. D. Garside (Edinburgh University Press, Edinburgh, 1993 (1816)).

——*The Bride of Lammermoor*. Edinburgh edition of the Waverley Novels, Vol. 7. (Edinburgh University Press, Edinburgh, 1995 (1819)).

——*Letters on Demonology and Witchcraft* (William Tegg, London., 1868).

Scott-Moncrieff, W. G. (ed.), *The Records of the Proceedings of the Justiciary Court, 1661–1678.* Vols. I. and II (Scottish History Society, Edinburgh, 1905).

Sharp, L. W. (ed.), *Early Letters of Robert Wodrow 1698–1709* (Scottish History Society, Edinburgh, 1937).

Tanner, J. R. (ed), *Correspondence of Samuel Pepys 1679–1700* (G. Bell, London, 1926).

Taylor, L. B. (ed.), *Aberdeen Council Letters: 1552–1681* 6 Vols. (Oxford University Press, London, 1942–61).

The Acts of the Parliament of Scotland Vol. VI Part II. 1648–1660. Vol. II 1424–1567; Vol. IV. 1593–1623; Vol. VI p. I 1643–1647; Vol. VI Part II. 1648–1660; Vol. VII. 1661–1669; Vol. VIII. 1670–1686 (for Lords Commissioners of H. M. Treasury, 1872)

The Bannatyne Ms., The Dunvegan Castle Muniments, National Archives of Scotland. Ref: 2950/691, s5.57, 1–3.

The Celtic Magazine 1876–1877.

The Dunvegan Castle Muniments NAS Ref. 2950/683/24.909.4.

The Exchequer Rolls of Scotland (1899) Vol. XX. 1569–1579 NAS.

The Free-Holder 1716.

The Glasgow Herald.

The Guardian ed. J. C. Stephens (The University Press of Kentucky, 1982).

The Highlander.

The Lounger: A Periodical Paper Published at Edinburgh in the Years 1785 and 1786. Three Vols.

The Records of the Commissioners of the General Assembly of the Church of Scotland, 1646–1647 (Mitchell. F. and Christie, J. (eds). (Scottish History Society, Edinburgh, 1892)).

The Seaforth Muniments. National Archives of Scotland. Ref: GD46/15.

The Seaforth Papers. National Archives of Scotland. Ref. F415.080.

The Seaforth Papers. National Library of Scotland. Ms. 6396.

The Seaforth Papers. National Library of Scotland. Ms. 6400.

Thomas, L-A., unpublished and untitled manuscript on personal second sight experiences (nd).

Thomas, P. (ed.), *Mercurius Politicus: The English Revolution III Newsletters During the Civil War*. Vols. 5 and 6. (Cornmarket Press, London, reprint 1971).

Timony, M., *Red Brian Carabine's Prophecy and Other Interesting Historical Matter* (M. H. Gill, Dublin, 1906).

Tod, A. (ed.), *Elizabeth Grant of Rothiemurchus: Memoirs of a Highland Lady* (Canongate Classics, Edinburgh, 1988 (1898)).

Toland, J., 'Toland's Marginalia' in Martin's *Description of the Western Islands of Scotland* British Library, ref: c. 45.c.1.

Warrants for the Arrest of Witches, October, 1577 and January, 1578 NAS Ref: E/7 fol. 76(v)–68(r) and NAS Ref: GD 93/92.

Wesley, J., *The Works of the Rev. John Wesley*. 17 Vols. (John Jones, London, 1809–1813).

West Highland Free Press.

Whitelock, B., *Memorials of the English Affairs* (Bulstrode Whitelock, Oxford, 1853 (1732)).

Whytt, R., 'An Account of the Earthquake felt at Glasgow and Dumbarton: Also of a Shower of Dust falling on a Ship Between Shetland and Iceland; in a Letter From Dr Robert Whytt, Professor of Medicine at The University of Edinburgh, to John Pringle, M.D. F.R.S. Edinburgh, February 10, 1756.' *Philosophical Transactions of the Royal Society* Vol. XLIX Part II (1755) pp. 509–511.

Wodrow, R., *Analecta: or Materials for a History of Remarkable Providences; Mostly Relating to Scotch Ministers and Christians*. Four Vols. (Maitland Club, Glasgow, 1842–1843).

——*Early Letters of Robert Wodrow 1698–1703*. Ed. L. W. Sharp (Scottish Historical Society, Edinburgh, 1937).

Wood, A., *What is Mesmerism: An Attempt to Explain its Phenomena* (Sutherland and Knox, Edinburgh, 1851).

Wood, J. Maxwell, *Witchcraft and Superstitious Records in South East District of Scotland* (EP Publishing, Wakefield, 1975).

Wood, W., *Ms Essays and Papers of Wendy Wood*. NLS, Acc. 8197, Files 10–14.

Secondary sources

Abercrombie, J., *Inquiries Concerning the Intellectual Powers and the Investigation of Truth* (John Murray, London, 1846).

Aitken. G. A. (ed.), *The History of the Life and Adventures of Mr Duncan Campbell*, Vol. IV of Romances and Narratives by Daniel Defoe (Dent, London, 1895).

Alston, D., 'The Fallen Meteor: Hugh Miller and Local Tradition' in *Hugh Miller and the Controversies of Victorian Science* edited by Michael Shortland (Clarendon Press, Oxford, 1996) pp. 206–209.

Anon., 'Coinneach Odhar: The Great Island Seer and Prophet,' *The Clan MacLeod Magazine* (1947) pp. 411–413.

Anon, 'Second Sight,' *Tocher* No. 6 (1972) pp. 192–200.

Armstrong, R. A., *A Gaelic Dictionary in Two Parts* (Duncan, London, 1825).

Aubrey, J., *Miscellanies upon Various Subjects* (London, 1784 (1696))

Bain, R., *History of the Ancient Province of Ross* (Pefferside Press, Dingwall, 1899).

Baine, R. M., *Daniel Defoe and the Supernatural* (University of Georgia Press, Athens, 1968).

Baker, H., *Employment for the Microscope* (Dodsley, London, 1753).

——*The Microscope Made Easy, etc.* (Dodsley, London, 1743).

Barron, J., *The Northern Highlands in the Nineteenth Century: Newspaper Index and Annals* 3 Vols. (R. Carruthers, Inverness, 1903–1913).

Barry, J., Hester, M. and Roberts, G. (eds), *Witchcraft in Early Modern Europe* (Cambridge University Press, Cambridge, 1996).

Bascom, W., 'The Forms of Folklore: Prose Narratives,' in *Journal of American Folklore* No. 78 (1965) pp. 3–20.

Bauman, R. (ed.), *Folklore, Cultural Performances and Popular Entertainments* (Oxford University Press, New York and London, 1992).

Baxendale, J and Pawling, C., *Narrating the Thirties: A Decade in the Making, 1930 to the Present* (Macmillan, Basingstoke, 1996)

Beaumont, J., *An Historical, Physiological and Theological Treatise on Spirits, Apparitions, Witchcrafts, and Other Magical Practices...With a refutation of Dr Becker's World bewitch'd etc* (London, 1705).

Ben-Amos, D., 'Folktale' in *Folklore, Cultural Performances and Popular Entertainments* edited by R. Bauman (Oxford University Press, New York and London, 1992) pp. 101–118.

——(ed.), *Folklore Genres* (University of Texas Press, Austin and London, 1976).

Bennett, J. H., *The Mesmeric Mania of 1851* (Sutherland and Knox, Edinburgh, 1851).

Bennett, M., 'Second Sight and Seers in the New World,' a paper presented at the seminar on second sight at Tulloch Castle, Dingwall, 15 September 2001, during the BSF.

Black, G. F., *A Calendar of Cases of Witchcraft in Scotland 1510–1727* (The New York Public Library, New York, 1938).

Black, R., 'A Century of Coded Messages' in *West Highland Free Press* (13 February 1998) p. 19.

——'How Did Thomas Become the Messiah?' in *West Highland Free Press* (30 January 1998) p. 21.

——'The Messiah of the Gael' in *West Highland Free Press* (16 January 1998) p. 19.

——(ed.), *An Lasair: An Anthology of 18th Century Scottish Verse* (Birlinn, Edinburgh, 2001).

Blair, D. B., *Coinneach Odhar am Foisaiche*. Abridged extracts from Alexander Mackenzie's *Prophecies of the Brahan Seer* serialised in *Mac-Talla*, an all-Gaelic weekly newspaper published in Cape Breton (Sydney, Cape Breton, 1900).

Blanchard, R., 'Richard Steele and The Secretary of The SPCK' in C. Camden (ed.), *Restoration and Eighteenth Century Literature* (University of Chicago Press, Chicago, 1963) pp. 287–295.

Brahan Seer Celebratory Booklet (Brahan Seer Festival, Dingwall, 2001).

Brannan, R. L., *Under the Management of Mr Charles Dickens: His Production of 'The Frozen Deep'* (Cornell University Press, Ithaca, 1966).

Breuilly, J., 'The National Idea in Modern German History,' in J. Breuilly (ed.), *The State of Germany: The National Idea in the Making, Unmaking and Remaking of a Modern Nation-state* (Longman, London and New York, 1992) pp. 1–28.

Briggs, R., 'Many Reasons Why: Witchcraft and the Problem of Multiple Explanation' in J. Barry, M. Hester and G. Roberts (eds), *Witchcraft in Early Modern Europe* (Cambridge University Press, Cambridge, 1996).

Broadie, A., *The Scottish Enlightenment* (Birlinn, Edinburgh, 2001).

Brotherstone, T. and Ditchburn, D. (eds), *Freedom and Authority: Scotland c1050 – c1650* (Tuckwell Press, East Lothian, 2000).

Bruford, A., *Scottish Oral History Group Newsletter* No. 2 (October, 1979).

Burke, P., *Varieties of Cultural History* (Polity Press, Cambridge, 1997).

——*Popular Culture in Early Modern Europe* (Temple Smith, London, 1978).

Busst. A. J. L., 'Scottish Second Sight: The Rise and Fall of a European Myth,' in *European Romantic Review* Vol. 5, part 2 (1995) pp. 149–177.

Campbell, J. G., *Superstitions of the Highlands and Islands of Scotland* (James Maclehose, Glasgow, 1900).

Campbell, J. L. (ed.), *A Collection of Highland Rites and Customes: Copied by Edward Lhuyd From The Manuscript of The Rev James Kirkwood (1650–1709) and Annotated by Him With the Aid of The Rev John Beaton* (D. S. Brewer, Cambridge, for the Folklore Society, 1975).

——and Hall, T. H., *Strange Things* (Routledge and Keegan, Paul, London, 1968).

Carr, Wm., 'The Unification of Germany,' in Breuilly (ed.), *The State of Germany: The National Idea in the Making, Unmaking and Remaking of a Modern Nation-state* (Longman, London and New York, 1992) pp. 80–102.

Carruthers, R., *The Highland Note-Book or Sketches and Anecdotes* (Black, Edinburgh, 1843).

——'Review of "The Seaforth Papers; Letters from 1796 to 1843"' in *The North British Review* Vol. 39 (Aug–November, 1863) pp. 318–356.

——(ed.), *A Biographical Dictionary of Eminent Scotsmen* (Blackie, Edinburgh, 1860).

Chambers, R., *Domestic Annals of Scotland* 3 Vols. (W. & R. Chambers, Edinburgh, 1858/1861).

——*Popular Rhymes of Scotland* (Chambers, Edinburgh, 1890 (1826)).

Chapman, M., *The Gaelic Vision in Scottish Culture* (Croom Helm, London, 1978).

Chartier, R., *The Cultural Uses of Print in Early Modern France,* Trs. by L. G. Cochrane (Princeton University Press, Princeton, 1987).

Cheape, H., *Tartan: The Highland Habit* (National Museums of Scotland, Edinburgh, 1991).

Clark, S., 'King James's Daemonologie: Witchcraft and Kingship' in *The Damned Art,* ed. S. Anglo (Routledge, London, 1977).

Cohn, S. A., 'A Historical Review of Second Sight: The Collectors, Their Accounts and Ideas' in *Scottish Studies* Vol. 33 (1999) pp. 146–185.

——'A Survey on Scottish Second Sight' in *Journal of the Society for Psychical Research* Vol. 59, No. 836 (1994) pp. 385–400.

——'The Theory and History of Inherited Second Sight,' a paper presented at the seminar on second sight at Tulloch Castle, Dingwall, 15 September 2001, during the BSF.

Collins English Dictionary (London, 1995)

Corson, J. C., *Notes and Index to Sir Herbert Grierson's Edition of the Letters of Sir Walter Scott* (Clarendon Press, Oxford, 1979).

Cowan, E. J. (ed.), *The People's Past: Scottish Folk, Scottish History* (Polygon, Edinburgh, 1991).

——(ed.), *The Ballad in Scottish History* (Tuckwell Press, East Linton, 2000).

——'The Covenanting Tradition in Scottish History,' in E. J. Cowan & R. J. Finlay (eds), *Scottish History: The Power of the Past* (Edinburgh University Press, Edinburgh, 2002) pp. 121–145.

——& Finlay, R. J. (eds), *Scottish History: The Power of the Past* (Edinburgh University Press, Edinburgh, 2002).

——& Henderson, L., 'The Last of the Witches? The Survival of Scottish Witch Belief,' in J. Goodare (ed.), *The Scottish Witch-hunt in Context* (Manchester University Press, Manchester, 2002) pp. 198–217.

Curry, P., *Prophecy and Power: Astrology in Early Modern England* (Polity Press, Cambridge, 1989).

Daiches, D., Jones, P. and Jones, J. (eds), *A Hotbed of Genius: The Scottish Enlightenment 1730–1790* (Saltire Society, Edinburgh, 1986).

Dalyell, J. G., *The Darker Superstitions of Scotland Founded on a Series of Annual Journeys* (Waugh and Innes, Edinburgh, 1834).

Daniel, S. H., *John Toland, His Methods, Manners, and Mind* (McGill-Queen's University Press, Kingston and Montreal, 1984).

Davison, J., *Discourses on Prophecy: In Which are Considered Its Structure, Use and Inspiration* (James Parker, Oxford and London, 1870).

De Certeau, M. (trs. by S. F. Rendal), *The Practice of Everyday Life* (Berkeley, Los Angeles, London, 1984)

Dégh, L. and Vázsonyi, A., 'Legend and Belief,' in *Folklore Genres* edited by D. Ben-Amos (University of Texas Press, Austin and London, 1976) pp. 93–123.

Dempster, Miss, 'Folk-Lore of Sutherlandshire' in *The Folk-Lore Journal*, Vol. 6. (1888) pp. 149–189.

Donaldson, M. F. M., *Wanderings in the Western Highlands and Islands* (Gardner, Paisley, 1920).

Dow, F. D., *Cromwellian Scotland* (John Donald, Edinburgh, 1979)

Duffin, C., 'Fixing Tradition: Making History from Ballad Texts,' in E. J. Cowan (ed.), *The Ballad in Scottish History* (Tuckwell Press, East Linton, 2000), pp. 19–35.

Dunbar. J. T., *History of Highland Dress: A Definitive Study of the History of Scottish Costume and Tartan,* with an Appendix on Early Scottish Dyes by Annette Kok (B. T. Batsford, London, 1979 (1962)).

Dunn, C. W., *Highland Settler: A Portrait of the Scottish Gael in Cape Breton and Eastern Nova Scotia* (Breton Books, Cape Breton Island, 1991)

Dwelly's Illustrated Gaelic to English Dictionary (Gairm, Glasgow, 1994).

Dyche, T. and Pardon, W. (eds), *A New General Dictionary* 10th edition (Ware, London, 1760).

Ewan, E. and Meikle, M. M. (eds), *Women in Scotland c.1100–c.1750* (Tuckwell Press, East Linton, 1999).

Farquharson, A., 'Highlanders at Home and Abroad,' TGSI Vol. III (1873/4) pp. 9–25. p. 9.

Fielding, P., *Writing and Orality: Nationality, Culture, and Nineteenth-Century Scottish Fiction* (Clarendon Press, Oxford, 1996).

Finnegan, R., *Oral Tradition and the Verbal Arts* (Routledge, London and New York, 1992).

Forbes, J., *Mesmerism True – Mesmerism False: A Critical Examination of the Facts, Claims and Pretensions of Animal Magnetism* (Churchill, London, 1845).

Gaelic Chapbooks in NLS Collections. Six texts of ballad/songs at Shelfmark L. C. 2879, and one text of ballad/song at shelfmark Hall. 133. h.3 (Printed for Peter Turner, Inverary).

Geneva, A., *Astrology and the Seventeenth Century Mind: William Lilly and the Language of the Stars* (Manchester University Press, Manchester, 1995).

Gillies, Wm. (ed.), *Gaelic and Scotland: Alba agus a'Ghàidhlig* (Edinburgh University Press, Edinburgh, 1989)

Glendening, J., *The High Road: Romantic Tourism, Scotland, and Literature, 1720–1820* (Macmillan, Basingstoke, 1997).

Goodare, J., 'The Aberdeen Witchcraft Panic of 1597' *Northern Scotland, the Journal for the Centre of Scottish Studies* Vol. 21 (2001) pp. 17–37.

——(ed.), *The Scottish Witch-hunt in Context* (Manchester University Press, Manchester, 2002).

——'Women and the Witch-hunt in Scotland' *Social History* Vol. 23. No. 3 (1998) pp. 288–308.

Goodrich-Freer, A., 'Second Sight in the Highlands' in TGSI Vol. 21 (1896) pp. 105–115.

Goody, J., *The Power of the Written Tradition* (Smithsonian Institution Press, Washington and London, 2000).

Gregory, A., 'Witchcraft and "Good Neighbourhood" in Early Seventeenth-Century Rye,' *Past and Present* No. 133 (1991) pp. 31–66.

Harvey, W., *Scottish Chapbook Literature* (Alexander Gardner, Paisley, 1903).

Hemingway, A., *Landscape Imagery and Urban Culture in Early Nineteenth-Century Britain* (Cambridge University Press, Cambridge, 1992).

Henderson, L., 'The Road to Elfland: Fairy Belief and the Child Ballads,' in E. J. Cowan (ed.), *The Ballad in Scottish History* (Tuckwell Press, East Linton, 2000), pp. 54–69.

——& Cowan, E., *Scottish Fairy Belief: A History* (Tuckwell Press, East Linton, 2001).

Hewitt, D. S., 'The Survey of the Letters of Sir Walter Scott' *Scottish Literary Journal: A Review of Studies in Scottish Language and Literature* Vol. 7, No. 1 (1980) pp. 7–18.

Hibbert, S., *Sketches of the Philosophy of Apparitions* (Oliver and Boyd, Edinburgh, 1825).

Hill. G. B. and Powell, L. F. (eds), *Boswell's Life of Johnson* Six Vols. (Clarendon Press, Oxford, 1934–1950).

Hobsbawm, E. and Ranger, T. (eds), *The Invention of Tradition* (Cambridge University Press, Cambridge, 1983).

Hogg, J., *The Three Perils of Man: War, Women and Witchcraft*, ed. D. Gifford (Edinburgh, 1996).

Hollinshead, R., *Scottish Chronicles, A Complete History and Description of Scotland* (Arbroath, 1805).

Howie, J., *The Scots Worthies, Containing a Brief Historical Account of the Most Eminent Noblemen, Gentlemen, Ministers, and Others Who Testified or Suffered for the Cause of Reformation in Scotland, from the Beginning of the Sixteenth Century, to the Year 1688* (W. R. McPhun, Glasgow, 1775 (1845)).

Hunter, M., *Robert Boyle (1627–91): Scrupulosity and Science* (The Boydell Press, Woodbridge, 2002).

Innes, C., *The Brahan Seer Trail* (Ross-Shire Journal, Dingwall, 2003 (1997)).

Jordanova, L., *History in Practice* (Arnold, London, 2000)

Journal of the Society for Psychical Research Vol. 63, No. 855 (1999).

Langewiesche, D., 'Germany and the National Question in 1848,' in J. Breuilly (ed.), *The State of Germany: The National Idea in the Making, Unmaking and Remaking of a Modern Nation-state* (Longman, London and New York, 1992) pp. 60–79.

Larner, C., *A Source Book of Scottish Witchcraft* (Department of Sociology, University of Glasgow, Glasgow, 1977).

——*Enemies of God* (Chatto and Windus, London, 1981).
——*Witchcraft and Religion* (Basil Blackwell, Oxford, 1984).
——'Witch Beliefs & Witch Hunting in England & Scotland.' *History Today* Vol. 31 (1981) pp. 32–36.
Lee. E., *Animal Magnetism* (Churchill, London, 1843).
Levack, B. P., 'The Great Scottish Witch Hunt of 1661–1662' *The Journal of British Studies* Vol. XX. (1980) pp. 90–108.
——'State-Building and Witch Hunting in Early Modern Europe' in J. Barry, M. Hester and G. Roberts (eds), *Witchcraft in Early Modern Europe* (Cambridge University Press, Cambridge, 1996) pp. 96–115.
MacCrow, B. G., *Kintail Scrapbook* (Oliver and Boyd, Edinburgh, 1948).
MacDonald, M., 'Were there TWO Brahan Seers?' *The Scots Magazine* (October, 1969) pp. 34–38.
Macdonald, S., *Reimagining Culture: Histories, Identities and the Gaelic Renaissance* (Berg, Oxford and New York, 1997).
MacDowall, C. G., *The Chanonry of Ross: An Account of Fortrose and Rosemarkie and the Cathedral Kirk of Ross* (Inverness, 1963).
MacEchern, D., 'Highland Second Sight' TGSI Vol. 29 (1919) pp. 290–314.
Macgregor, A. A., *Over the Sea to Skye* (W. and R. Chambers, London, 1926).
——*The Peat-Fire Flame: Folk-tales and Traditions of the Highlands and Islands* (Moray Press, Edinburgh, 1937).
MacInnes, J., 'Religion in Gaelic Society' in TGSI No 52 (1982) pp. 222–242.
——'The Seer in Gaelic Tradition' in H. E. Davidson's *The Seer in Celtic and Other Traditions* (John Donald, Edinburgh, 1989) pp. 10–24.
——'The Panegyric Code in Gaelic Poetry and its Historical Background' in TGSI Vol. 50 (1978) pp. 435–498.
——'The Gaelic Perceptions of the Lowlands' in William Gillies' (ed.) *Gaelic and Scotland: Alba agus a'Ghàidhlig* (Edinburgh University Press, Edinburgh, 1989) pp. 89–100.

Mackenzie, A., *History of the Mackenzies, with Genealogies of the Principal Families of the Name* (A. and W. Mackenzie, Inverness, 1894).

——*History of the Munros of Fowlis* (A. and W. Mackenzie, Inverness, 1898).

Mackenzie, D., 'The Brahan Seer' in L. Spence (ed.), *An Encyclopaedia of Occultism: A Compendium of Information on the Occult Sciences, Occult Personalities, Psychic Science, Magic, Demonology, Spiritism and Mysticism* (Routledge, London, 1920).

Mackenzie, H., *The Lounger, a Periodical Paper Published in Edinburgh* Vol. III (1786).

——*The Works of Henry Mackenzie*. 8 Vols (Constable, Edinburgh, 1808).

Mackenzie, J., *Sar-Obair Nam Bard Gaelach: The Beauties of Gaelic Poetry and Lives of the Highland Bards* (Norman Macleod, Edinburgh, 1904 (1841)).

Mackenzie, O., *A Hundred Years in The Highlands* (Geoffrey Bles, London, 1949 (1921)).

Mackenzie, W. M., 'The Truth about the "Brahan Seer"', *The Glasgow Herald* (25 January 1936).

Maclennan, A. B., *The Petty Seer* (Highland News, Inverness, 1894).

MacLeod of MacLeod, R. C., *The MacLeods of Dunvegan: From the Time of Leod to the End of the Seventeenth Century* (Privately printed for the Clan MacLeod Society, 1927).

——*The Island Clans During Six Centuries* (Robert Carruthers, Edinburgh, 1930).

——*The Macleods: Their History and Traditions* (Privately printed for the Clan MacLeod Society, 192-?)

MacLeod, D., *Memoir of Norman Macleod, D. D.*, 2 Vols. (Daldy, Ilbister, London, 1876)

Macrae, N., *The Romance of a Royal Burgh: Dingwall's Story of a Thousand Years* (EP Publishing, Wakefield, 1974 (1923)).

Maidment J. (ed.), 'Representation by Sherif-Depute of Ross to the Commissioners of the Privy Council Anent the Witches of Kilernan,' in *Reliquie Scoticae: Scottish Remains in Prose and Verse* (T. G. Stevenson, Edinburgh, 1828) pp. 1–4.

——*Analecta Scotica* Two Vols. (T. G. Stevenson, Edinburgh, 1834).
——(ed.), *The Spottiswoode Miscellany* (Spottiswoode Society, Edinburgh, 1845).
Marshall, R. K., *Women in Scotland 1660–1780* (The Trustees of the National Galleries of Scotland, Edinburgh, 1979).
——*Virgins and Viragos, a History of Women in Scotland from 1080 to 1980* (Collins, London., 1983).
Marwick, J. D., *List of Markets and Fairs Now and Formerly Held in Scotland* (The Royal Commissioners of Market Rights and Tolls, Glasgow, 1890)
Matheson, Wm., 'The Historical Coinneach Odhar and Some Prophecies Attributed to Him.' TGSI Vol. 46 (1968) pp. 66–88.
Maxwell-Stuart, P. G., 'The Fear of the King is Death: James VI and the Witches of East Lothian,' in *Fear in Early Modern Society*, W. G. Naphy and P. Roberts (eds) (Manchester University Press, Manchester and New York, 1997).
——*Satan's Conspiracy: Magic and Witchcraft in Sixteenth-Century Scotland* (Tuckwell Press, East Lothian, 2001).
——'Witchcraft and the Kirk in Aberdeenshire, 1596–97,' *Northern Scotland, the Journal for the Centre of Scottish Studies* Vol. 18 (1998) pp. 1–14.
——*Witchcraft in Europe and the New World 1400–1800* (Palgrave, Basingstoke, 2001).
McArthur, C., 'Culloden: A Pre-emtive Strike,' *Scottish Affairs* No. 9 (1994) pp. 97–126.
[McCrie, T.], *A Vindication of the Scottish Covenanters: Consisting of A Review of the First Series of the 'Tales of My Landlord,' Extracted from the Christian Instructor for 1817* (Glasgow, 1824), pp. 4, 33–34.
McGuinness, P., Harrison, A. and Kearney, R. (eds), *John Toland's Christianity not Mysterious: Texts, Associated Works and Critical Essays* (The Lilliput Press, Dublin, 1997 (1696)).
McKean, T. A., *Hebridean Song-Maker: Iain Macneacail of the Isle of Skye* (Polygon, Edinburgh, 1997).
McKerracher, A. C., 'The Lady of Lawers,' *The Scots Magazine* Vol. 117, No. 3 (1982) pp. 253–260.

McLachlan, H. V. and Swales, J. K., 'Stereotypes and Scottish Witchcraft,' *Contemporary Review* Vol. 234. part 1357 (1979) pp. 88–94.

Meek, D. E. (ed.), *Tuath is Tighearna: An Anthology of Gaelic Poetry of Social and Political Protest from the Clearances to the Land Agitation (1800–1890)* (Scottish Academic Press for Scottish Gaelic Texts Society, Edinburgh, 1995).

Milne, D., 'Notices of Earthquake-Shocks Felt in Great Britain, and Especially in Scotland, with Inferences Suggested by These Notices as to the Causes of Such Shocks,' *Edinburgh New Philosophical Journal* Vol. 31 (1841) pp. 92–122.

Morrison, Wm. and Macrae, N., *Highland Second Sight* (George Souter, Dingwall, 1908).

Murdoch, J., 'The Clan System' TGSI Vol. I (1871) pp. 31–43.

Murray, J. A. H., *The Romance and Prophecies of Thomas of Erceldoune* (Early English text Society, London, 1875).

Nabakov, P. (ed.), *Native American Testimony* (Penguin, New York, 1991).

Napier, M., *Memorials and Letters Illustrative of the Life and Times of John Graham of Claverhouse, Viscount Dundee*, 3 Vols. (Edinburgh, 1862).

Newton, M., *A Handbook of the Scottish Gaelic World* (Four Courts Press, Dublin, 2000).

Nicolson, A., *Gaelic Proverbs* (Maclachlan and Stewart, Edinburgh, 1881).

Nicolson, A., *A History of Skye: A Record of the Families, the Social Conditions, and the Literature of the Island* (Maclaren, Glasgow, 1930).

Normand, L. and Roberts, G. (eds), *Witchcraft in Early Modern Scotland: James VI's Demonology and the North Berwick Witches* (University of Exeter Press, Exeter, 2000).

Parsons, C. O., *Witchcraft and Demonology in Scott's Fiction* (Oliver and Boyd, Edinburgh and London, 1964).

Paul, J. B. (ed.), *The Scots Peerage: A History of the Noble Families of Scotland* 9 Vols. (Douglas, Edinburgh, 1904–1914)

Pierce, C. E., *The Religious Life of Samuel Johnson* (The Athlone Press, London, 1983).

Pinches, R. (ed.), *Burke's Family Index* (Burke's Peerage, London, 1976).

Prebble, J., *The King's Jaunt: George IV in Scotland, August 1822 'One and Twenty Daft Days'* (Birlinn, Edinburgh, 2000 (1988))

Reid, R. W., *Illustrated Catalogue of the Anthropological Museum, Marischal College, University of Aberdeen* (Aberdeen University Press, Aberdeen 1912).

Ross, A., *The Folklore of the Scottish Highlands* (B. T. Batsford, London, 1976).

Ross, A. M., *History of the Clan Ross* (A. M. Ross for Subscribers, Dingwall, 1932).

Ross, J. R., *The Great Clan Ross* (John Deyell Ltd, Canada, 1968).

Russell, B., *A History of Western Philosophy* (Unwin, London, 1988).

Sanderson, S., *The Secret Commonwealth & a Short Treatise of Charms and Spels by Robert Kirk* (D. S. Brewer, Cambridge, for the Folklore Society, 1976).

Scott, H. (ed.), *Fasti Ecclesiae Scoticanae; The Succession of Ministers in the Parish Churches of Scotland* (William Paterson, Edinburgh, 1870).

Scribner, B., 'Is a History of Popular Culture Possible?' *History of European Ideas* Vol. 10 (2) (1989) pp. 175–191.

Sharpe, C. K., *A Historical Account of the Belief in Witchcraft in Scotland* (Hamilton, Adand, London, 1884).

Simpson, J., '"The Weird Sisters Wandering": Burlesque Witchery in Montgomerie's *Flyting*,' in *Folklore* 106 (1995) pp. 9 –20.

Sinclair, J., *The Statistical Account of Scotland 1791–1799: Inverness-shire, Ross and Cromarty* Vol. XVIII (EP Publishing, Wakefield, 1981 (1791–1799)).

Smith, A., *A Summer in Skye* (Nimmo, Hay and Mitchell, Edinburgh, 1912 (1866)).

Smout, C., 'Tours in the Scottish Highlands From the Eighteenth to the Twentieth Centuries,' *Northern Scotland*, Vol. 5 No. 2 (1983) pp. 99–121.

Stafford, F., *The Sublime Savage; a Study of James Macpherson and the Poems of Ossian* (Edinburgh University Press, Edinburgh, 1988).
Stainton, M. W. writing as 'M. A. (Oxon.),' *Second Sight: Problems Connected with Prophetic Vision, and Records Illustrative of the Gift, Especially Derived From an Old Work Not Now Available for General Use* (1889).
Stevenson, D. *The Origins of Freemasonry: Scotland's Century, 1590–1710* (Cambridge University Press, Cambridge and New York, 1988).
Stiùbhart, D. U., 'Women and Gender in Early Modern Western Gàidhealtachd' in E. Ewan and M. Meikle (eds), *Women in Scotland c1100–1750* (Tuckwell Press, East Linton, 1999).
Sutherland, E., *Ravens and Black Rain: The Story of Highland Second Sight* (Corgi, London, 1985).
——'Second Sight and Some Seers' in *The Brahan Seer Celebratory Booklet* (Dingwall, 2001).
Swire, O. F., *The Highlands and Their Legends* (Oliver and Boyd, Edinburgh and London, 1963).
——*Skye, the Island and its Legends* (Blackie, Glasgow, 1961).
——*The Outer Hebrides and their Legends* (Oliver and Boyd, Edinburgh and London, 1966).
Thomas, K., *Religion and the Decline of Magic* (Penguin, London, 1973).
Thompson, P., *The Voice of the Past: Oral History* (Oxford University Press, Oxford, 1978).
Thomson, D. S., 'The Gaelic Oral Tradition,' *The Proceedings of the Scottish Anthropological and Folklore Society* Vol. V, No. 1 (1954) pp. 1–17.
Thorndike, L., *Michael Scot* (Nelson, London and Edinburgh, 1965).
Trevor-Roper, H., 'The Invention of Tradition: the Highland Tradition of Scotland,' in E. Hobsbawm and T. Ranger (eds), *The Invention of Tradition* (Cambridge University Press, Cambridge, 1983) pp. 15–41.
Vansina, J., *Oral Tradition as History* (The University of Wisconsin Press, Madison, 1985).
Vines, C., *Objections to Animal Magnetism or Mesmerism* (Blackwell, Reading, 1845).

Winter, A., *Mesmerised: Powers of Mind in Victorian Britain* (University of Chicago Press, Chicago and London, 1998).

Withers, C., 'The Historical Creation of the Scottish Highlands,' *The Manufacture of Scottish History* edited by I. Donnachie and C. Whatley (Polygon, Edinburgh, 1992) pp. 143–156.

——*Gaelic Scotland: The Transformation of a Cultural Region* (Routledge, London and New York, 1988).

Womack, P., *Improvement and Romance: Constructing the Myths of the Highlands* (Macmillan, Basingstoke., 1989).

Wood, W., *Yours Sincerely for Scotland: The Autobiography of a Patriot* (Barker, London, 1970).

Wormald, J., 'The Witches, the Devil and the King,' in T. Brotherstone and D. Ditchburn (eds), *Freedom and Authority: Scotland c1050 – c1650* (Tuckwell Press, East Lothian, 2000) pp. 165–180.

www.brahanseer.co.uk/news/pages/the_story

www.travelscotland.co.uk/features/seer_festival

Index

International Studies in Folklore and Ethnology

SERIES EDITOR
Anne O'Connor

This series seeks to contribute to the current vibrant multidisciplinary academic debate regarding folklore and ethnology. The definition of both folklore and ethnology is a constant challenge, and the history of the development of the disciplines differs from one country to another. Folklore is at once dynamic process, shared communication and performance, and ethnology embraces context and folklife. So while these research areas continue to experience dramatic transformation, in terms of methodology, theoretical approaches as well as practical engagement with people and cultures, this series focuses on the evolving study of traditional and popular cultures, in all contexts and across all geographies of time and space. As folklore and ethnology reach across boundaries and become manifest in (new) cultural contexts through the enabling power of global communications and re-imaginings, this series therefore provides an international forum for continuing debate.

Through a mixture of edited collections and single-author monographs, this series aims to re-evaluate contemporary critical thought as well as exploring new directions and theories, thus making a significant contribution to these disciplines which are fundamental to our understanding of contemporary culture and identity.

Vol. 1 Alex Sutherland
The Brahan Seer: The Making of a Legend
282 pages. 2009.
ISBN: 978-3-03911-868-7